The University Unthought

Why is it important to have a revolutionary critical pedagogy? What are the new inter/disciplinary engagements possible within the university? What will it be like to live and learn in this university of the future?

Drawing on these essential questions, this volume explores the political future(s) of the university. It does not take a simplistic recourse to the tenets of liberal democracy, but seeks a more engaged positioning of the university space within everyday practices of the social. It cross-examines the history of this 'ideal' university's relationship with the banal everyday, the 'apolitical' outside and what exceeds intellectual reason, to finally question if such historicizing of the university is necessary at all.

Along with its companion *The Idea of the University: Histories and Contexts*, this brave new intervention makes a compelling foray into the political promise of the university. It will be of interest to academics, educators and students of the social sciences and humanities. It will also be of use to policy-makers and education analysts, and be central to the concerns of any citizen.

Debaditya Bhattacharya teaches literature at Kazi Nazrul University, India. He has previously taught at Sri Venkateswara College, University of Delhi, India (2010–2012), Central University of South Bihar, India (2013–2015) and Nivedita College, University of Calcutta, India (2015–2018). Debaditya's doctoral work engaged with the relationship between literature and death, and with specific reference to the testimonial speech-act. He researches on continental philosophy, and writes on contemporary modes of political articulation as well as practices of mobilization in the Indian context. His current interests cohere around a social-economic history of higher education, with specific attention to Indian policy contexts. He is co-editor of *Sentiment, Politics, Censorship: The State of Hurt* (2016).

The university is in crisis everywhere. Pushed by the demand for new technology-driven skills and hugely expanded aspirations for college degrees, the traditional university is being squeezed by a mercenary sector that supplies education for profit and shrinking state support. These two volumes, containing essays by a stellar list of contributors, provide the most comprehensive discussion I have seen of this crisis, particularly in India but also covering the neighbouring countries and the global scene.

—**Partha Chatterjee**
*Professor of Anthropology, Columbia University,
New York, USA, and Honorary Professor, Centre for
Studies in Social Sciences, Kolkata, India*

These landmark volumes offer a veritable smorgasbord of deep and original thinking about the question of what a university is for. A stellar cast of essayists explores the university's historical embeddedness in the nation-state, critiques its present imbrication with global capital, and provides a richly imagined manifesto for its future.

—**Niraja Gopal Jayal**
*Professor, Centre for the Study of Law and Governance,
Jawaharlal Nehru University, New Delhi, India*

This invaluable and extraordinarily thought-provoking collection offers many critical readings of not only the idea but also the ideology of the university in the global south, and especially India. It not only brings out the 'consecration' of nationalist and neoliberal commonsense in the university today, but also provides a vocabulary to challenge and question this consecration. One of the great pleasures of the collection is also the tension and implicit conversation between the various readings, which differ from each other, sometimes subtly and sometimes emphatically. An indispensable set of volumes for anybody concerned about the stakes of 'higher' education today.

—**Ajay Skaria**
*Professor, Department of History/Institute of
Global Studies, University of Minnesota, USA*

Asked to blurb these volumes, I made the mistake of reading them. They are such rich collections I have no idea where to start my praise. Suffice to say that they are must-reads for anyone seeking to understand the programs of governments, corporations, and international agencies to de-educate the global citizenry in the name of economic efficiency. As a U.S. reader, I was particularly enlightened by the careful analyses of higher education in India, whose education systems will have a major influence on the planet's future. Seen from here, the first volume could be called 'Provincializing America'. The second shows that another higher education is possible. Superb work that will help policy turn the corner.

—**Christopher Newfield**
*Professor, Department of English, University
of California-Santa Barbara, USA*

The University Unthought
Notes for a Future

Edited by Debaditya Bhattacharya

LONDON AND NEW YORK

First published 2019
by Routledge
2 Park Square, Milton Park, Abingdon, Oxon OX14 4RN

and by Routledge
711 Third Avenue, New York, NY 10017

Routledge is an imprint of the Taylor & Francis Group, an informa business

© 2019 selection and editorial matter, Debaditya Bhattacharya; individual chapters, the contributors

The right of Debaditya Bhattacharya to be identified as the author of the editorial material, and of the authors for their individual chapters, has been asserted in accordance with sections 77 and 78 of the Copyright, Designs and Patents Act 1988.

The views and opinions expressed in this book are solely those of the authors and do not necessarily reflect those of the publisher. The text representations and analyses are intended here to serve general educational and informational purposes and not obligatory upon any party. The authors and publisher have made every effort to ensure that the information presented in the book was correct at the time of press, but do not assume and hereby disclaim any liability with respect to the accuracy, completeness, reliability, suitability, selection and inclusion of the contents of this book and any implied warranties or guarantees. The authors and publisher make no representations or warranties of any kind to any person or entity for any loss, including, but not limited to special, incidental or consequential damage, or disruption – physical, psychological, emotional, or otherwise – alleged to have been caused, directly or indirectly, by omissions or any other related cause.

All rights reserved. No part of this book may be reprinted or reproduced or utilised in any form or by any electronic, mechanical, or other means, now known or hereafter invented, including photocopying and recording, or in any information storage or retrieval system, without permission in writing from the publishers.

Trademark notice: Product or corporate names may be trademarks or registered trademarks, and are used only for identification and explanation without intent to infringe.

British Library Cataloguing-in-Publication Data
A catalogue record for this book is available from the British Library

Library of Congress Cataloging-in-Publication Data
A catalog record has been requested for this book

ISBN: 978-1-138-06732-5 (hbk)
ISBN: 978-0-429-44197-4 (ebk)

Typeset in Sabon
by Apex CoVantage, LLC

. . . to those who dare against the dying of the light.

Contents

List of contributors ix
Preface and acknowledgments xiv

Introduction
What 'use' is the liberal ruse? Debating the 'idea' of
the university 1
DEBADITYA BHATTACHARYA

PART I
Beyond nostalgias 39

1 The provocations of the public university in
  contemporary India 41
  JANAKI NAIR

2 Decolonizing the university 62
  ADITYA NIGAM

3 The crisis of the public university 74
  SUPRIYA CHAUDHURI

PART II
'Cultures' of thinking and doing 91

4 The idea of a university and the invention of culture
  in colonial/postcolonial India 93
  MOSARRAP HOSSAIN KHAN

5	Scientific research productivity in the Indian university sector DHRUBA J. SAIKIA AND ROWENA ROBINSON	105
6	In search of a scientific public sphere SHOBHIT MAHAJAN	126

PART III
Imagining an 'other' university 143

7	What if the university is a *parrot's training*? ANUP DHAR	145
8	Academic freedom and the ownership of knowledge LAWRENCE LIANG	163
9	Between disciplines and interdisciplines: the university of *in*-discipline DEBADITYA BHATTACHARYA	183

PART IV
Drafting manifestos for change 209

10	The commoditization of education PRABHAT PATNAIK	211
11	Neoliberal savagery and the assault on higher education as a democratic public sphere HENRY A. GIROUX	222
12	The university in question ARI SITAS	237
13	Revolutionary critical pedagogy: staking a claim against the macrostructural unconscious PETER MCLAREN	246

Index 269

Contributors

Supriya Chaudhuri is Professor of English (Emerita) at Jadavpur University, Kolkata, India. Her research interests include English and European Renaissance literature, cultural history, modernism and critical theory. Among her recent publications are *Commodities and Culture in the Colonial World* (Routledge 2017); *Reconsidering English Studies in Indian Higher Education* (2015); and chapters in *A Companion to Virginia Woolf* (Blackwell, 2016); *Celebrating Shakespeare: Commemoration and Cultural Memory* (2015); and *A History of the Indian Novel in English* (2015). She has written and engaged publicly with issues of higher education, the future of the humanities, arts, culture and the nation.

Anup Dhar is Professor of Philosophy in the School of Liberal Studies and Director of the Centre for Development Practice, Ambedkar University Delhi, India. He works at the interface of the Marxian political and Lacanian psychoanalysis, which offers him a way to rethink questions of 'transformative social praxis' in largely adivasi (and dalit) contexts in central India. Some of his co-authored books include *Dislocation and Resettlement in Development: From Third World to World of the Third* (2009) and *The Indian Economy in Transition: Globalization, Capitalism and Development* (2015). His co-edited books include *Breaking the Silo: Integrated Science Education in India* (2017) and *Psychoanalysis in the Indian Terroir: Emerging Themes in Culture, Family, and Childhood* (2018). He has also co-edited a special double issue of *Rethinking Marxism* titled "Marxism and Spirituality" Vol. 28, No. 3–4. (2016). He is the editor of *CUSP: Journal of Studies in Culture, Subjectivity, Psyche* (http://cuspthejournal.com/). He is also a member of the editorial board of *Rethinking Marxism* (http://rethinkingmarxism.org/ [2016–2019]).

x Contributors

Henry A. Giroux is University Professor for Scholarship in the Public Interest at McMaster University in Hamilton, Ontario, Canada. His many books include *Border Crossing, 2nd edition* (2005); *Beyond the Spectacle of Terrorism: Global Uncertainty and the Challenge of the New Media* (2006); *The University in Chains: Confronting the Military-Industrial-Academic Complex* (2007); *Against the Terror of Neoliberalism* (2008); *Youth in a Suspect Society: Democracy or Disposability?*(2009); *On Critical Pedagogy* (2011); *Zombie Politics in the Age of Casino Capitalism* (2016); *America's Addiction to Terrorism* (2016); *America at War with Itself* (2016); *The Public in Peril: Trump and the Menace of American Authoritarianism* (2017) and *American Nightmare: Facing the Challenge of Fascism* (2018).

Mosarrap Hossain Khan received his doctorate from the Department of English, New York University, USA. Currently, he is assistant professor at Lovely Professional University, Punjab, India. His areas of research include South Asian literature and culture, postcolonial theory, religion and secularism, and theories of everyday life. He is a founding editor at *Café Dissensus*.

Lawrence Liang is Professor in the School of Law, Governance and Citizenship at Ambedkar University Delhi, India. He worked with the Alternative Law Forum, which he helped co-found. He also moonlights as a film and media scholar. He has recently finished a book on libraries and the future of reading and is completing another one on law and justice in Indian cinema. He writes for a number of places, including *e-flux* and *Kafila*, and has taught and lectured at many universities in India, the US, and Europe. He is the author of *The Public is Watching: Sex, Laws and Videotape* and *A Guide to Open Content Licenses*.

Shobhit Mahajan is Professor of Physics and Astrophysics at the University of Delhi, India. He regularly writes for newspapers and magazines on a variety of issues and was associated with the science and environmental fortnightly *Down to Earth* for over ten years as a Special Contributor in Physical Sciences. He has written more than a dozen popular books on science and technology which have been published by Scholastic Inc., Penguin and H.F. Ullmann. He is also the author of two textbooks for undergraduate and postgraduate students.

Peter McLaren is Distinguished Professor in Critical Studies, Co-Director of the Paulo Freire Democratic Project, and International Ambassador for Global Ethics and Social Justice at the Attallah

College of Educational Studies, Chapman University, USA. He is the author and editor of over fifty books, including *Schooling as a Ritual Performance* (1986), *Life in Schools* (1989), *Critical Pedagogy and Predatory Culture* (1994), *Revolutionary Multiculturalism* (1997), *Che Guevara, Paulo Freire, and the Pedagogy of Revolution* (2000), and *Pedagogy of Insurrection: From Resurrection to Revolution* (2015). His writings have been translated into 30 languages.

Janaki Nair is Professor at the Centre for Historical Studies, Jawaharlal Nehru University, New Delhi, India. Her areas of academic interest span across labour and urban history, legal history, feminism and women's history, and visual cultures and traditions. Her publications include *Women and Law in Colonial India: A Social History* (1996), *Miners and Millhands: Work, Culture and Politics in Princely Mysore* (1998), *The Promise of the Metropolis: Bangalore's Twentieth Century* (2005) and *Mysore Modern: Reconceptualising the Region under Princely Rule* (2011), among others. She has actively organized and written in the public media against sustained onslaughts on Indian higher education. She has also been instrumental in archiving the teach-in 'nationalism lectures' in JNU, in the form of an edited collection *What the Nation Really Needs to Know* (2016).

Aditya Nigam is Professor at Centre for the Study of Developing Societies (CSDS), New Delhi, India. His recent research has been concerned with the decolonization of social and political theory. In particular, he is interested in theorizing the contemporary experience of politics, populism and democracy in the non-West – treating the non-West as the ground for 'doing theory', rather than a field for application or testing of standard frameworks derived from the Western experience. He is the author of *The Insurrection of Little Selves: The Crisis of Secular Nationalism in India* (2006), *Power and Contestation: India Since 1989* (with Nivedita Menon; 2007), *After Utopia: Modernity and Socialism and the Postcolony* (2010), and *Desire Named Development* (2011). He also works with the CSDS's Indian Languages Programme and its Hindi journal *Pratiman*. He comments regularly on contemporary political issues on the blog *Kafila*.

Prabhat Patnaik is Professor Emeritus at the Centre for Economic Studies and Planning at Jawaharlal Nehru University, New Delhi, India. His books include *Time, Inflation and Growth* (1988), *Economics*

xii *Contributors*

and *Egalitarianism* (1990), *Whatever Happened to Imperialism and Other Essays* (1995), *Accumulation and Stability Under Capitalism* (1997), *The Value of Money* (2008), *The Retreat to Unfreedom* (2003), *Re-envisioning Socialism* (2011) and *Theory of Imperialism* (2016; with Utsa Patnaik). He has recently co-authored a volume on the political economy of the recent demonetization experiment in India, titled *Demonetisation Decoded: A Critique of India's Currency Experiment* (2017). He is the editor of the journal *Social Scientist*.

Rowena Robinson is Professor of Sociology at the Department of Humanities and Social Sciences, Indian Institute of Technology (IIT) Bombay and has taught earlier at University of Delhi and Jawaharlal Nehru University, New Delhi, India. Among other publications, she is author of *Boundaries of Religion* (2013) and *Tremors of Violence* (2005) and editor of *Minority Studies* (2012). She is co-editor with Marianus Joseph Kujur of *Margins of Faith: Dalit and Tribal Christianity in India* (2010) and with Sathianathan Clarke of *Religious conversion in India: modes, motivations and meanings* (2003). She has also published several journal articles in the areas of ethnic conflict, Christianity and issues of constitutional law.

Dhruba J Saikia was a Professor at the National Centre for Radio Astrophysics of the Tata Institute of Fundamental Research (TIFR) and is presently a Visiting Professor at the Inter-University Centre for Astronomy and Astrophysics (IUCAA). His research interests are in different aspects of extragalactic astronomy and astrophysics, especially active galaxies, and more recently on education, with an emphasis on higher education. Besides TIFR, he has been engaged in research and/or teaching at the Jodrell Bank Observatory of the University of Manchester; National Radio Astronomy Observatory USA; Queen's University at Kingston, Canada; Australia Telescope National Facility (CASS) of CSIRO Australia, the University of Western Australia and Cotton University, India. He has published about 150 research papers in leading journals, and co-edited two volumes: *Low-Frequency Radio Universe* (2009) with D. A. Green, Y. Gupta and T. Venturi; *Fluid Flows to Black Holes, A tribute to S Chandrasekhar on His Birth Centenary* (2013) with Virginia Trimble. He was the Editor of the *Bulletin of the Astronomical Society of India* and the Founding Vice-Chancellor of Cotton University at Guwahati. He is a Fellow of the National Academy of Sciences, India.

Ari Sitas is a creative socialist thinker, activist, poet, dramatist and one of the key intellectuals of the post-1980s generation in South Africa. He is a professor and the head of the Sociology Department at the University of Cape Town, South Africa. He also chairs the National Institute for the Humanities and the Social Sciences in South Africa and leads a multi-institutional project in Afro-Asia studying the flows of people, slaves and music (7th-15th centuries AD). He and an ensemble of other scholars are working on a sequel to *Gauging and Engaging Deviance, 1600–2000*, recently published by Tulika Press in India, titled *Scripts of Defiance*. His other publications include *The Mandela Decade: Labour, Culture and Society in Post-Apartheid South Africa* (2010) and *The Ethic of Reconciliation* (2008). At the moment, he is working on his latest oratorio, which is a via dolorosa of our contemporary period and is to be staged by India's foremost theatrical director, Anuradha Kapur.

Preface and acknowledgments

Let me open this collective of two companion volumes – *The University Unthought: Notes for a Future* and *The Idea of the University: Histories and Contexts* – on an intensely personal note.

Early in 2017, a cousin brother of mine (living in the northeastern state of Tripura) scraped together all of his life's savings to finance his son's higher education. He hadn't been a 'successful' father by any means, and had barely managed to put his son through a government-run secondary school in Agartala – all the while complaining about the failing 'quality' of public education in a then-communist-ruled state and the thriving racket of private tuitions. He still tried saving up a meagre fortune for what lay ahead, and eventually decided to chase my nephew's desire for a professional programme in a private technical college in Bangalore. There were 'rumours' about this college not having the necessary affiliations, and – on probing further – I realized that the off-campus affiliating university was embroiled in litigation with regulatory bodies over the extent of its territorial jurisdiction. This is a routinely familiar story, and one that shrouds the inception and future of several private colleges and universities in a strange mist of confusion. The courts of the country have, on a number of occasions, issued injunctions against such for-profit institutions of higher education and deemed them illegal. I went about my usual rounds of cautionary counsel with my brother's family, till they landed in Bangalore for the necessary admission formalities. The warnings were ignored, the loan papers signed, the money arranged, the papers filled out, the son admitted – and on his way back to the hotel that evening, my brother suffered a cardiac arrest and died before he could be taken to the hospital. I went over, and cremated the body.

Perhaps, medically speaking, there wasn't really a connection between the depletion of a bank account, a debt bond, an only son's education and a father's untimely death. I also know that this story has little news value, and perhaps even lesser discursive value for the ceremony of a 'preface'. There are far more poignant stories that scream out of the graves and remains of many a lost life and lost career, or a promise of a future never even dared and dreamt. Recounting this rather personal episode here might apparently hold only a cathartic significance, but I believe this chronicle of a death retold sounds an adequate dirge to all that is dying with/within the 'idea' of the university today. To crisply put it, the death is of the public university, and the constitutive 'publicness' that helped it survive.

It is fairly understandable why now is a good time to get talking about the 'idea of the university', given the everyday onslaughts on both its liberal traditions of autonomy and its radical possibilities for a different politics. The legacies of social exclusion made possible by the university's histories of 'disinterested' intellectual labour also call for relentless questioning.

There has been substantial academic work on the neoliberal university (relating its history with questions of democracy and the exact policy directions in higher education) in the European and North American contexts, but very little concerted research – plumbing positions from different disciplines – exists in the Indian context. Journalistic pieces or op-ed articles have come out regularly in print and electronic media on recent incidents as well as legislative implications of policy, expressing the massive discomfiture of acclaimed scholars, public intellectuals and activists over current trends in public-funded higher education the world over. However, attempts to bring together thoughts from within varied disciplinary 'silos' about the perceived 'crisis' of university education are largely wanting. Furthermore, the recent political resurgence of right-wing forces across continents provokes greater alarm and is accompanied by routine incidents of social-economic discrimination on university campuses or state-sponsored clampdowns. It is this climate of rabid anti-intellectualism that makes a renewed historiographic intervention necessary and timely.

While the triumphalist intrusion of the Hindu Right into spaces of the Indian academia has called for intense solidarity movements over the past few years, the neoliberal directions in policy are neither new nor tied to the electoral fortunes of specific party-regimes or political actors. In fact, as we all know, cultural conservatism has been an old and trusted ally of ruthless corporatization – advertising the 'free marketplace' of 'excellence' – and this is as true of the Anglo-American academy as of a 'third-world' economy committed to 'developmental' agendas. Our resistance movements thus need to forge international alliances in the cause of generating a creative-critical archive that could reimagine a progressive politics of higher education across the world – in terms of quality, access and the principles of social justice. Equally important is the need to measure the pits and promises of tertiary education against the historical mutations charted by primary and secondary levels of schooling, in grossly unequal contexts of privilege and opportunity.

It also warrants remembering that the university today does not merely call for specialized academic-analytical discourse alone, but also personal reflections/reminiscences of change as well as journalistic reportage of events. At a time when the mainstream public media have been unabashedly beholden to corporate-political patronage and have routinely run state-engineered propaganda by 'doctoring' sentiment against public university communities, it is imperative that popular opinion be exposed to forms of ethical-critical reporting. Also, when the state has tried hard to outlaw all modes and means of expressing alternative opinion as constitutive of 'sedition', one may only call forth the ghosts of 'experience' to rewrite history away from populist prejudice. Consequently, this has been made part of the rationale of these volumes – since, now more than ever, it is crucial to strike a chord among non-academic constituencies of public opinion.

The content of these two volumes will therefore include some reflective or impressionistic pieces, coming from authors who range across academia and 'serious' journalism or occupy the cusp between the two. There is a deliberate convergence of objective, critical work with the form of testimonials and manifestos – spanning the recollected pasts and imaginable futures of the university. With contributors from widely variant professional persuasions and areas of scholarly interest – and, yet, tied by their physical proximity with the everyday contortions of university structures! – these volumes hope to take the reader through a broad spectrum of writing genres. The literary is pitted against the statistical, policy analysis is coupled with historical minutiae, the archival is played out alongside the memoir, and a terseness of expression often juxtaposed with shades of argumentative vigour. This is a necessary politics of discourse, in order to reach out to diverse publics – who might associate better with truth-claims based on first-hand contexts of experience.

Now, to come to the task of acknowledging debts, there have been so many that every attempt at cataloguing them will only leave me terribly indebted to an agony of unfair selection. As every editor worth her salt knows, an anthology is like a performance – the mettle of which is not her doing at all. The individual actors might only be thanked evermore for filling the hours of the evening with their magic, and the failings may squarely be laid on the one who conceptualized the possible alchemy of their labours. The actual 'work' exceeds the final event of the performance – and likewise, for these books, it covered the space of years. Never a moment between the darkness of the womb and the light of day, in this passage towards the final object in your hands now, has been dulled by the lack of patience or the impatience of achievement. I can only blame the infirmity of language for not being able to thank the authors with any degree of completeness. They remain the promise of this collective, and the reason for its being there at all.

Perhaps a collective on the university has been in the hatching, ever since – by one of those many permutations of privilege – one walked into the precincts of one such space. It has raged through the years of sitting within classrooms and looking at their windowed outsides, writing examinations and seeking revaluations, marching with comrades into imaginary struggles and real ones, living the first throb of democracy at student union elections, mixing excitement and dread in the aftermath of conversations and impassioned arguments. We did not change the world, as we thought we would through our phantasmal trysts with the university – and, which is why this collective shaped up while we walked the streets with our colleagues, raised slogans, held placards over our heads, taught and unlearnt the ways of the classroom, lived the life of an 'ad hoc' teacher, clenched our teeth through daily routines of indignity, gulped down our angst, sometimes in silence and sometimes in incoherent blabber, fought at teachers' council meetings and through petty proceedings of committees, and then braced up for the next day's struggle. Every time, there was hope laced along the ends of the night that passed. The first thought of compiling or converting these hopes into these volumes was chanced upon, when – in the early months of 2015 and just before leaving a university job in Bihar – I participated in a discussion with students on the 'idea of the university'. My talk on the occasion was intended as a parting rebuttal to a university that cared too little for what its idea stood for. Kamlanand Jha, a senior colleague and a most trusted comrade, urged me to consider expanding that immediate cathartic outburst into the stuff of a book. And thus it began!

I knew from the beginning that this 'book' cannot be a monograph, because there was so much outside of my experience of the university that needed to be accounted for. When Rohith Vemula left a nation sleepwalking into a bloodied 'collective conscience' and the cries of sedition rent newspaper columns, I collaborated with *Cafe Dissensus Magazine* to bring out an online archive of essays on the theme in

September 2016. Most of my collaborators from that edition have unquestioningly stayed on since, while the editors of the webzine – Mosarrap Hossain Khan and Mary Ann Chacko – have been exceptionally nice to hint at a book future for the work thus shared.

Over time, conversations with Ajay Skaria, Romila Thapar, Niraja Gopal Jayal, Apoorvanand, Pranab Bardhan, Geetha Nambissan, Ravindra Karnena, Chirashree Dasgupta, Ayesha Kidwai, Tejaswini Niranjana, Franson Manjali, Vinita Chandra, Upal Chakrabarti and Sukanya Sarbadhikary added much to the act of thinking through these volumes and strengthened the resolve behind them. Back in Bihar – where I (un)learnt more about the university than its metropolitan monumentality assures – Yogesh Pratap Shekhar, Richa, Shanker Asish Dutt, Vinay Kanth, Daisy Narayan, Muniba Sami, Anuj Lugun, Prashant Thakur, Kanupriya Jha, Samta Rai, Amrit Ghoshal, Prabhat Jha and Abhyuday have braved the agony of many a debate with soldierly resilience. Coming to teach at a fairly nondescript college in Kolkata and slipping into a relationship with the university that gets more rarefied by the day, friends and colleagues – Nilanjana Sen, Sudakshina Ghosh, Piyalee Das Sharma and Joyita Mitra, being but a few – remained as the sounding-board for ideas and worldly failures. Through all these leaps and shifts, snatches of conversations with Partha Chatterjee, Harbans Mukhia, Sundar Sarukkai, Tanika Sarkar, Rochelle Pinto, Jawed Naqvi, Saugata Bhaduri, Simi Malhotra, GJV Prasad and Anton Bech Jorgensen have meant a world of encouragement and permanent solidarity.

The most intimate alliances are best left unsaid. But, were it not for Rina Ramdev, the university may have never been a place for me to want to belong to. She is what redeems the work of ideas beyond the realm of the odious, with her abiding friendship. My students have been fellow travellers through the dense recesses of every 'idea' – and so will they continue to inspire every other. Kalpana Jha has been a living workshop of the imagination; and, because she escaped the life of the university, she taught me out of my disillusionments with it. My family has stuck with me, despite not knowing why these years have felt like an exercise in calculated disengagement. I can only assure them here of my constancy.

Shoma Choudhury, from Routledge, has been at the receiving end of my frenzied outbursts on email – and has, evidently, still not given up. I cannot thank her enough for this wonderful bond of collegiality and faith. Brinda Sen, from the editorial team, still continues to battle the storm out. There have been four anonymous reviewers, who – at various points in the preparation of these two volumes – have helped me with the most insightful suggestions and criticism. Their comments ring through my wakeful moments of anticipation, as the volumes go to print.

Janaki Nair's essay appeared in an earlier version in *Economic and Political Weekly* (Vol. 52, No. 37) in September 2017. Peter McLaren's clarion call to revolutionary critical pedagogy uses chapter excerpts from his book *Pedagogy of Insurrection* (Peter Lang 2015). The original publisher of either piece deserves the warmth of gratitude, for handling paperwork without its habitual burden of cruelty.

Postscript: Through my childhood years, I responded to the interlocutors of 'ambition' by saying that I want to become an educationist. When queried why, I self-assuredly said – without the faintest clue of what it meant – that I want to better the state of education in the country. Now, for some inexplicable reason, I hate that word – 'educationist'. Perhaps because I know there is none by that name. I dedicate this book to all who did not want to become 'educationists'.

Debaditya Bhattacharya
2 January 2018

Introduction
What 'use' is the liberal ruse? Debating the 'idea' of the university

Debaditya Bhattacharya

The nation 'in' the university

Walter Benjamin, in his 1915 essay 'The Life of Students', passionately rues the infiltration of the 'vocational spirit' into the university's life of creative *eros*. The burden of proof conferred by demands of 'utility' and confirmed with the calculated welfarism of "socially relevant labor" makes for Benjamin's charge against the independent student-associations (*Freie Studentenschaften*) in German universities of his time (Benjamin 2011 [1915]: 201). He persuasively builds a case against the liberal imagination of political voluntarism as social 'returns on investment' made by the state, and maintains:

> [T]he true sign of corruption is not the collusion of the university and the state (something that is by no means incompatible with honest barbarity), but the theory and guarantee of academic freedom, when in reality people assume with brutal complacence that the aim of study is to steer its disciples to a socially adapted individuality and service to the state.
>
> (ibid.: 199)

The drive towards a "concept of duty" (ibid.: 200) as the social-professional rationale of university education and its consequent alliance with what has severally been understood as 'nation-building' is what Benjamin alerts us to the dangers of. Not only is the construal of such a service ethic as the primary 'responsibility' of university life utterly self-seeking in its bourgeois demonstrations of efficient citizenship, but it also goes on to configure ontologies of 'value' within a civic-nationalist moral norm of 'virtue'. In this, the university becomes a claimant for both public affect and moral priority through assured dividends on welfare spending. The liberal penchant worked into the constitution of the university, Benjamin discerningly hints, is the guise for its invasion by the vocational. Socially relevant labour is not the unique litmus of legitimacy designed by a neoliberal state, as we now tend to believe – but has been quite silently at work since the shaping up of the liberal 'project' of the university. That two of modernity's most prominent institutions – the nation-state and the university – were historically united in their time of birth is no mere accident, but obviously mirrors the cultural-political logic of the Enlightenment. Entrepreneurial vocationalism as *debt-and-duty* has since held the promise of a historical destiny for the liberal-democratic university, and it is here that the "theory and guarantee of academic freedom" has failed its originary condition of 'autonomy'.

What is especially significant about Benjamin's critique of the relationship between university communities and the state is that it decisively pre-empts the neoliberal onslaught as not a break with the liberal past (as is most often presumed!), but merely a continuation of it. It suggests that, while traditions of liberalism demanded a counterfeiting of the ethical in a purely 'economic' (though, disguised as 'social') contract between the individual and the state, the neoliberal order only substituted the state with a global market. To that extent, the state is only made to arbitrate between the self-investments of the individual and the claims of global capital. The university consequently no longer manufactures an ethic of social work as apprenticeship to national economy, but decisively prepares both human resource and infrastructural goods for free auctioning in a global flexible marketplace of 'work'. Socially necessary labour is no longer patented by the state, but must be made globally relevant as credit-capital.

In my introductory essay for the first volume, titled 'The university in history: from *idea* to impossibility', I have elaborately charted this course of substitutions that has transformed the university's relationship with the 'nation/trans-nation' dyad. From Frederick Wilhelm III's co-optation of the Humboldtian university within a recuperative project of national glory for the then war-ravaged Prussia to the current race for 'world-class' universities as global benchmark within transnational labour-markets, the previous volume begins by making a historical case around the perceived 'uses' of higher education.

Adding to this, nearly five decades of history in the Euro-Atlantic world bear out the truth in Benjamin's prophecy with proximate symptoms of a 'crisis' (World Bank 1994, 1996, 1997, 2002). Subsequently, the setting up of the World Trade Organization (WTO) in 1995 and its formulation of a General Agreement on Trade in Services (GATS) officialized what William Tabb calls a "World Take Over" of education as a potential tradable service with immense investment opportunities for global corporations (Tabb 2000: 1–18). The GATS framework effectively made way for a multilateral import-export economy to substitute the essentially public character of knowledge-institutions across the world (Altbach 2001; Education International 2000). The considerably low Gross Enrolment Ratio (GER) of higher education in India, accompanied by its being among the nations with lowest GDP rates of public spending in the sector, made it seem especially profitable for prospects of transnational trade through inclusion within the GATS arrangements (WTO 1998: 6, 2010: 13–4). The Doha Round of WTO negotiations in 2001 saw India 'offering' up its higher education sector to corporate finance capital, pending 'commitment' and a consequent lowering of subsidies to deregulate public institutions while creating a 'level playing field' for global-international corporations. The recent policy moves towards slackening the grasp of a central regulatory body like the University Grants Commission (UGC) – first, by promising an order of 'graded' financial autonomy to 'top' higher educational institutions (GoI 2018a, 2018b) and then by proposing a complete seizure of funding authority from the regulator (GoI 2018c) – only lengthen the WTO's shadow over Indian public education sectors.

The nation *in place of* the state

The structural adjustments unleashed by what John Williamson termed the "Washington Consensus" of 1989 called upon the debt-burdened third world economies to curb state controls on the social sector (including education and health services), and open up their markets to private corporations as means to greater loan sanctions from the World Bank and International Monetary Fund (IMF). It was argued that an effective deregulation of public services would not only earn greater national returns (and therefore, better 'growth'-dividends) through foreign capital inflows, but would also help overcome the debt-crisis with assured global credit (Williamson 1990). Successively, the Indian economic policy regime marked a paradigm-shift by relinquishing state ownership of public infrastructures and allowing entry of private players as both patron and provider of non-profit social goods. As early as in 1995, the Indian government tabled a *Private Universities (Establishment and Regulation) Bill* with a declared policy intention to stem the 'mushrooming' of private self-financing institutions of higher education in the country, but in the process laying out guidelines for the "incorporation" of more such colleges in those sciences and technology disciplines which promised commercial application (GoI 1995: 1). Though the Bill was forced into dormancy in the Upper House of the Parliament before being withdrawn in 2007, several state assemblies (such as Gujarat, Himachal Pradesh, Uttar Pradesh, Chhattisgarh, Maharashtra and Andhra Pradesh) went on to enact similar legislation in the intervening years – thus lending credence and legitimacy to private corporate investment in higher education. In April 2000, a "special subject group on policy framework for private investment in education" – headed by corporate tycoons Mukesh Ambani and Kumarmangalam Birla – submitted its report for reform-planning initiatives to the Prime Minister's Council on Trade and Industry (Ambani and Birla 2003: 840–5). Infamously known as the *Ambani-Birla Report*, it unequivocally pitted the primary and secondary education sectors against higher education and argued for a diversion of public funds from the latter to the former. Underlying an apparent concern for the gaping 'quality' deficit within government schools was the urgency of a call to reduce state subsidies for colleges and universities, thus enabling increased private financing of the sector. The *Report* further re-configured tertiary education in a "knowledge-based society" (ibid.: 841) as far from being a public good, since the benefits of it were assumed to be realized through higher private lifetime incomes of the student. Historically, this marked a shift of financial priorities for the erstwhile welfare state by re-positioning its commitment from funding institutions to funding individuals (through loan assistance and financial aid packages).

The University Grants Commission – tasked with grant disbursals in the field of general higher education – followed up this insidious policy move from a subsidy model of public provisioning to a loan/scholarship-based relief package model by envisioning a *Model Universities Act* in 2004. Urging universities to generate their own revenues through industrial collaborations and philanthropic partnerships (*The Times of India* 2004), this public document aimed at bringing all universities of the country under a 'model' code of stealthy privatization – in complete disregard for divergent socio-economic contexts or material inequities. In the face of stiff opposition from teachers and students alike, the subsequent United Progressive Alliance (UPA-I) government withdrew the UGC's portentous recommendations, but only to have the Prime Minister appoint a National Knowledge Commission (NKC) in 2005 under the chairmanship of yet another corporate stakeholder in the telecommunications industry. The NKC drafted a flurry of *Reports* in 2006, 2007 and 2009 – with a view to reaping the "demographic dividend" (GoI 2009a: 3) of the country and bolstering

Introduction 5

a "knowledge economy" (ibid.: 15) that would "involve diversifying the sources of financing to encourage private participation, philanthropic contributions and industry linkages" (ibid.: 14). It also spoke of reducing the "current barriers to entry" (ibid.: 14) of private players by easing regulations and merging governance bodies (much in line with what we see happening now!), while at the same time consigning the non-revenue-generating disciplines like humanities and liberal arts to policy oblivion.

The final nail in the coffin of public-funded higher education was proposed in the form of a *Foreign Educational Institutions (Regulation of Entry and Operations) Bill 2010* – and later re-introduced in the Parliament as the *Foreign Education Providers Bill 2013* (GoI 2010). Working at the behest of the Doha agreement of 2001 and preparing ground for the WTO's Tenth Ministerial Conference in 2015, this draft legislation sought to allow foreign universities to set up offshore campuses in India and thus massively curtail the state's financial liabilities in the field of higher education. Disguised as a measure for restricting foreign exchange outflows from the national economy and preventing students from going abroad in search for 'world class' opportunities, this Bill was an attempt at outsourcing constitutional commitments of 'access' and 'quality' to the charge of global 'competition' (Vaidhyasubramaniam 2010).

While this history of policy reform will animate much more meticulous discussion in following chapters, the contemporary moment might cursorily appear as an ideological rupture. I want to argue, however, that it is instead an apotheosis of a long-unfolding theatre of legislative planning. With the recent electoral rise of the Hindu Right in India, the sustained assault on public universities in the name of their being 'anti-national' or 'seditious' spaces is in fact an accurate instance of how transnational economic designs are executed under the guise of an aggressive cultural nationalism. It is no paradox that universities are being used as a site for manufacturing a certain hegemonic consensus, because that has historically been their function as part of a bourgeois public sphere. Insofar as they are made to foist an immanent fantasy of the 'national' as imaginative test of loyalty and precondition of citizenship, the calculated jingoism of Hindutva disavows the public good of higher education as ranged against the funding state and therefore better left to global forces of competition. The populist narratives played out by the public media around how such institutions contribute to a 'waste' of taxpayers' money and must therefore be shut down, coupled with the government's active attempts to scrap research fellowships or increase teaching workload

6 *Debaditya Bhattacharya*

or cut down teaching jobs in public institutions, explain the policy underpinnings of the contemporary moment.

An explanatory anecdote from recent history might serve to put things in perspective here. For the second year in a row in India, the National Institutional Ranking Framework (NIRF) – an annual audit-mechanism for rating 'performance' of higher educational institutions, as empowered by the *Draft Educational Policy 2016* – ended up ensconcing as the 'best' those same universities which have routinely and spectacularly incurred the 'nationalist' wrath of the current government. For example – IIT Madras, the identified precursor to the rhetorical monstrosity called the 'anti-national' through an attempted de-recognition of a student study-circle in early 2015, was granted the topmost position among engineering institutes. Much in the same vein, Jawaharlal Nehru University (which saw the arrests of student-scholars on trumped up charges of sedition) was named second, Jadavpur University (which continues to witness orchestrated clashes by right-wing lumpen elements) was ranked fifth, Hyderabad Central University (which drove an institutionally boycotted Dalit scholar to suicide on provocations of ruling-party legislators) came seventh, and Delhi University (which recently flashed up scenes of violent assault and vandalism in response to an academic seminar) was rated eighth among all universities. As I have maintained elsewhere, the simultaneous branding of dissenting spaces as the 'best' institutions of the country and by the same government that persecuted them – though seemingly rife with contradiction – is actually united in terms of policy intent (Bhattacharya 2018). This sudden deluge of accolades for those perceived as "rogue" institutions – through highest-ever NAAC ratings, Visitor's Awards, National Board of Accreditation (NBA) approvals and NIRF laurels – begs being read in the light of possible futures charted by the T.S.R. Subramanian Committee Report on New Education Policy (2016a). Section 7.5 of the Report, while lauding the "initiative recently taken to rank top Universities in the country" (2016a: 144), hints at the exact policy implications of 'high ratings':

> On the upper end of the scale, A or I represents the best in its class in India. The institutions in this bracket would have total autonomy in all respects, including fixing faculty salaries, fee structure, entering into collaborations, etc. . . . In other words, there shall be a direct positive correlation between the quality of institution and the grant of autonomy, along with which there will be collateral responsibility to sustain that quality.
>
> (ibid.: 143, Clause 7.5.19)

Introduction 7

The ideological scourge of the 'anti-national' is finally legitimized through its coincidence with the NIRF's glorious mandate, and in the process paving way for a delinking of the 'best' institutions from state financial support. Early in 2018, the Human Resource Development (HRD) minister's ceremonious anointing of 62 of such 'best' higher educational institutions as deserving of complete autonomy (ToI 2018) – whereby, they might open new courses or departments or off-campus centres at will, run short-term certificate or skill-based programmes, hike student fees, enter into private partnerships, admit foreign students and recruit foreign faculty at higher salaries, on the sole condition that "no demand for fund is made from the government" (GoI 2018a: 8–9, Clauses 4.2–4.11) – makes policy into a consummate tool of avenging public education for ideological non-compliance. The impoverishment of revenue for 'performing' institutions is made part of official policy through an imminent push towards self-financing measures, and the seat cuts in JNU or the proposed 1100 percent fee-hike in Panjab University (PU) are but underwritten as natural policy outcomes for seditious spaces.

This second volume in a two-part archive on the university is occasioned as much by the need to rethink the consecration of 'nationalistic' common sense at the altar of transnational capital, as by the forms of resistance generated by such a structural collusion of interests. The twinning of 'saffronization' and 'financialization' in the imminent fortunes of the university is neither new nor unprecedented, and must of course produce in its wake the rage of a resolute defiance. The broad sweep of more than two centuries of university reform – beginning with the origins of the modern European university to its first Indian imports in the colonial context, from the caste/class consensus in English-language instruction to post-independence policy directions (Radhakrishnan recommendations, Kothari Commission, National Policy on Education 2016 etc.), from the provincial trajectories of state universities to the impact of state politics on higher education – has been surveyed in historical detail through the chapters in the first volume. Much of the collective labour of our reflections there has consisted in exhuming the contradictions that belie this transition from the liberal consensus to the neoliberal compromise, in the global political economy of higher education. What follows in this essay is different – in that it seeks to pitch the question of the university's 'use' on an alternative register. Shunning the policy demand for demonstrating utility at the level of disciplinary intersections with the flows of capital, I maintain that there is a radically *other* means of building a *university of use*.

Drafting a manifesto for this 'other' university requires us to move beyond rehearsed idioms of despair and defence. The surviving variety of opposition directed at the repressive neoliberal university has, across contexts, taken recourse to a nostalgia for its liberal past. The progressive intellectual response – couched in demands for freedom, 'reasonableness' and a return to the welfare model – is framed in a constitutional resort to rights discourses and the tenets of liberal humanism (Nussbaum 2010; Readings 1996; Beteille 2014; Newman 2000, 2001; Hovey 1999; Currie and Newson 1998; Smith and Webster 1997; Newson 1998; Rothblatt 1997; Soley 1995). There is a consequent romanticization of the elite humanist quest for truth as an internal condition for democracy, and in the process liberalism is peddled as the political laboratory of social justice. The structural exclusions repeated by centuries of national-bourgeois hegemony are wished away through 'apolitical' fantasies of the welfarist state, and the university's own legacy of class solidarities is left untouched by the charge of historical injustice. Forms of resistance, in their easy preference for nostalgic essentialisms about a not-so-distant past, remain far from challenging *status quoisms* that have made the university live out its own dangers. To advocate a return to the *aporias* of liberal democracy as inherently suited to the valorous ideal of academic autonomy not only misses Benjamin's caution about the co-implication of neoliberalism, but prescribes the disease for its own cure.

In resisting the leash of a competitive global market that ties higher education to its foreseeable futures, what is forwarded by liberal fantasies of 'academic freedom' is a structural pretence of non-interventionist governance that has already pre-programmed the university's afterlife to exalted advertisements of national 'service' and 'growth'. The nation is reified as the ontological essence of the university's being-in-the-world, whether in the abstract cause of a cultural regeneration or a more positivist ethic of economic self-help.

An erotic education: re-imagining the nation

It is this imagination of a 'national university' – teleologically oriented towards a normative consciousness of nationhood, and working to promote the bureaucratic interests of the state – that the pedagogue in Rabindranath Tagore shunned as a distinctively European legacy. Soon after his initial encounters with rural agricultural labour and the low-caste/Muslim tenants working on his family estates in Shilaidaha and Patisar, Tagore began taking an active interest in how the extant colonial machinery of education was geared towards producing

Introduction 9

specific forms of social exclusion and institutional regimes of disconnect. Struck by the degree to which formal learning had become an instrument of economic mobility and utilitarian opportunism wielded by the city-bred *'bhadralok'* (genteel) communities – and much to the disadvantage of the rural outcaste – Tagore relentlessly argued for a re-evaluation of educational systems within the country (1997 [1937]: 490–1). Beginning his reflections with an essay originally published in Bengali in the magazine *Sadhana*, titled 'Shikshar Her-pher' (The Discrepancies of Education), he rejected the argument in favour of English-language education as inherently unsuited to the majority of student populations deprived of any access to social capital (Tagore 1988 [1892]: 565–72). The linguistic alienation, he went on to contend, did of course grant a nominal sense of superiority to those already entitled to positions of social privilege and now seeking induction into the lower orders of colonial bureaucracy; but only served to further push the disenfranchised away from a life of dignity and collective self-determination.

Tagore's critique of the seemingly 'anti-colonial' demand for a 'national education' system consisted in the latter's ideological reliance on a Western import. That a national university – modelled on the idea of its European counterpart – cannot but work along narrow definitions of national self-interest is what carried the charge of his vehement disapproval. Based as it was on a contractual bond of loyalty to the imperial interests of a ruling elite and its consequent championing of orthodox cultural traditions as part of a civilizational mission, Tagore believed that the nationalist demand for *Swadeshi* infrastructures was hardly short of legitimizing the colonial imagination of a 'nation' (Chattopadhyay 2000: 155). Risking the ire of popular sentiment at the peak of India's struggle for political independence, the poet insistently recoiled from the possible injustices of founding a 'national' institution. He writes in an essay detailing the cardinal lineaments of 'The Centre of Indian Culture' (1919):

> Lately, most of our attempts to establish national schools and universities were made with the idea that it was external independence which was needed. We forget that the same weakness in our character, or in our circumstances, which inevitably draws us on to the slippery slope of imitation, will pursue us when our independence is merely of the outside. For then our freedom will become the freedom to imitate the foreign institutions, thus bringing our evil fortune under the influence of the conjunction of two malignant planets – those of imitation and the badness of

imitation – producing a machine-made University, which is made with a bad machine. . . . [A]s soon as the idea of a University enters our mind, the idea of a Cambridge University, Oxford University, and a host of other European Universities, rushes in at the same time and fills the whole space. We then imagine that our salvation lies in a selection of the best points of each patched together in an eclectic perfection. . . . An impatient craving for result and an unfortunate weakness for imitation have led us to cherish just such an unnatural desire for a National University, full-fledged from its very birth.

(Tagore 1996 [1919]: 470–1)

Notwithstanding the communicative infirmities of a borrowed pedagogy and the socio-historical differences threatening a loaned 'idea' of the university, Tagore saw in this odd transposition a far more sinister influence of the Western iconography of the 'nation'. That the European university was imbued with a triumphalist egoism of national 'progress' and could consequently translate into a spirit of aggressive materialistic pursuit (which Benjamin calls the 'vocational spirit'!) is where Rabindranath's primary objections lay. In his cautionary distance from the spectre of the 'national' institution, one finds an emphatic rejection of both manipulated class-interest as well as the sublime *call* of sacrificial duty. To conjure the 'nation' as the absolute horizon of knowledge-practice within the university would automatically commission routines of intellectual conscription in the service of the state. Furthermore, such a bureaucratic commitment to the structures and procedures of power would inhibit, if not completely destroy, the most essential *parrhesiac* exercise of what Tagore calls the "courage of thought" (1996 [1922]: 562). He warns us:

The main source of all forms of voluntary slavery is the desire of gain. It is difficult to fight against this when modern civilization is tainted with such a universal contamination of avarice. I have realized it myself in the little boys of my own school. For the first few years there is no trouble. But as soon as the upper class is reached, their worldly wisdom - the malady of the aged - begins to assert itself. They rebelliously insist that they must no longer learn, but rather pass examinations. Professions in the modern age are more numerous and lucrative than ever before. They need specialization of training and knowledge, tempting education to yield its spiritual freedom to the claims of utilitarian ambitions.

(ibid.: 561)

The "modern civilization" that Tagore denounces as contaminated by "claims of utilitarian ambitions" is what completes his precise estimate of the European 'national spirit'; and it is this scourge that he hopes to escape by imagining the birth of a 'world university' in Visva Bharati. Having modelled a school in Shantiniketan around the contours of the '*tapovan ashram*' and stressing on an indispensable element of freedom from institutional convention (Chattopadhyay 2000: 123), Tagore first expressed his nascent desire for opening a university in a letter to his son Rathindranath. Written on 11 October 1916 – within a year of Benjamin's note to German students, lamenting the gradual disappearance of "any immediate creativity that is unconnected with official position" (Benjamin 2011 [1915]: 203) – Tagore reinstated the need to move away from screechy proposals for a 'national university' and its conjoined ideal of patriotic self-giving:

> I have it in mind to make Shantiniketan the connecting thread between India and the world. I have to found a world centre for the study of humanity there. The days of petty nationalism are numbered – let the first step towards universal union occur in the fields of Bolpur. I want to make that place somewhere beyond the limits of nation and geography – the first flag of victorious universal humanism will be planted there. To rid the world of the suffocating coils of national pride will be the task of my remaining years.
>
> (1997 [1916]: 179)

The 'task' assumed a real form in the foundation of Tagore's university by December 1918, though it was only to be officially inaugurated three years later. It was the first of its kind in India – centred around an *ashram* school in the rural countryside, and thus staging the *provincial* as the ground for its own transgression in a meeting of the world's cultures. The pastoralism of its rural setting was, for Rabindranath, both an antidote to the modern race of 'national progress' as well as a necessary lesson for the collective unconscious of rustic sociality to open itself up to the differences of an 'international' dialogue. Also, the strategic confluence of an apparatus of elementary education with the highest goals of intellectual striving in the university hit at the roots of a crucial pedagogical disconnect that plagued the institutional life of education across the world. The apparent unconcern within university infrastructures towards conditions of prior socialization and their incumbent hierarchies of access to intellectual rights is what Rabindranath attempted to address, by making his school act as the imaginative basis for his university. Just as the coupling of distant (and unconnected) 'levels' of cognitive competence within the machinery of education served a rare promise of social inclusion along previously uncharted routes, so did Tagore's insistence on a "meeting of the East and the West" (1996 [1922]: 556) in a spirit of egalitarian comradeship urge a critical re-examination of the nationalist project as self-consciously exclusionary. The bard saw the university as a fit site for "not a meeting of individuals, but of various human races" – and in the course of which, all forms of collective cultural practice "must find both their freedom of self-expression and their bond of federation" (ibid.: 556). He was even loath to use the word 'University' in describing his fledgling institution to European collaborators, since the burden of historical memory around the term invoked a need for structures of national-bureaucratic control and regimentation. Wary as he was of letting his call for ideational freedom and worldwide cooperation be swamped by regulatory infrastructures that passed for the colonial 'idea' of the university, Tagore pointedly responded to Sir William Rothenstein's proposal to form a board of trustees for Visva Bharati in April 1921:

> [W]hen I sent my appeal to western people for an International Institution in India I made use of the word 'University' for the sake of convenience. But that word not only has an inner meaning but outer associations in minds of those who use it, and that fact tortures my idea into its own rigid shape. It is unfortunate. I should not allow my idea to be pinned to a word like a dead butterfly for a foreign museum. It must be known not by a definition, but by its own life growth. I saved my Shantiniketan from being trampled into smoothness by the steam roller of your education department. . . . [M]y bird must still retain its freedom of wings and not be turned into a sumptuous non-entity by any controlling agency outside its own living organism. I know that the idea of an International University is complex, but I must make it simple in my own way. I shall be content if it attracts round it men who have neither name nor worldly means, but who have the mind and faith, who are to create a great future with their dreams. Very likely I shall never be able to work in harmony with a board of trustees, influential and highly respectable, for I am a vagabond at heart. But the powerful people of the world, the lords of the earth, may make it difficult for me to carry out my work.
>
> (1997 [1921]: 265–6)

Tagore's "idea of an International University", while resolutely opposed to every hint of an imperial inheritance, was to be paradoxically rooted in its own immediate contexts of "life growth" as much as it sought to provide ceaseless "intellectual hospitality" (1996 [1922]: 559) to the world outside. It was through this message of unconstrained cooperation with scholars from all nations that the poet-educator of Visva Bharati strove to "prepare the grand field for the co-ordination of the cultures of the world, where each will give to and take from the other" (1996 [1919]: 485). The governing logic of such a knowledge-exchange, far from being competitively aimed at establishing priority-claims, was to enable a respectful egalitarianism of difference – and not just a liberal-humanist politics of tolerance. It is for this reason that Tagore refused to heed Gandhi's call for non-cooperation and instead launched a reasoned critique of cultural isolationism as philosophically oriented towards an ethic of violence. Even in the heyday of the nationalist movement urging a complete boycott of colonial institutions of education, the political thinker in Rabindranath issued a public disavowal of what he poignantly phrased as "these organisations of National Egoism" (2001 [1921]: 55). In a series of letters addressed to C.F. Andrews (between late 1920 and early 1921, excerpts from which were later published in the *Modern Review* of May 1921), Tagore expressed his urgent distrust of the methods employed by Gandhi and reaffirmed his faith in the unstinted policy of cooperation as the only condition of possibility for his university:

> We have no word for Nation in our language. When we borrow this word from other people, it never fits us. . . . But I know Shantiniketan will not bring forth its fullness of flower and fruit if, through me, it does not send its roots to the western soil. . . . The idea of non-cooperation is political asceticism. Our students are bringing their offering of sacrifices to what? Not to a fuller education but to non-education. It has at its back a fierce joy of annihilation. . . [which] in its passive moral form is asceticism and in its active moral form is violence. . . . Therefore I feel that the true India is an idea and not a mere geographical fact. I have come into touch with this idea in far away places of Europe and my loyalty was drawn to it in persons who belonged to different countries from mine. . . . Therefore my one prayer is: let India stand for the *cooperation* of all peoples of the world. . . . I should feel proud of my humanity when I can acknowledge the poets and artists of other countries as mine own. Let me feel with unalloyed gladness that all the great glories of man are mine. . . . When we have the

intellectual capital of our own, the commerce of thought with the outer world becomes natural and fully profitable. But to say that such commerce is inherently wrong, is to encourage the worst form of provincialism, productive of nothing but intellectual indigence.

(2001 [1920–1921]: 55–62)

The attitude of 'provincialism' that Rabindranath perceived as the logical culmination of non-cooperative nationalism was never at odds with the utilitarian-pragmatic ends of modern education – committed as it was to a routine supply of "clerks, deputy magistrates, pleaders, or physicians" (1996 [1919]: 473) – because it merely attempted to wrest control of an alien idea of the university. Nor did it posit an alternative ethic of communitarian exchange against the colonial touchstone of the 'nation'. Quite on the contrary, Tagore prophetically (and indeed instructively for our times!) identified its fantasies for a 'National University' as "only another name for a Hindu university" (ibid.: 490). The cultural mission appropriated by a nationalist order of resistance could not but breed, in the long run, a fascistic self-aggrandisement of dominant intellectual traditions and a ruthless indifference to minority representations of history. Such an eventuality irked Tagore out of any residual sympathy with the agitational politics of *Swadeshi*, in that it increasingly anticipated the retrogressive forces of a genocidal culturalism.

There was of course no element of surprise in the climate of wholesale censure that Tagore's public positions occasioned – not only from journalistic communities of opinion, but also among considerably large sections of the contemporary intelligentsia. As early as in 1917 – while Rabindranath was still working out his tentative proposal for Visva Bharati in stark defiance of the *Swadeshi* agenda for cultural purism – Chittaranjan Das launched a virulent tirade in his Presidential address at the Bengal Provincial Conference. Recalling excerpts from Tagore's lectures on nationalism in the USA, decrying the collusion of the 'nation' with a politics of cultural militancy and economic self-interest, Das made out a case of treacherous infidelity and delusive 'punditry' against the poet:

> Some 'Pandits' in Europe are said to have discovered that the nation-idea is entirely imaginary. . . . As a necessary consequence, some of our own people have got hold of the idea and are seeking to pooh-pooh our nascent desire for national life on the strength of this new-found theory of theirs. . . . Even Rabindranath, who had been the high-priest of the nation-idea at the inception of the

Swadesi Movement, is said to have laid considerable emphasis upon this new-old doctrine during his recent tour in America. . . . It seems to me, then, that the whole of this anti-nation idea is unsubstantial – based upon a vague and nebulous conception of universal humanity. Each nation must develop its latent manhood 'as a nation', ere it is possible to rouse within it a sense of true amity and togetherliness.

(Ghosh 1972: 28–9)

The "true amity and togetherliness" that Das saw forestalled in Tagore's sharpening critique of the 'nation-idea' was what the latter feared as a fanatic mandate for 'uniformity' and a forced assimilation of difference. The poet was well aware of its mystical appeal for 'self-sacrifice' – and surmised in it an irreducible will to violence despite the rhetorical garment of *ahimsa*'. He was determinedly against letting this spirit of 'annihilation' (as he calls it!) invade his idea of creative knowledge-practice at Visva Bharati – a point that even his trusted friend and historian Jadunath Sarkar came to express reservations about. In response to a letter from Tagore inviting the acclaimed scholar of history to join the governing committee of Visva Bharati in May 1922, Sarkar formulated a critique of the university's aesthetic internationalism as founded on unsure academic grounds. He articulated a degree of suspicion about the rigour and discipline of undergraduate training at Tagore's university, and diagnosed it as the result of a supercilious preoccupation with 'diversity' (Chakravarty 2011). Needless to say, Tagore was painfully wounded by such scepticism from one of his closest associates – and before long, this rift translated into an irredeemable estrangement between the two.

The rampant misgivings about Tagore's educational philosophy as fundamentally unhinged from concerns of the 'national' movement (as well as the nascent glimmers of a colony's self-articulation as 'nation-state') are, however, farthest from the truth. Rabindranth too contributed his share to this body of hermeneutic misappropriations around his work in Shantiniketan, through consistent references to his own world of belief under vacuous Enlightenment rubrics like 'universal humanism', 'spiritual brotherhood of man' and 'internationalism'. The liberalism of intent that has thus been equated with the bard's conception of the university – as rooted in an abstract secular-modern ideal of *cosmopolitics* – falsifies much of its real purpose and purview. Scholarly and social scientific assessments of the 'Visva Bharati ideal' have laboriously strutted about in borrowed ideological abstractions like universalism or transnationalism (Bhattacharya 2014: 71–3; Majumdar

16 Debaditya Bhattacharya

2001), but only to overlook the relentless insistence in Rabindranath's pedagogical practice to an immediate agenda of social justice.

Material histories of intellectual privilege and production were in fact at the heart of Tagore's structural experiments with the university – and to dilute the socially transgressive potential of his pedagogy in a metaphysics of 'spiritual unity' is an act of definite injustice. We shall have occasion to talk about this in the very next section, but for now it must suffice to say that the 'world university' of Tagorean imagination does not in any way pre-empt an auctioning of the 'nation' unto a Darwinist global order of *efficient survivability*. Instead, it resolutely stands in resistance to the logic of competitive self-sustenance that now guides the life of the public university. To talk of Visva Bharati as simply embodying a principle of 'internationalist cooperation' unwittingly calls forth an absurd analogy with the current fortunes of higher education – but this is a patent manipulation of discourse!

It is true that Tagore was deeply distrustful of the trajectories of 'nation-building' evident in the West, and had already come to disavow allegiance to any such tendencies of collective self-expression by the time of the First World War (1996 [1917]: 419–66). The founding of a university became, for him, a means of reinventing the idea of the nation in stark contradistinction to the forces that moulded it in Europe. It was through Visva Bharati that Tagore proposed and worked out the manifesto for an alternative conception of nationhood as a community bound by the power of *eros*. The ethical basis for constituting such a nation was to be an erotic engagement with the 'other' in and through education. It was to be *a pedagogy of love*, performed at the limits of one's knowledge of the self. Tagore was convinced that a nation committed to justice must have as its precondition the pain of self-knowledge. To *learn to love what lies at the limit* (of social experience) necessitates the agony of having to suffer the knowledge of one's own incompleteness. And it is through a historical apportioning of justice at this limit that one can eventually exceed the mystique of nationalism, and move towards a radically altered polity of what Benjamin calls the spirit of 'creative *eros*'. The university might embody the nation only insofar as it opens up the latter's relationship with the *aporetic* – and it is here that 'creativity' finds its true meaning by re-designating *the social as the infinite play of the erotic*. The re-configuring of relations of production as renewed sites of erotic investment is the only task of the Tagorean university.

> The power is where there is right, and where there is the dedication of love. It is *maya* to imagine that the gift of self-government

is somewhere outside us. It is like a fruit that the tree must produce itself through its own normal function, by the help of its inner resources. It is not a Chinese lantern, flimsily gaudy, that can be bought from a foreign second-hand shop to be hung on the tree to illuminate its fruitlessness. . . . Of course turning out songs is my proper work. But those who are unfortunate cannot afford to limit their choice to the works they can do; they must also bear the burdens of the tasks they can not do!

(Tagore 1921: 355–6)

Social inclusion at the university: practice or project?

It is well worth asking at this point: how exactly might the transgressive idea of the 'nation' take shape in the university? What are its practical modalities of expression, and through what means might those within the university execute such a transformation? In other words, what are the material implications of the university's commitment to social justice – apart from limited meritocratic structures of access into its insides? It is here that Tagore confronts questions about the 'use' of a university of his kind – and he repeatedly urges an earnest engagement with these questions. Though thoroughly dismissive of the utilitarian character of formal education and the 'success'-cult of aspirational materialism that it sets in motion, Rabindranath insisted that the university's demonstration of its own 'use' might work as an accurate antidote to the delirious self-seeking that results of it. In a much-quoted letter to Leonard Elmhirst, dated 19 December 1937, the poet incisively recalled:

> It is well known that the education which is prevalent in our country is extremely meagre in the spread of its area and barren in its quality. Unfortunately, this is all that is available for us and the artificial standard set up is proudly considered respectable. Outside the *bhadralok* class, pathetic in its struggle to affix university labels to the names of its members, there is a vast obscure multitude who cannot even dream of such a costly ambition. With them we have our best opportunity if we know how to *use* it there, and there only can we be free to offer to our country the best kind of all-round culture not mutilated by the official dictators.
>
> (Tagore 1997 [1937]: 490–1)

The official diktats of 'accountability' and 'social relevance' that now seek to bulldoze public universities into self-financed service-counters or advisory appendages for industrial corporations are what Rabindranath prophetically cautions us against, by urging the university to escape its respectable idealism of mere 'disinterestedness'. That knowledge is opaque to the quantitative logics of production has nauseatingly eaten into the commonsense-imagination of the university today, as much as it has invited top-down bureaucratic efforts at rationalization. Discerningly, Tagore alerted us to this possibility of the university being turned against its idea by external prescriptions of 'goals' and 'objectives', since the time of his early lectures on Visva Bharati. He repeatedly stressed the need for the institution to participate in the economic life of the nation, lest the contingent forces of economy begin to manufacture a role for it (1996 [1919]: 490). What he meant was that the university must be in a direct and constant communion with the life that it excludes – in other words, with a self-consciousness of its intellectual entitlements and an ethical investment in forms of *work* that exceed such relations of privilege. If this be ignored, 'economic life' translates into 'employability' – the 'vocational spirit' of liberal higher education that I began by referring to.

In his essay 'An Eastern University', Tagore writes about the 'use' of a pedagogy of love:

> [T]here should be some common sharing of life with the tillers of the soil and the humble workers in the neighbouring villages; studying their crafts, inviting them to the feasts, joining them in works of co-operation for communal welfare; and in our intercourse we should be guided, not by moral maxims or the condescension of social superiority, but by natural sympathy of life for life, and by the sheer necessity of love's sacrifice for its own sake.
>
> (1996 [1922]: 568)

Importantly enough, this co-operative principle of university life – as envisioned here – is a commitment to social justice as distinct from a call to 'social service', because its "motive force is not the greed of profit" (ibid.: 567). It was in pursuance of this rationale of the 'university's use' that Tagore deliberately founded Visva Bharati in a provincial location (far from urban-industrial communities of labour) and made his school of rural children coming from neighbouring villages remain the guiding force behind his university. However, he did not stop at that. In February 1922, he inaugurated the Institute of Rural Reconstruction in a plot of village land adjacent to the Shantiniketan campus, which was to be later named as Sriniketan. Through a confluence of instructors from across the world, including Leonard K. Elmhirst, Arthur Geddes and Kim Taro Kasahara, the Sriniketan experiment was imagined as an organic extension of the university into the worlds of disparate rural experience. A combination of agricultural research, cottage industrial training, public health measures, elementary and adult education in night schools as well as varied forms of popular entertainment inserted the constituencies of intellectual practice at the university within local material contexts of dispossession. The opening of Shiksha Satra in 1924, with a declared intention of fighting structural manifestations of social injustice by providing free educational opportunities to children of the village folk, and the Lok Shiksha Sansad in 1937 to further the cause of mass education in the distance mode – completed Tagore's vision of the university's 'lifeworld'. The privileged insulation of higher education was sought to be constantly called into question through unmediated encounters with the reality of a life 'outside' its own enclosures. Because, as Tagore maintained in his essay 'Palli-Seva':

> When our college students study economics and ethnology, they rely entirely on European scholarship to learn about their own villages. The rural people mean nothing to us because we regard them as *chhotolok*, meaning, literally, small people. Given such contempt for their own village people, it is not surprising that educated Indians prefer to learn about their country's history and society from the Europeans. There have been many an ethnological 'movement' among our common people. Our educated class is ignorant about those. It takes no interest in its native environment because it does not have to study it to pass examinations.
> (Tagore 1926: 64–5)

However, this ritual initiation of the university student into 'native environments' of social production was neither to be peddled as philanthropic intention nor as an exercise in vocational skill training. The modern university's habitual oscillations between a consecrative nationalism and economic pragmatism can unproblematically balance a fascist demand for 'service' with a token exhibition of what, in our times, has come to be hailed as 'corporate social responsibility'.

If a transformative re-imagining of the nation was to be the 'use' of the university, it cannot re-fashion the privilege of 'access' as either an obligatory call to patriotic duty or to self-expiation in 'conscientious' economic desire. It must live up to its 'ideal', which – as Tagore put it – "is not specially set apart to be doled out as famine ration carefully calculated to be just good enough for emaciated life and dwarfed mentality" (1997 [1937]: 490). Instead, the university must own up to its collusion with structures of historical injustice – and, exceed itself unto an ethical striving for the 'outside'. In this alone might it embody a spirit of critique, as intimately folded into a future of *difference*. This erotic work of education – as I previously elucidated – is not the charge of 'selfless' philanthropy, just as it cannot be the basis for employability *by other means*. Tagore was keenly conscious that the ethic of 'selflessness' is only an extreme form of possessive individualism – where the incorporeal subject of 'service' becomes the name for a metaphysical essence of belonging. Hence, the university's compulsory encounter with 'otherness' is no social service agenda – it must, unequivocally and unalterably, be apprenticed to the cause of social justice. It must institute a living relationship with spaces

> fast degenerating into serfdom, compelled to offer to the ungrateful towns cheerless and unintelligent labour for work carried on in an unhealthy and impoverished environment. The object of Sriniketan is to bring back life in its completeness into the villages, making them self-reliant and self-respectful, acquainted with the cultural tradition of their own country, and competent to make an efficient use of the modern resources for the improvement of their physical, intellectual and economic condition.
> (Tagore 1928: 1)

Almost a hundred years into the Tagorean 'experiment' with rural life as being at the centre of the university's pedagogical mission, its dream for a future has been veritably converted into a tragic pathology. The organic life of the university that Rabindranath proposed as a form of embodied practice has now taken on the charge of 'social relevance' by an altogether different route of skill development. As a result, the university's erotic investments in a project of rural reconstruction stand inverted in a maniacal hunger for developmental economics. Instead of being entrenched in a default relationship with alterity – that is, an *agonism* of social relations as the means to a transgressive imagination of the nation – the current-day university has yielded to the universalizing tendencies of the global labour market. Advocating a wholesale vocationalization of higher education, quantum measures of skill 'output' have come to mediate the relationship between a symbolically disenfranchised rural populace and the largely elite-metropolitan university (GoI 2008a, 2009a, 2009b, 2015b). In this, concerns for rural development have conveniently coincided with increasing

Introduction 21

numbers of higher education institutions (HEIs), but only insofar as the metric for social justice is made incumbent on a greater reproducibility of existing social relations. The more the amount of skill training and the more the magnitude of expendable/outsourceable labour, the more likely is a statistical flourish of national 'growth' indicators (GoI 2015b, 2015c; Agarwal 2017: 134; World Bank 2006). The policy-dictated euphoria over rural self-empowerment through access to university education is all about creasing out the disparities of social capital through a uniform standard of employable 'skills' (Sabharwal and Kannan 2017: 100–1).

In all of this, the implosion of the idea of the university in a sovereign fetish over the exchange value of 'knowledge' takes one back to a larger game of numbers. The striking profligacy of governmental interest in tying the fortunes of higher education to vocational skills training – since the National Knowledge Commission's recommendation for merging the latter with "mainstream education system" (2009a: 14), Delhi University's experimental introduction of a Four Year Undergraduate Programme (FYUP) in 2013 with an added year of application-oriented cognitive coursework, or more recently, the establishment of a Ministry of Skill Development and Entrepreneurship (MSDE) in 2014 and then the National Policy on Skill Development in July 2015 – relates to a race for greater Gross Enrolment Ratios (GER) in the Indian context (MHRD 2014: 15–20; GoI 2015b). That a democratic promise of 'access' must proportionately bolster a numerical indexing of 'development', through greater evidence of institutional enrolments, is part of the neoliberal university's *raison d'être*. But, the fact that the affordability and accessibility of institutional learning no longer cohere in a principle of social justice is borne out by a deeper look at these numbers. In a country where 93 percent of its workforce is employed in the informal sector (NSSO 2001a; NSSO 2001b; Unni 2002: Table 3; GoI 2008b) – with no guarantee of a regularized pay, social security, humane working conditions or leave entitlements – would mass vocational education really facilitate a life of dignified employment or even bargaining powers to that effect? With recent Labour Bureau Surveys fixing the composition of skilled labour at a meagre 2 percent of roughly 470 million of the country's working population (GoI 2014a, 2015a) and the demographic fraction with vocational/skill training ranging between 5.4 and 6.8 percent (GoI 2016b, 2015a, 2014b), there is already a surplus of available skills in the job market that evidently fail the employability test. Put plainly, there is more than triple the amount of skills than there are jobs to absorb them (Varma 2015). In such a situation, institutional incentives for skill-development programmes will further compound a reserve pool of qualified labour that must either be left to the contingencies of the unorganized sector, or be forced to offset its opportunity costs through a vicious cycle of ceaseless debt. Yet, the Indian government's invitation to 'top' institutions to honour their newly achieved glory of 'autonomy' by starting self-financed "skill courses, consistent with the National Skills Qualification Framework" (GoI 2018a: 8) – and its plans for overhauling the regulatory framework with a permanent ex officio installation of an MSDE representative (GoI 2018c: 2) – betoken the paradoxes of state reform. Without embarking on policy initiatives of capacity-building within the formal economy, the current thrust on wholesale vocationalization can only aggravate the 'crisis' in the lure of entrepreneurial 'self-help'. Additionally, in the absence of proportionate inductions by the job market, regimes of institutional skill training are likely to accentuate wage disparities between massive sections of the skilled workforce – by deeming the lack of formal recognition as tantamount to a lack of technical competence. The internal conflicts of interest within communities of identical labour automatically strengthen the sway of capital, by creating self-warring factions within marginalized social groups.

Tellingly, Tagore had – by the end of his life – grown disillusioned with his own imaginative claims around the university as an alternative public sphere. The reflexive potential of an erotic subjectification that he helped found in Visva Bharati – by moving away from the colonial origins of the university – was already giving way to a cognitive homogeneity of *unfreedom* by the late 1930s. He regretted the ideological incursions of 'competence' and commensurate 'progress', that increasingly sought to vocationalize a pedagogy based on the performative *promise* of love. The university, he could succinctly predict, was returning to its destinal foreignness of *purpose* from *method* – while the principle of entrepreneurial self-interest had overtaken the life of the mind as a life dedicated to the 'state'. But, despite these depressing glimpses into an imminent future for his university, Tagore was mightily confident that his project of rural reconstruction would continue to hold out the promise of a different education. Having severally called it "an education for fullness" (Mukherjee 2013 [1962]), he said in the above-cited letter to Elmhirst in 1937:

> I myself attach much more significance to the educational possibilities of Shiksha Satra than to the school and college at Shantiniketan which are everyday becoming more and more like so many schools and colleges elsewhere in this country, borrowed cages

that treat the students' minds as captive birds whose sole human value is judged according to the mechanical repetition of lessons, prescribed by an educational dispensation foreign to the soil. It would indeed give me great joy if Sriniketan could at last make use of its opportunities to realise my dream.

(ibid.: 491)

Those "educational possibilities" – in as far as they have bred our era of skill development missions as the unquestionable culmination of the 'inclusive' university – have tragically spent the Tagorean dream of 'social justice' in statistics and vision documents.

Confronting utility: a politics of the future

Following on the lessons from Benjamin and Tagore, this volume argues that a politics of the university's future must necessarily begin from a premise of self-critique. The traditions of liberal wisdom and economies of meritocratic access and social privilege that the 'idea' of the university has instituted in a relationship of narcissistic self-absorption must, by default, become the conditions of thinking its own political future. Public discourse about the university needs to exceed the enchantments of a self-image, especially when infrastructural networks of knowledge-dissemination have always been sites of reproducing relations of power – between the caste-elite male and the subaltern, the global-metropolitan and the suburban-rural, the exact sciences and philosophy, the intellectual and non-intellectual communities of labour. The task of progressive politics is to work the question of access into an awareness of the class, caste and gendered nature of all levels of education, without mystifying the university as an achieved idea[l] of freedom.

Also, it begs reiterating that the history of the university has never been immune to questions of 'use'. From the medieval instantiation of the *universitas* as a corporate body seeking to protect the interests of the ecclesiastical elite to the Kantian faculties of academic instruction securing the disinterested rationale of an Enlightenment modernity, institutions of 'higher' learning have always contributed to the making of a *useful* class of citizens and their material relations of production. It suits no purpose therefore to argue for a pristine chastity of the right to intellectual labour – because that veers perilously close to what government reports and commissions insidiously urge for in 'depoliticizing' campus spaces. Nor does the postmodern exhilaration of a 'secret surplus' in the insurrectionary power of classroom pedagogies go much further, in their singular disregard for the political economy of structural change. It remains for our universities to confront the fetish of 'utility' by neither playing unto the state's drive towards a bureaucratized managerial order of 'anti-politics' nor its penchant for 'reform' and innovation.

Instead, it needs to be reiterated *ad nauseam* that the 'use' of the university is in emphatically politicizing the right to reason and intellectual labour, rather than insisting on its own singular appropriation of it. In this, the university is called upon to bear witness to its own liminalities as a structural precondition for social justice. The raptures of a self-possessed *insiderism* that the university's call to freedom and autonomy has amounted to must give in to a parasitic alliance with the banal 'outsides' of reason – not just in polemical spectres, but in engaged political activism against the theoretical-liberal 'idea of the university'. This does not, however, vindicate the vocational as a means of reconnecting the university with the realm of material practice, because the 'Skill India' programmes of contemporary lore only serve to commodify the tactical contingencies of everyday practice into [abstract] socially necessary labour-time. In so doing, the drive towards vocationalization normalizes the history of social-intellectual deprivation as the very condition of possibility of economic mobility. The 'welfare-reforms' regime of the liberal university is therefore particularly suited to repeating the horrors of systemic inequity through its devious ploys of 'democratic access' and 'employability'. A university without the political mission of interrogating its own ontologies – that is, a mission of radical self-transformation – is a university of no 'use', and is indeed a useless 'idea'.

It is with this agony of self-questioning that we hope to have put together a public archive of resistance, radically questioning the "idea" of the university – not as the expression of an aspirational class-unconscious, but as the promise of a time of justice. We only hope to leave the reader in excruciating doubt. And with it, a pledge for intimate solidarity, not to 'save' the idea of the university but to fight it towards a progressive future.

Is defending the university enough?

The essays collected here will variously attempt to work around this "idea" of the university, from its historical origins to current debates on its existence and sustenance in a neoliberal India. Given the systematic attempt at curtailing public spending on higher education since the late 1970s in Europe and America and consequently within postcolonial developing countries through the 1990s onwards, what is at stake is not just the physical-institutional infrastructures of higher education, but the very "idea" of the university in terms of its politics and pedagogy. What is this "idea" of the university that we are out to defend? Does the work of defence preclude the task of rearranging the idea itself? This being the first question that we invite readers to reflect upon, it is important for us to challenge the Humboldtian-Newmanian or the liberal-humanist 'ideal' of academic exchange that has long overshadowed debates on the *true* nature of the modern university.

The attempt here is thus to hint at the political future(s) of the university, not by a simplistic recourse to the tenets of liberal democracy but through a more engaged positioning of the university space within everyday practices of the social. Is the university, as we often like to believe, to be protected as a privileged safety valve of *dissensual* consciousness – or must it rather be conceived outside of the romantic logic of Enlightenment emancipation? Is the university, by virtue of its civic enclosures and largely urban-metropolitan roots as well as a merit-based economy of access, protected against the incursions of the 'commons' as a ghetto of proprietorial intellectual activity? Can the 'idea' of the university alone invoke greater safeguards against power, when all other spheres of social-cultural production are increasingly giving way? What is the history of this 'ideal' university's relationship with the banal everyday, the 'apolitical' outside and what exceeds intellectual reason – and is such historicizing necessary at all? How has this 'inside-outside' dichotomy in relation to the university been used by policy-makers to delegitimize intellectual production for its social-material disconnect on the one hand, and its potential for political alliance on the other? Insofar as organized state attempts at linking university education with skill development agendas claim a noble convergence of the spheres of the social and the pedagogical, how far does it carry its pledge to social justice?

Notwithstanding the all-too-popular commonsense-charges of elitism and exceptionalism levelled at the university community, how would we want the current-day public university to enable a 'democratic intuition of the other'? In this sense, how does one re-bind the 'cognitive training of distinctions' thought to be the proper task of the university with the banal practices of democracy, without easy recourse to a Cartesian argument of rational debate and inquiry? What is the role of the non-urban/non-metropolitan university in achieving this, or for that matter the communities of non-intellectual labour within university spaces? How do the institutes of technology and management or law and medical schools relate to this 'idea' of the university, in routinely mobilizing 'merit' as capital investment for standards of accountability in human resource and public service? In a WTO-governed economy of education-as-tradable-service and its beneficiaries as clientele, what are the exact material/infrastructural/policy challenges that we are up against? How does the private university, while often espousing the liberal principle of academic-administrative autonomy, stand with regard to the future/s of a politics of higher education? Recent incidents in the institutional murder of a Dalit student in Hyderabad Central University, the forced disappearance of a Muslim student from another university campus, the arrest and planned witch-hunt of student leaders as well as teachers in university campuses across India, the steep fee-hike in the Indian Institutes of Technology, the threat of withdrawal of research fellowships, the curtailing of project grants leading to a shutdown of research organizations, the whole-scale contractualization of teaching posts, the planting of ruling-party-stooges in positions of administrative authority within institutions of higher education in India might provide an entry-point into conversations ploughed from across the world.

Reading hope into resolve: narrating futures

What follows in the pages of this collection is an intensely passionate conjecture on the *forms* of possibility engendered by the public university, though with critical attentiveness to its specific roots and iterations. Against a backdrop of the precise historical trajectories of the Indian public university, Janaki Nair poses a set of keen questions about its continuing relevance in both serving as well as critiquing state formations. While worldwide trends in higher education portend a future for the 'idea' of the university – as being surmounted by market principles and a managerial economy of outcomes – the Indian context begs to be read in the light of its own pasts and promises. The contemporary surfeit of state-sponsored clampdowns on intellectual spaces in the country, Nair argues, requires of us a reasoned debate about possible modes of defence. However, in our laudatory attempts at hailing traditions of academic autonomy, we must renew the university's pledge to self-reflection as a 'public good'. What and who constitutes this 'publicness' of its character, and how might an engaged positioning of such institutions within democratic agendas of public interest revive their future potential? It is within such frames of critical re-assessment that public perceptions around the Indian university – as increasingly a site of 'provocation', anxiety and control – may be productively addressed.

Aditya Nigam sounds a significant strain in his essay 'Decolonizing the University', by maintaining that the entire history of post-independence educational policy in India has been unthinkingly commissioned by an allegiance to colonial economic modernity. Having borrowed the disciplinary apparatuses of intellectual inquiry from Western self-definitions of the 'modern', the Indian university is either fated to an insufficient search for global relevance or to jingoistic priority-claims around a fiction of the 'indigenous' past. While the former resonates in policy attempts to conscribe universities to a transnational order of capital, the latter reflects most corrosively in the rhetorical harvest of Hindutva. Nigam observes that a true "swaraj in ideas" cannot reproduce the modes of Western self-presentation in hollow conjurings of a mythical 'norm', but must involve an act of intense theoretical labour in understanding the needs of our present and determining our future on our own terms. These terms mandate intellectual alliances beyond normative frames of reference, and the decolonization of the university – both in terms of the content and language of knowledge production – might potentially be the stage for it.

Supriya Chaudhuri sees in the 'crisis' of the Indian public university not only the all-too-visible attempt by ruling-party hegemonies to appropriate regimes of intellectual production, but also (and more importantly) the lingering policy imbalances of a Nehruvian legacy. The large-scale bureaucratization of the academy, as the practical underside of state funding, has increasingly eroded the *parrhesiac* potential of university communities – till the recent NPE draft goes on to unabashedly propose a centralized mechanism of faculty recruitment from cadre-based education services. Commenting on the recent re-invention of liberal arts education within exorbitantly priced private university curricula, Chaudhuri urges a serious engagement with the 'new humanities' from within public-funded institutions of higher education today. It is only through the interconnectedness of these disciplines that the public nature of the public university may now be realized, in forging an alliance with all 'other' meanings and possibilities of the human as the *pre*-condition of democracy.

The European liberal university, in its present appropriation by an order of technocratic managerialism, has rightfully provoked widespread angst and alarm. Yet – as Mosarrap Hossain Khan argues – much of this anxiety within progressive-liberal circles of the international academia is laced with a lament for the loss of the university's national cultural mission, as envisioned in the Humboldtian instance. Khan goes on to contend that the case of India is distinctly more complex – in that its history of the European import of a 'liberal humanist' university has never quite confronted the question of 'national culture'. It is this discursive project, long aborted by India's colonial encounters with knowledge-institutions, that now seems to have been taken up by Hindutva forces. The deep ambiguities within a Nehruvian paradigm of 'nation-building' – skirting away the irrational excesses of a postcolonial unconscious in the ill-translated overtones of a secular-industrial polity – are currently exhumed in the fascist fantasies of an 'invented' national culture.

Dhruba Jyoti Saikia and Rowena Robinson, in their meticulous analysis of scientific research conditions in India, investigate the structural reasons for 'quality' issues with journal publications from the university sector. Though, historically speaking, the best of scientific research has emerged from public universities through the first half of the twentieth century, policy measures of the post-independence period attempted a bifurcation of scientific training and research away from the universities and subsequently localized them within national laboratory-structures of independent institutes. Saikia and Robinson observe that the deliberate alienation of the university sector from effective goals of scientific knowledge-creation – through a combination of inadequate infrastructures, bureaucratic administrations and pedagogical inertia within teaching-learning processes – has fed into a culture of 'received' rote-learning with little impetus for critical inquiry-based science. This has been further aggravated by the menace of 'predatory journals', absurd regulatory frameworks and measures of individual 'output' that discourage collaborative engagement. The university's mission of disseminating scientific knowledge in larger public interest is marred by a systemic encouragement of 'safe' research and 'risk-aversion' – geared largely towards a personal ethic of 'advancement'.

Shobhit Mahajan begins by noting the demographic changes within student communities at public universities, following the implementation of affirmative action policies in India. In this, he sustainably builds a case against the detractors of caste-based reservation by analysing current data relating to the historical composition of university entrants. However, Mahajan contends that a token policy of structural 'access' does little to correct historical prejudice, insofar as infrastructures of communication and social capital are stacked against the marginalized. For the university to really open itself up to those systemically excluded from its precincts, there needs to be institutional encouragement of a public culture of science. Scientists and scientific workers within universities are called upon to disenchant and demystify the language of specialization. The author insists on broad-based knowledge-coalitions working in the vernacular languages to design quality textbooks, deliver public lectures and turn the sciences towards the everyday life of democratic citizenship.

In moving beyond the need for a protectionist discourse on the university, Anup Dhar raises some wonderfully pertinent questions about the future of the extant university-imagination in his essay. Can the university become a site for a "post-capitalist *praxis*", and not just an "anti-capitalist *critique*"? How might the standard surviving expression of the university become adequate to a form of educational experience that *does* more than critical knowledge production – or, in fact, produces a triadic epistemological adventure of 'knowing-being-doing'? Praxis – as what Dhar accurately identifies as the "foreclosed of the university-imagination" – is precisely the Tagorean formulation of a radical critique of colonial education systems in Shantiniketan and Sriniketan. A form of pedagogy that works with and through (and not *on*) the slave's knowledge-praxis could, in Tagore's worldview, bridge the life-worlds of the subaltern and the theoretical alienation of cognitivist learning. It is here that Lacan's Discourse of the University betrays its alliance with the Master's Discourse, as opposed to its classical self-presentation as being on the side of the slave. Dhar titillatingly postulates the 'idea' of Development Practice (currently embodied through an M.Phil. programme at Ambedkar University Delhi) as consisting in an attempt to re-vision the university as a mode of 'action*ing* research' and 'righting/writing wrongs' – a movement towards transformative praxis!

In an extremely significant intervention, Lawrence Liang turns the debate on academic freedom to issues around the ownership of knowledge and questions of intellectual property. The larger policy drive towards privatization of education sits all too well with a politics of patenting and copyright within the domain of academic knowledge, in this age of monopoly print-capital. Liang offers a pointed critique of how the circumscription of knowledge as 'property' goes against the Kantian idea of the university, as a space of substantive freedom from all forms of control. Taking off from the two landmark judgments of the Delhi High Court in relation to the DU photocopying case, the author goes on to engage with the specific import of 'fair dealing' exceptions within copyright law and their interpretive amplitude in favour of an equitable access to knowledge. For societies working with a history of graded dispossessions with regard to social capital, imagining the university as a collegial community of public knowledge is a resolute reclamation of it.

My essay in the volume works around a specific paradox that governs the current fate and possible futures of interdisciplinary intellectual practice within the university. How is it that the contemporary historical moment is simultaneously witness to a euphemistic extolling as well as a systematic hostility directed at the institutional practice of 'interdisciplinarity'? While the former attitude considers *certain* expressions of such academic practice as crucial to the cognitive 'competence' demanded by transnational labour-markets, the latter regards *certain other* forms of its practice within the university as redundant and therefore worthy of being defunded and allowed to perish. In trying to chart the motivations behind this 'curious' ambivalence of policy directions, I begin by looking at the origins of the scientific 'discipline' in Enlightenment Europe and its epistemological promise for a colonial project of control. Subsequently, the internally fraught history of academic specialization – in occasionally 'forging' ties with interdisciplinarity – has evolved divergent responses and crucial disjunctures with regard to the university's relationship with the social. I explore, in this essay, the ethico-political condition of interdisciplinary knowledge-practice as the 'dangerous' ground for re-imagining 'social justice'.

Prabhat Patnaik finally prepares the ground for a manifesto on Indian higher education, by marking out its historical transition from a state-funded welfare model to a neoliberal oligarchy of private economic interests. He contends that this period of transformation does not just produce a more flexible and exploitable labour-force for the international market, but also irredeemably converts the very nature of the intellectual 'input' that goes into manufacturing such a workforce. Faced with a complete disappearance of the use value of education – that is, its potential for democratic-critical inquiry and social sensitivity – within the profit-motives that govern its exchange in the international market, the university too is peddled as an *absolute* commodity. The successive weakening of a secular-democratic consensus as central to the idea of higher education makes the latter serve as an apology for communal-fascist forces, while being harnessed to the empire of global finance capital. Addressing income-wealth inequalities through capital controls and a thoroughgoing overhaul of the economic policy framework, Patnaik suggests, might be the only route to "reviving" university systems.

Referring to organized onslaughts on the democratic-civic potential of higher education as a war on "memory, agency and the political", Henry A. Giroux delves into contemporary forms of the American 'cultural consensus' with great immediacy. At a time when all critical

Introduction 31

public spheres aimed at training citizens into a practice of freedom and the struggle for justice are under threat, the university becomes the site of producing a version of self-aggrandizing 'commonsense'. The latter sees students as human capital and social relations as reproducing what Giroux calls the 'Walmart model' of production. The right-wing defence of such strategies of symbolic co-optation by the market is all too predictable, in order for a rule of hate and terror to gain legitimation from an unthinking citizenry. The systematic attacks on faculty tenure and academic autonomy across university campuses in the US foretell a heightened aggression against spaces of civic literacy in the era of Donald Trump. Giroux hints at a set of concrete measures that must make for a politics of radical resistance against this wholesale bartering of democracy for unfreedom – and in the process, force university workers to structure social movements as pedagogical campaigns.

A concise piece by Ari Sitas, 'The University in Question', works through a further set of incisive pointers that map the destinal possibilities in/of the university. Having framed his reflections within the overarching narrative of a fiscal-political 'crisis', Sitas expresses concern about the imaginative poverty of popular idioms of resistance. What is missing from campus struggles, against both political authoritarianism and corporate fundamentalism, is a radically alternative idea of the university – and in the absence of which, most movements languish in a romantic-mythical ideal of a welfarist past. Such symbolic articulations of a golden 'norm' not only achieve a strategic elision of the material histories of the university, but also foreclose the imaginative fecundity of political passion by looking for neat theoretical touchstones. It begs of our present conjuncture, therefore, to question the fundamental assumptions and matrices of monastic/imperial power that went into the fashioning of the university – and which might now become the basis for a re-conceptualization of its purpose and practice.

Continuing the urgency of a plea, Peter McLaren ends by arguing for a material practice of revolutionary critical pedagogy as the only viable 'task' of the university. The transnational consolidation of capital, he argues, works by manufacturing a fiction of the market as the hope of an equitable future as well as the ubiquitous law of nature. The function of critical pedagogy, in taking off from Paulo Freire's work, lies in enabling a movement from this false consciousness to critical self-consciousness. The critical educator – counterposed against the figure of the 'neutral' academic – must perform the political role of an 'activist-interventionist' by exposing the myth of the market as founding the default rule of inequity. Consequently, McLaren insists that the space of pedagogical insurrections within the classroom might become the condition of a return to *true community* – by welding theory with an immediate agenda of historical justice. The ruthless subsumption of social hierarchies within a humanism of individual 'nature', and the infinite reproduction of 'value' as the norm of consumption are what critical pedagogy must confront and unconceal as the structural premise of capitalist desire.

The historical 'unthought': returning to *The Idea of the University*

Having briefly surveyed the range of themes and convictions that occasion the political-emotional charge of essays included in this volume, I place this work in the custody of all who care to think (about) the university. There is reasonable consensus about this being the time to think the university anew, not just rethink it. And in this task, we open the future of higher education to what I have named as the domain of the 'unthought'. The infinity that threatens the 'unthought' – as the formative unconscious of institutional reason – is what must be imagined as the democratic condition of a university. Its most proper rationale is in training its 'initiates' into a practice of imagining and engaging with *ir*-rationality on its own terms. The foreclosures of knowledge – with regard to both the subject and object of university learning – must open into a manifesto for our collective futures. The university must indeed be 'politically' unthought, for it to be materially viable to resist the onslaughts of the present. The 'Notes for a Future', as what are contained in these pages, do not signify a visible *mise-en-scène* for a university in 2020 (as empty political rhetoric goes!), but it hints at issues that must be imaginatively attended to if the university is to be seen through to a future.

It definitely begs being reiterated that our anticipated futures – for the institution that all of us, contributors to this volume, belong to in different ways and through divergent disciplinary rites of passage – cannot be identical. A vision for a desired future cannot be an excuse for naive imitative idealism; it must be achieved through close and critical conversations with our differential histories, modernities and traditions. Though the forces of transnational capital work to elide our particular relationships with and experiences of the public university, the responsibility of resistance lies in choosing the exact trajectories of change that are historically warranted. In all of this, what is of utmost concern is how to reclaim the 'public-ness' of the public university – while working within contesting imaginations and orderings of space, place, nation, culture and necessity. Heeding such a need for historical perspective, this volume feeds into another companion anthology titled *The Idea of the University: Histories and Contexts*. The latter seeks to provide a glimpse into the historical discourses that have driven material-epistemological transformations within specific university-settings, without risking them into a linear narrative.

Let me conclude with a direct reference to a populist political archive around the university. Soon after the advance GDP estimates for India were tailored to offset the corrosive impact of a demonetization drive – a move that banned 86 percent of legal tender circulating in the national economy and brought untold misery to millions working in the informal sector, in the name of curbing 'black money' – the Prime Minister went on record to brandish his success as consisting in the power of "hard work" over "Harvard" (Verma 2017). Implicit in this utterance is a rhetorical fiction of his own 'self-made' persona (*"garib ma ka beta"*, meaning "a poor mother's son") as reliant on an ethic of hard work as opposed to a Harvard education – the latter eminently an allusion to Amartya Sen and other noted home-grown economists who publicly condemned the demonetization project as logically facile and financially unviable. Interestingly, this 'Harvard-hard work' dichotomy does more than is apparent in the PM's self-congratulatory ruckus. The polemical construction in fact rests on antagonizing the idea of higher education (or an intellectual profession) as ranged against a populist ethic of uncritical, unquestioning 'hard work' that contributes 'in real terms' to the interests of the economy. The word-play deviously likens the 'liberal' research university – or more pertinently, 'foreign'-educated public intellectuals – to a palpable threat against national interests of 'work' and economic growth. Implicit in this is a provocation to public perceptions around the 'best' of universities as still being inadequate and grossly irrelevant to the material realities of life and 'work' – and therefore, better subjected to the scorn of the state or its clutches of control. The university professor is also, at the same time, peddled as an elite self-absorbed 'work'-shirker enjoying the unworthy privilege of public audience.

Coming from the Prime Minister, if this be regarded as a portent for what lies ahead in the life of the university, it is time we stand up and be counted. The alternative is not so much a death of the university as of its futures!

References

Agarwal, Megha. 2017. 'Skill Development in India: The Supply Side Story', in Devesh Kapur and Pratap Bhanu Mehta (eds.) *Navigating the Labyrinth: Perspectives on India's Higher Education* (pp. 132–56). Hyderabad: Orient Blackswan.

Altbach, Philip G. 2001. 'Higher Education and the WTO: Globalization Run Amok', *International Higher Education*, 23: 2–4.

Ambani, Mukesh and Birla, Kumarmangalam. 2003. 'Report on a Policy Framework for Reforms in Education', *Journal of Indian School of Political Economy*, 15(4): 840–5.

Benjamin, Walter. 2011 [1915]. 'The Life of Students' (trans.) Rodney Livingstone, in *Early Writings: 1910–1917* (pp. 197–210). Cambridge, MA: Belknap Press.

Beteille, Andre. 2014. *Universities at the Crossroads*. New Delhi: Oxford University Press.

Bhattacharya, Debaditya. 2018. 'Who's Afraid of Academic Freedom? The Illiberal Pulls of the Public University in India', in Apoorvanand (ed.) *Essays on Academic Freedom*. New Delhi: forthcoming.

Bhattacharya, Kumkum. 2014. *Rabindranath Tagore: Adventure of Ideas and Innovative Practices in Education*. Heidelberg, New York: Springer.

Chakravarty, Bikash. 2011. *Byahata Sakhya: Rabindranath O Jadunath Sarkar*. Calcutta: Visva-Bharati.

Chattopadhyay, Bratin. 2000. *On Education and Rabindranath*. Calcutta: Subarnarekha.

Currie, Jan and Newson, Janice. (eds.) 1998. *Universities and Globalization: Critical Perspectives*. Thousand Oaks, CA: Sage.

Education International. 2000. 'The WTO and the Millennium Round. What is at stake for Public Education?' Available at http://files.eric.ed.gov/fulltext/ED438281.pdf (accessed on 31 December 2017).

Ghosh, Yatindrakumar. (ed.) 1972. *Bengal Provincial Conference 1917, Calcutta Session (A Report)*. Calcutta: Adhyayan.

Government of India. 1995. *The Private Universities (Establishment and Regulation) Bill*. New Delhi: Ministry of Human Resource Development.

———. 2008a. *Eleventh Five Year Plan 2007–12: Education, Volume II: Social Sector*. New Delhi: Planning Commission of India.

———. 2008b. *Economic Survey 2007–2008: Social Sectors*. New Delhi: Ministry of Finance.

———. 2009a. *National Knowledge Commission Report to the Nation 2006–2009*. New Delhi: National Knowledge Commission.

———. 2009b. *National Policy on Skill Development*. New Delhi: Ministry of Labour and Employment.

———. 2010. *The Foreign Educational Institutions (Regulation of Entry and Operations) Bill*. New Delhi: Ministry of Human Resource Development.

———. 2014a. *Report on Employment-Unemployment Survey, Volume I, 2013–14*. Chandigarh: Labour Bureau.

———. 2014b. *Report on Education, Skill Development and Labour Force, Volume III, 2013–14*. Chandigarh: Labour Bureau.

———. 2015a. *Economic Survey 2014–15*. New Delhi: Ministry of Finance.

———. 2015b. *National Policy on Skill Development and Entrepreneurship*. New Delhi: Ministry for Skill Development and Entrepreneurship. Available at www.skilldevelopment.gov.in/National-Policy-2015.html (accessed on 31 December 2017).

———. 2015c. *Skill Development and Employment are major Challenges: Economic Survey*. New Delhi: Press Information Bureau, Ministry of Finance.

———.2016a. *National Policy on Education 2016: Report of the Committee for Evolution of the New Education Policy. 2016*. New Delhi: Ministry for Human Resource Development (MHRD)

——— 2016b. *Report on Education, Skill Development and Labour Force, Volume III, 2015–16*. Chandigarh: Labour Bureau.

——— 2018a. 'University Grants Commission [Categorisation of Universities (Only) for Grant of Graded Autonomy] Regulations', in *The Gazette of India* (February 12). New Delhi: Ministry of Human Resource Development.

——— 2018b. 'University Grants Commission (Conferment of Autonomous Status upon Colleges and Measures for Maintenance of Standards in Autonomous Colleges) Regulations', in *The Gazette of India* (February 12). New Delhi: Ministry of Human Resource Development.

——— 2018c. *Draft Higher Education Commission of India (Repeal of University Grants Commission Act) Act 2018*. New Delhi: Ministry of Human Resource Development. Available at http://mhrd.gov.in/sites/upload_files/mhrd/files/HE_CoI_India_2018_act.pdf (accessed on 1 July 2018).

Hovey, Harold A. 1999. *State Spending for Higher Education in the Next Decade. The Battle to Sustain Current Support*. The National Center for Public Policy and Higher Education. Available at http://files.eric.ed.gov/fulltext/ED439633.pdf (accessed on 31 December 2017).

Majumdar, Arun. 2001. *Rabindranath-er Visva-Bharati ebong Bangali Modhyobitto Mon*. Kolkata: Subarnarekha.

Ministry of Human Resource Development. (MHRD) and Confederation of Indian Industry (CII). 2014. 'FDI in Indian Higher Education', in *Annual Status of Higher Education in States and Union Territories in India 2014* (pp. 15–20). New Delhi: CII.

Mukherjee, Himangshu B. 2013 [1962]. *Education for Fullness: A Study of the Educational Thought and Experiment of Rabindranath Tagore*. New Delhi: Routledge.

National Sample Survey Organisation (NSSO). 2001a. *Employment-Unemployment Situation in India, 1999–2000, Part I*, 55th Round. New Delhi: GoI.

———. 2001b. *Informal Sector in India, 1999–2000*, 55th Round. New Delhi: GoI.

Newman, Frank. 2000. 'Saving Higher Education's Soul'. Available at http://nerche.org/futuresproject/publications/soul.pdf (accessed on 31 December 2017).

Newman, Frank and Couturier, Lara. 2001. 'The New Competitive Arena: Market Forces Invade the Academy'. Available at http://nerche.org/futuresproject/publications/new_competitive_arena.pdf (accessed on 31 December 2017).
Newson, Janice. 1998. 'The Corporate-Linked University: From Social Project to Market Force', *Canadian Journal of Communication*, 23: 107–24.
Nussbaum, Martha C. 2010. *Not for Profit: Why Democracy Needs the Humanities*. Princeton, NJ: Princeton University Press.
'Protest against UGC Act continues'. 2004. *The Times of India* (January 22). Available at https://timesofindia.indiatimes.com/city/delhi/Protest-against-UGC-act-continues/articleshow/439924.cms (accessed on 2 January 2018).
Readings, Bill. 1996. *The University in Ruins*. Cambridge, MA: Harvard University Press.
Rothblatt, Sheldon. 1997. *The Modern University and Its Discontents*. Cambridge: Cambridge University Press.
Sabharwal, Manish and Kannan, Srinivasan. 2017. 'The Case for Vocationalising Higher Education', in Devesh Kapur and Pratap Bhanu Mehta (eds.) *Navigating the Labyrinth: Perspectives on India's Higher Education* (pp. 132–56). Hyderabad: Orient Blackswan.
Smith, Anthony and Webster, Frank. (eds.) 1997. *The Postmodern University? Contested Visions of Higher Education in Society*. Buckingham: Open University Press and SRHE.
Soley, Lawrence C. 1995. *Leasing the Ivory Tower: The Corporate Takeover of Academia*. Boston, MA: South End Press.
Tabb, William K. 2000. 'The World Trade Organization? Stop World Take Over', *Monthly Review*, 51(10): 1–18.
Tagore, Rabindranath. 1921. 'On Constructive Work – A Letter', *Modern Review*, March: 355–6.
———. 1928. 'Sriniketan: The Institute of Rural Reconstruction', in *Visva-Bharati Bulletin* No. 11. Calcutta: Visva-Bharati.
———. 1988 [1892]. 'Shikshar Her-pher', in *Rabindra Rachanabali Volume VI* (pp. 565–72). Calcutta: Visva-Bharati.
———. 1996 [1917]. 'Nationalism Lectures', in Sisir Kumar Das (ed.) *The English Writings of Rabindranath Tagore, Volume Two: Plays, Stories, Essays* (pp. 417–66). New Delhi: Sahitya Akademi.
———. 1996 [1919]. 'The Centre of Indian Culture', in Sisir Kumar Das (ed.) *The English Writings of Rabindranath Tagore, Volume Two: Plays, Stories, Essays* (pp. 417–66). (pp. 467–91). New Delhi: Sahitya Akademi.
———. 1996 [1922]. 'An Eastern University', in Sisir Kumar Das (ed.) *The English Writings of Rabindranath Tagore, Volume Two: Plays, Stories, Essays* (pp. 556–69). New Delhi: Sahitya Akademi.
———. 1997 [1916]. 'Letter to Rathindranath Tagore, dated 11 October 1916', in Krishna Dutta and Andrew Robinson (eds.) *Selected Letters of Rabindranath Tagore* (pp. 178–9). Cambridge: Cambridge University Press.

———. 1997 [1921] 'Letter to Sir William Rothenstein, dated 24 April 1921', in Krishna Dutta and Andrew Robinson (eds.) *Selected Letters of Rabindranath Tagore* (pp. 264–6). Cambridge: Cambridge University Press.

———. 1997 [1937]. 'Letter to Leonard Knight Elmhirst, dated 19 December 1937', in Krishna Dutta and Andrew Robinson (eds.) *Selected Letters of Rabindranath Tagore* (pp. 490–2). Cambridge: Cambridge University Press.

———. 2001 [1920–1921]. 'Tagore's Reflections on Non-Cooperation and Cooperation: Letters to Charles Freer Andrews', in Sabyasachi Bhattacharya (ed. and trans.) *The Mahatma and the Poet: Letters and Debates Between Gandhi and Tagore* (pp. 54–62). New Delhi: National Book Trust.

———. 2006 [1926]. 'Palli-Seva', *Palli Prakriti* (trans.) Uma Das Gupta, in *Rabindranath Tagore: My Life in My Words* (pp. 64–5). New Delhi: Penguin.

'UGC grants full autonomy to 62 higher educational institutes; JNU, BHU, AMU in the list'. 2018. *The Times of India* (March 20), Available at https://timesofindia.indiatimes.com/home/education/news/ugc-grants-full-autonomy-to-62-higher-educational-institutes-jnu-bhu-amu-in-the-list/articleshow/63387456.cms (accessed on 5 July 2018).

Unni, Jeemol. 2002. 'Size, Contribution and Characteristics of Informal Employment in India', in *Country Case Study*. Geneva: International Labour Organization.

Vaidhyasubramaniam, S. 2010. 'Foreign Universities Bill, an Unprescribed Pill', *The Hindu* (1 August). Available at www.thehindu.com/opinion/open-page/Foreign-universities-bill-an-unprescribed-pill/article13264704.ece (accessed on 2 January 2018).

Varma, Subodh. 2015. 'Survey: Even Among Skilled Workers Joblessness Is High', *The Times of India* (July 20). Available at https://timesofindia.indiatimes.com/india/Survey-Even-among-skilled-workers-joblessness-is-high/articleshow/48138599.cms (accessed on 2 January 2018).

Verma, Lalmani. 2017. 'Harvard vs Hard Work: With GDP Data, PM Narendra Modi Snubs Note Ban Critics', *The Indian Express*, 2 March. Available at http://indianexpress.com/elections/uttar-pradesh-assembly-elections-2017/harvard-vs-hard-work-with-gdp-data-pm-modi-snubs-noteban-critics-4550000/ (accessed on 2 January 2018).

Williamson, John. 1990. *Latin American Adjustment: How Much Has Happened?* Washington, DC: Institute for International Economics.

World Bank. 1994. *Higher Education: The Lessons of Experience*. Washington, DC.

———. 1996. *From Plan to Market: World Development Report*. Washington, DC.

———. 1997. *The State in a Changing World: World Development Report*. Washington, DC.

———. 2002. *Constructing Knowledge Societies: New Challenges for Tertiary Education*. Washington, DC.

———. 2006. *Skill Development in India: The Vocational Education and Training System*. Washington, DC.

World Trade Organization. 1998. 'Education Services: Background Note by the Secretariat'. No. S/C/W/49. Available at www.wto.org/english/tratop_e/serv_e/w49.doc (accessed on 31 December 2017).

———. 2010. 'Education Services: Background Note by the Secretariat'. No. S/C/W/313. Available athttps://docs.wto.org/dol2fe/Pages/FE_Search/FE_S_S009-DP.aspx?language=E&CatalogueIdList=119349,79546,63271,89964,41567&CurrentCatalogueIdIndex=1&FullTextHash=&HasEnglishRecord=True&HasFrenchRecord=True&HasSpanishRecord=True (accessed on 31 December 2017).

Part I
Beyond nostalgias

1 The provocations of the public university in contemporary India*

Janaki Nair

> The characteristic gift of the university is the gift of an interval.
> – Michael Oakeshott

The news that the overall enrolment of eligible Indians (age group 18–23 years) has increased from 27.5 million in 2010–11 to 35.7 million in 2016–17, and of the consequent rise in the Gross Enrolment Ratio (GER, the proportion of those in the relevant age group enrolling in Higher Education) from 19.4 percent in 2010–11 to 25.2 in 2016–17 is news of no small achievement. Releasing the report of the All India Survey on Higher Education for 2016–17, the Ministry of Human Resources, which oversees higher education, also took pride in the fact that the gap between men and women is narrowing since the latter today constitute over 46 percent of those in higher education.[1]

Still, such information reaches us precisely at the time when there have been direct and indirect attacks on the public university as an idea and as an institution. The last two years have also seen a massive pushback, by students and teachers, against the attempt to challenge or dismantle the public university system, and the opportunities it had offered to Dalits, women, tribals, ethnic minorities, to define a new future. The large numbers therefore tell us little about the dramatic ways in which universities and colleges are changing, not just in their composition but in their goals and achievements, with serious consequences for the future of Indian intellection itself. As such, Oakeshott's evocation of the idea of the university as the 'gift of an interval' may sound like something from a distant and luxurious (not to say, elitist) past, as if about an impossible institution. No doubt, there is a serious need for hard and collective thinking, as is attempted in this volume, about the future of the Indian public university in particular, and higher education in general, if we are not to lose all that has been so painstakingly achieved.

* * *

For some time now, intellectuals in different parts of the globe have sounded the death knell of the university, and the public university in particular, as we have known it (Eagleton 2015; Vernon nd; Chaudhuri 2016). The threat today is posed not just by market forces, and managerial approaches to higher education, but by the dramatically transformed demands of the "knowledge economy", and the vastly altered ways in which both teaching and research are conducted (Chaudhuri 2011). It has also compromised, if not undermined, the precious autonomy that is vital to its existence (U. Kumar 2016). Today, above all, we need to ask: what is the university? What has its place been in our part of the world (Arunima 2016)? And who is it for?

We have come a long way from the medieval description of the university as "wisdom's workshop".[2] In its Western incarnation, the university had moved from being a space that served the church, to becoming a secular institution, one that came to serve the developmental goals of the nation-state, old and new. The university, right from the late nineteenth century, was seen as a public good, a space for creating and upholding democracy, and – as at least one scholar, David Theo Goldberg, has recently pointed out – a space that enabled social mobility, or "middle classness".[3] But here too, especially in the twentieth century, the gnawing pressures of aligning knowledge production and teaching practice to the needs of the market have been difficult to resist.

What – or who – is the university for?

In a country like India, the modern university traced a different historical trajectory. The Indian university is a radically modern creation, bearing no trace of any earlier forms of knowledge production or teaching practice, names like Nalanda notwithstanding. It was the creation of a colonial power in the nineteenth century. For long serving the purposes of a colonial regime's need for a modern bureaucratic elite, the Indian university in its national-modern phase continued to produce an intellectual aristocracy. Yet, from its historical arrival as a space of exclusion and elite formation, it has come a very long way in the past few decades to represent a vital institutional space for ensuring social mobility, especially for those for whom education is the only form of capital when access to other material resources, such as property, are non-existent or limited.

In India today, we are also faced with the often paralysing problem of governmental control, a hyper-politicization of governance mechanisms that undermine institutional autonomy. At the same time, primarily as a result of reservation policies and support for higher education through fellowships (especially, but not only, the non-NET fellowships),[4] the student body has been democratized in fundamental and important ways. The public university as a space that is created and supported by the state is, therefore, a highly politicized and fractious realm, both for faculty and student bodies. As the president of Jawaharlal Nehru University Students' Union (JNUSU), Kanhaiya Kumar asked at the start of the tumultuous events that engulfed JNU in February 2016, "What is a university for? A university is there to critically analyse society's 'common conscience'. To promote critical thinking. If universities fail in this job, there can be no nation, there will be no people's participation" (K. Kumar 2016).

Disentangling the enabling role of the state from more pernicious modes of interference is therefore the inaugural task: we must ask, with what resources might we argue for the continued relevance of the university as a public good? And what kind of defence of its autonomy can be made? Despite the stressful changes that are taking place, the Indian university is a place that is simultaneously withdrawn and engaged; it is simultaneously serving and criticizing society and state, and therefore is a vital place of self-reflection; it is a place for simultaneously achieving goals of openness and equality while reaffirming some hierarchies and styles of distinction. Let us remember that JNU, for instance, not only produces a hyper-visible, if small, number of political activists of all stripes, and nurtures vigorous discussions of political ideologies of all hues; it also produces a much larger number of those who uphold and promote the system, as bureaucrats, economists, educators, members of the judiciary, participants in the media and, not least, mainstream politicians. It is this duplex function that characterizes the public university today.

Also, we should remember that the public Indian university has been a politicized space from its very founding. At first, it both produced and challenged the "rule of racial difference" that was the hallmark of colonial rule (Seth 2015; Lelyveld 2003; Renold 2005; Datla 2013). In the early twentieth century, it began to be recognized as a space for the redressal of caste inequalities, as for instance in measures that were pioneered by the Mysore State in 1918. Finally, from the 1920s at least, it became an important site of nationalist and revolutionary agitation (Altbach 1970a, 1970b; Carreau 1969; Singh 1991). Today, it is the site of state-mandated equality of a kind, while simultaneously highlighting, producing and foregrounding new inequalities.

The student movements of the pre-independence period were linked, and not opposed, to larger nationalist or communist parties, and were not necessarily engaged in intergenerational conflicts. Today, there is greater engagement with university-related issues: hostels, fellowships, deprivation points, grading systems; even, though far more rarely, course structures. Less often are they anti-government (hence both the Hyderabad Central University and JNU events of 2016 are different from the struggles at the Film and Television Institute of India in 2015, for being openly critical of the Indian state and its policies). Today, we are seeing something like a war, with questions of caste, ethnicity, or university norms being deployed or exploited by both state and private interests, as happened in Hyderabad.

Certainly, many social and moral goals of equality have been achieved in the university as an institution since independence. The "intellectual" effects of this democratic churning are increasingly being felt only now, and have presented some intractable problems. This contradictory promise of equality is making the university a provocation, as pressures from within and without are bringing the very idea of the university to a crisis.

I am not, here, going to recount any details of recent student protests/struggles directly (which are no doubt critical events), so much as look at the setting within which a range of political positions are articulated (Nigam 1986; Deshpande 2016; Chatterjee 2016; Bhushan 2016). Therefore, I will take even the quotidian as the political; namely, what a space like the university – and the residential university in particular – has enabled. Such an evaluation of the Indian university must recount both its academic and non-academic achievements: the university both as a site of academic excellence and as a site of equity, freedom and reshaped socialities.

Let me begin with a few statistics: India has 46 central universities, 350 state universities, 245 private universities and 122 deemed universities, making a total of 763 universities, with 38,000-plus affiliating colleges (UGC nd). The total number of those in higher education, as recounted at the outset, is over 35 million, a number greater than the population of Iraq or Canada. Women constitute nearly half of all in higher education: the continued male-gendered tone of the New Education Policy chaired by T.S.R. Subramanian cannot but be a sign of surprising blindness to this achievement (MHRD 2016).

The public university and the 'politics of presence'

Let us start, therefore, by acknowledging the achievements of the higher education system. Why is it necessary to begin by pointing to the Indian public university's achievements beyond the purely academic? Because the public university may be the most inclusive of all institutions in contemporary India, in terms of representing female, Dalit, Scheduled Tribe (ST), Other Backward Class (OBC), and now third gender populations, with many Dalit/OBCs also getting into general seats. Most other institutions do not reflect this kind of representation. Take, for instance, the legislatures and the Parliament, where there is a shameful representation of women or minorities; take the judiciary, or the bureaucracy, where Muslims are largely absent; or the world of basic science, from which lower castes and women are largely excluded (Subramanian 2007).

Nevertheless, we have come a long way from how Vivek Dhareshwar characterized the reaction to the Mandal proposals in 1990–91: where the "secular" meritorious Indian was made possible only by disavowing caste (Dhareshwar 1993). After 2006, when OBC reservations to higher education were implemented, a new national common sense has emerged – often, though not always – with very positive, unexpected outcomes.[5] In the decades between the Mandal agitation (which was led by upper-caste students against the policies of reservation) and the present, a great deal has been achieved. I teach at a university that has long had a remarkable policy of weightages (acknowledged even by JNU's most grudging admirers), allowing people from various underprivileged backgrounds and locations to find a hope of higher education (JNU nd).[6] At another public university, the Kannada University, Hampi, where I recently was, I met legions of students from relatively poor and underprivileged backgrounds, including a large proportion of first-generation learners.

The representativeness of the Indian university is far less impressive when it comes to faculty recruitment. A huge backlog of unfilled positions, including several hundred reserved posts, especially in more specialized institutions such as Indian Institutes of Technology (IITs) and Indian Institutes of Management (IIMs), continues to persist (*Forward Press* 2016). We should ask ourselves the sobering question of why we are witness to possibly more than one lost generation of students who are yet to take their place as teachers, between the implementation of reservations in the 1950s and today. Why have we failed to create a sizeable class of intellectuals who can take up mentoring, teaching and research from among the newly empowered groups and classes?

In other words, the greatest achievement of contemporary India has been in ensuring the entry of Dalits, OBCs, women, and ethnic and sexual minorities to universities: a "politics of presence". The greatest failure has been in ensuring that such an entry is enhanced by systems that will make up for centuries of discrimination. There are too many who are being failed right out of the system due to their inadequate language skills, unfamiliarity with tools and methods, or simply the tremendous hostility to their very presence.

Clearly, new and unresolved problems are being produced by that very politics of presence. This is why the passionate plea of the New Education Policy document for disallowing politics and political groups based on caste/region/ethnicity is grotesquely out of sync with conditions in the Indian university today.[7] To ask the students who enter the portals of an institution of higher learning to set aside the marks of disprivilege is to pretend that the university is a non-social zone, unmarked by difference and hierarchy. The politics of presence alone, ensured by various deprivation policies, would have been manageable; what has made the university an ungovernable space today is that these policies are yielding unanticipated results and, in the absence of institutional measures for redressing continuing inequalities, are failing the very groups they are supposed to enable. To speak, then, of educational goals in isolation, or even of the question of educational excellence, is to grievously misjudge the basic heterogeneities that constitute the public university today.

Mastering the masters' language

Let us take two of the most well-known instances of the opportunities and predicaments that are faced by the non-elite student of the Indian university today. It is a parable for our times that Rohith Vemula's brilliant mastery of English, the language of all meaningful higher education in India today, was allowed to be expressed only in his tragic suicide note. The subject position of the student today may no longer be defined by an entry into an alienating English-speaking world, but by a mastery of it. But, as the Rohith Vemula case has demonstrated, it is the most profound and eloquent example of the limitations of such mastery in the absence of other supportive structures.

Fortunately, this is not the whole story. At one and the same time, thankfully, the higher education system in India has allowed for a direct rebuttal of the hegemonic stance of English; we have all witnessed the astounding oratorial skills of Kanhaiya Kumar in Hindi, which has succeeded in redrafting the very language of politics.

It is this potent mixture of attainments and possibilities, yearnings and dissatisfactions, which has made the public university, in its very inclusivity, appear as a place that is meeting all kinds of other (read: non-intellectual) desires and goals than it was intended for. Let us stay with the example of language. English has posed a debilitating block to non-English speakers since it is as yet the only meaningful language of higher education in India. As many have pointed out, English in India is not just a language. It is, at one and the same time, a judicial/legal apparatus, a political system, a semiotics of modernity – all of these, and more. It is a substance that even defies and exceeds the use of terms like "cultural capital" (Dhareshwar 1993; Pandey 2016).[8] Too little has been done by university administrators and teachers to either generate a body of material that will make systematic thinking in Indian languages possible, or equip those who are severely disadvantaged with the skills to use English creatively. A rare but important example was the work of Sharmila Rege in the University of Pune in encouraging true bilinguality in the classroom and in generating texts for mostly first-generation English speakers. But this is regrettably too exceptional in our university campuses.

The rhetoric of academic excellence

It will not do, as one member of the audience where I presented an early version of this article in Bengaluru pointed out, to remain silent on the question of academic excellence and whether it is compatible with the idea of accessibility of higher education to wider communities of Indians. How can it be configured in the democratizing space of the public university? If the university is to strike a fine balance between scholarship (the accumulation of knowledge) and education (teaching students), do we need to create standards for the evaluation of knowledge production/teaching that hold teachers as well as administrators accountable to the wider university public? Regrettably, not enough discussion about accountability has occurred in Indian scholarship on research and teaching. Instead of exploiting the creative tensions between the two, the teaching community has capitulated to the game of numericals, which, in the name of transparency, has probably done more damage to the assessment of teacher abilities and training.[9]

Joining the chorus for an audit culture that measures outcomes and processes of research and learning – and extends what is probably workable for the natural or physical sciences to the humanities and social sciences – are those clamouring for ranking, both nationally and internationally. What prospects does this hold out for an assessment of academic excellence? Craig Calhoun has observed:

> The rhetoric of excellence underwent a transformation which evacuated much specific meaning (and especially Aristotelian heritage) from the notion of "excellence", treating it as a term of commensuration, like price, rather than the quality of doing well in very different and largely incommensurable dimensions of life. But the theme that came to the fore was not altogether new: it was the pursuit of recognition and especially the positional good of being seen to be better than others.
>
> (2006: 9)

The new obsession with institutional rankings cannot recognize the particularities of the Indian university system, which is the second largest in the world and also extremely diverse.[10] Most of our universities – like Aligarh Muslim University, Banaras Hindu University or JNU, for example – were set up to address different objectives and have, over the years, developed their own unique and innovative ways. Focusing only on a common set of indicators will not do justice to the exercise of evaluating the performance of Indian universities.

Furthermore, teaching and learning processes in the social sciences, humanities and languages are gradual and incremental; so ranking systems which focus on citation indexes, or laboratory-industry interfaces, cannot be applied to social sciences and hard sciences alike.

Goading universities to compete with each other could even be counterproductive. Diversities exist among the different disciplines in terms of opportunities of funding and publication, differences in perspectives. Ranking, as indeed academic performance indicators, would lead to institutional homogenization and distortion in disciplinary balance, as institutions (and individuals) strategize to achieve what is being measured. Finally, since ranking places greater emphasis on research, teaching – which is so crucial in the context of massification of Indian higher education – is likely to get sidelined.

However, much is happening within universities that is exhilarating even if we accept the serious limits that are imposed by a mere politics of presence. In the Indian setting, the considerable ways in which universities transform lives is not necessarily measurable by internationally derived ranking/evaluation systems.

The transforming power of the university

The public university today is a space that is transforming, not conserving, social relations, perhaps in ways that may be reaching the point of ungovernability. Let us take the case of gender relations, and the university as the site of the most massive contemporary transformation of relationships between the sexes that are coded in strictly endogamous, caste and kin rule-respecting terms. Universities have become among the most important sites for resetting "the practical and passionate relationships" between the sexes and for exploring counter-heteronormative sexualities. Much of the violence against women to which we are increasingly witness is the result of ways in which such breaches of social protocol, often occasioned by access to higher education, are being managed, though usually unsuccessfully. (The college and the university are the spaces where many find long-term partners, and most go on to lead relatively undisturbed lives.)

Thus, there is both learning and unlearning in the university, since it is encountered as a new institutional space.[11] It represents that all-important interval, often allowing escape from the ties that bind, those suffocating categories to which one is socially consigned. This happens through a process of simultaneous avowal and disavowal. There is, on the one hand, a critical embrace of what lies beneath such categories (for example, in the choice of questions for research, in terms of archives that are created, in terms of methods that are refashioned, namely intellectual work as such). In the Kannada University, Hampi, I talked to students who are burning with a desire to know their pasts, or rather their communities' pasts: an Iruliga student, writing the history of his community in and around Ramanagara; a student from an agricultural background, researching the history of early modern agrarian relations in Chitradurga; someone is studying the roots of underdevelopment in the Hyderabad-Karnataka region; another studies the history of the Bal Basappa performing cult and its message of equality. No wonder Mahadev Shankanapura, the historian from Chamarajanagara, Karnataka, has said that he read the histories of India and found them wanting: they did not explain to him why he got where he was. That was a task for which he had to fashion new methodologies (Satyanarayana and Tharu 2013: 252).

But there is active disavowal of social origins as well, not just in the choice of subjects of study and research, but in the everyday life of the university and what it enables in this practical sense. Dearly held and received social habits are challenged in shared spaces, forums for debate, and in the process of coping with the tensions of proximity or adjacency. The university, and the residential university in particular, is a site of transformative encounters, with radically different forms of living, food cultures, religious and sexual practices. More than the classroom, perhaps, it is the hostel that amplifies these possibilities and predicaments.

Hostel life as instruction

Can the university continue to be a "gift of an interval", as it was once put by Michael Oakeshott, though perhaps not in the strictly academic sense he intended it? The importance of young adult socialization and the hostel as the site of such socialization has for too long been ignored, despite the acknowledgement of its transformative capacities. In Karnataka, there has long been a link between caste associations and their early recognition of the vital necessity of hostels for first-generation learners in particular. U. R. Ananthamurthy in his last work, *Hindutva athava Hind Swaraj*, among many others, has pointed to the very important link between the Dasoha tradition of the Lingayats, and the establishment of caste-specific hostels to meet the needs of those attending colleges and schools, enabling even poor students to study in cities and towns of Mysore/Karnataka. The landmark Miller Committee Report of 1919 in Mysore, which recommended reservations in educational institutions and in government jobs, had this to say:

> We see that out of 522 students accommodated in the government hostels, 435 are Brahmins and only 87 of other classes. We recommend that preference be given to the backward class pupils for admission into such institutions. . . . We deem it essential that hostels should be constructed in all taluk headquarters to encourage parents to send their children from the village elementary schools to the secondary schools. It is also necessary that in all hostels there should be at least three separate kitchens, two for vegetarians and one for non-vegetarians with a view to meet the convenience of all communities. . . . In the government hostels, a certain proportion of seats should be reserved for the backward class students, and we would fix it at not less than 50% unless the students forthcoming are less than that number. Private and communal hostels should receive the same grants as the government hostels do.
> (Report of the Committee to Consider Steps for Adequate Representation 1919: 10)

The provocations of the public university 51

In post-independence India, the hostel has shed some of its sectarian characteristics, particularly in the public university, and enabled all manner of new opportunities. Student demands have frequently focused on access to hostel space and, indeed, the continued use of hostel facilities for other kinds of access, especially to the city and its opportunities: Bangalore University, for instance, serves as the node for urbanizing students from four districts of Bengaluru Rural, Tumkur, Mandya and Hassan (recognizing that continued access to hostel facilities is what was leading many to serially pursue multiple degrees); Osmania University has recently refused hostel facilities to those seeking a second degree, which led to an instant drop in applications.

That is why the residential public university is an important entity to understand. Historically, the hostel has been a space for engaging with the "Indian social" in interesting, potentially democratizing but also segmenting, ways. It can be the centre of new forms of mobilization: the writer Siddalingaiah notes in his autobiography *Ooru keri* how students were largely mobilized from hostels during the *boosa* agitation of 1973 (2014: 67, 71, 100). It is the site of new forms of tolerance, but also forms of intolerance. There is a curious mix of rights-based discourses and cultural entitlements. To take the example of Kannada University, Hampi again, state funding for hostels in Karnataka has led to an interesting, perhaps unwitting, redrafting of caste identities. There are only two kinds of hostels at Hampi: the Scheduled Castes (SC)/ST students' hostel, and the OBC hostel, reflecting the role played by state institutions in redesignating "General Students" by invisibilizing them. The hostel is functioning in a number of interesting ways to pose a challenge to ascribed realities while simultaneously enabling the consolidation, and reassertion, of beleaguered community identities.

The multiple histories and uses of the hostel, the needs of first-generation learners, and of new urbanizers, have rarely generated creative responses; instead, they have most often led to the call for a return to some imagined neutral space, where agendas other than education may not be pursued. At the root of this call to return to the pursuit of intellectual goals alone is the growing hostility towards what Arvind Malagatti has described as the *Government Brahmana* (2014: 52). The *Government Brahmana* is taunted for being patronized by the state, and receiving undeserved handouts. Of course, anyone who reads that autobiography carefully, and indeed any of the Dalit autobiographies in Kannada, will realize that the humiliations of the Dalit do not end upon her entry into the space of the university; they continue in subtle and not so subtle ways. Yet the new righteousness of the "taxpayer" has been twinned with the big push towards privatization today.[12] There is a good chance that the public university, which legions of elites had accessed in both the pre- and post-independence periods before its accountability to the taxpayer was demanded, will go the way of the public health and schooling systems by being turned into a ghetto for those who can exercise no choices.

Privatization as panacea

The demand that the state withdraw from university education has been heard for a while now (Chattopadhyay 2010: 15–7). This is not simply because it is a space of extraordinary commercial opportunities – remember that the first recognition of "education as business" was in the capitation fee colleges and universities that mushroomed in the South, and in Western India, especially Andhra Pradesh, Karnataka, Tamil Nadu and Maharashtra from the 1970s. In 2000, the report of the Mukesh Ambani and Kumaramangalam Birla Committee called for full-fledged withdrawal of the state from encashable disciplines, such as science and technology, medical and business-related professions, leaving it to support only such unencashable disciplines as humanities, languages and social sciences (Birla and Ambani 2000).

The Mandal agitation by the upper castes of North India was a convenient forgetting of the inroads that had already been made into the category of "merit" by capitation fee colleges. This was necessary for the return of the "repressed", in the form of a renewed call to promote merit. Since then, the growing success of reservation programmes in bringing wider sections of Indian society into the university has led to public discourse being dominated by a different kind of objection to the achievements of higher education. The public university is increasingly seen as an undeserved privilege; some knowledges are not just irrelevant but positively dangerous (as the arts, humanities and social sciences); they are over-politicized and critical, therefore not engaged in real knowledge production. There is a new idealization of the university as a space of training, as "skill factories" rather than as laboratories for sustained and critical thought. The university is reduced, thus, to producing bits of human capital, of service to corporations and industry, fitting into society rather than questioning it.

As the idea of the university itself is under challenge, we are being asked to turn it from a robust, complicated, sometimes unpredictable "institution" into a more efficient "mechanism". The difference between institution and mechanism is not exaggerated here, and is at the source of the vast system of credentialling on an industrial scale that has already reached its epitome in the Vyapam scam. A vibrant market economy logic has seized hold of entrance exam aspirants: those who are calling for greater market interventions should first deal with the unruly ways in which the market has already intervened and reconstructed institutions of higher learning. There is, in short, a contradictory invocation of the market logic: even the New Education Policy (NEP) of 2016 wants entrepreneurial skills to be harnessed in higher education, and yet bemoans the commercialization of every aspect of education, including the surrogates who take entrance examinations. Mere hand-wringing does little to address the ironies of the current higher education scenario.

Some of the justifications offered for the sweeping changes which began to be announced by the Ministry of Human Resource Development (MHRD 2013) since 2014 are enhanced employability, skill development and seamless nationwide mobility for students. Great hopes are pinned on expanding higher education through deploying new technologies of disembodied teaching, in particular via Massive Online Open Courses, despite the disputable pedagogical outcomes of such technologies in teaching. We may admire, therefore, in this information-rich age, the prescience of T.S. Eliot for asking, as early as in 1934, "Where is the wisdom we have lost in knowledge? Where is the knowledge we have lost in information?"[13] The pursuit of learning cannot be the acquisition of information. This was recognized even at the modern university's founding. Speaking of the threat to institutions of learning posed by books and print culture, John Henry Newman (1909: 7, 9) had asked: "Why, you will ask, need we go up to knowledge, when knowledge comes down to us?" Newman, while acknowledging the democratizing potential of the printed word, nevertheless spoke of the insufficiency of print culture in substituting for knowledge; that can only be obtained, according to him, from the "teachers of wisdom" and from the "fullness [that] is in one place alone", namely the university.

But, as if the effect of educational "robber barons" on the life of the mind (and on unencashable disciplines) is not emaciating enough, intellectual life in India, both within and outside university spaces, is also facing a new onslaught from neo-nationalist anti-intellectualism.

The rise of a new anti-intellectualism

What do the political, commercial and administrative assaults on the public university, which have intensified in the past year, amount to? We are seeing the signs of a new wave of anti-intellectualism which will have a lasting impact on the way institutions of higher education will be run and managed. No doubt, India is participating in a global turn away from the older commitment of the university to a free pursuit of knowledge, and towards an increasing financialization of the university. Within this broad international trend, however, there is a concerted home-grown impulse towards an instrumentalization of knowledge not only to subserve economic ends, but national – cultural ones. Contrast the vision of Jawaharlal Nehru, who had emphasized the ideals of autonomy, experimentation and freedom in the university:

> A university stands for humanism. For tolerance, for reason, for the adventure of ideas and for the search for truth . . . if the universities discharge their duties adequately, then it is well for the nation and for the people.

How far we have travelled from these hopeful words! This futuristic vision of the university, propelled by misplaced optimism, may be compared with the inaugural statement of the NEP 2016, which articulates another vision:

> For two-thirds of mankind's history, India as one of the oldest and most glorious living civilisations in the world dominated the world scene in every respect – in philosophy, economics, trade, and culture as well as in education. If India does the things now required to be done, in 15 to 20 years Indian Education can be transformed. The rest of the 21st century could then belong to India.
>
> (MHRD 2016: Para 1.4.3)

The rhetoric of excellence, here buttressed by hyper-nationalism, looks outwards to international recognition: an imagined past becomes more and more urgent as visionary futures wane. This bears no resemblance to the pasts, the historical wounds, that faculty and students at the Kannada University, Hampi may be researching. The university must serve the state in more direct, celebratory, or useful ways as illustrated by the recently compiled list of 82 research topics for PhDs in Gujarat University.

Apart from the vigour with which we are seeing the construction of the "neo-nation", as much as we are contending with an unprecedented wave of anti-intellectualism, we are also inhabiting a post-truth society, and must be alert to its implications. We may, therefore, be at the same stage as Germany was in the 1930s, when, as Jurgen

Habermas pointed out in his critique of Heidegger, "intelligence" was devalued in favour of "spirit", and "analysis" was degraded to "authentic thought". I would therefore go further than Ramachandra Guha, who has asked why the Indian right (or the Indian conservatives) has not generated a new intellectual culture (Guha 2015). The current predicament is not merely that the right is striving, and failing, to replace erstwhile liberal/left scholars, good scholars, less-well known, or insignificant ones; what is happening now is an energetic closing of the Indian mind, and a call to replace real learning and thinking with a grab bag of pieties.

How to recover and preserve the space of hard-won freedoms, and even more hard-won equalities? The university as a space of engaged learning is increasingly being pushed towards policing and disciplining the mind. There is today a toxic mix of state, military, and neo-nationalist cultural power that wishes to confine, if not eradicate, freer forms of thought and expression. Soon after the 9 February 2016 incident in JNU, retired army generals made a proposal to bring guns and a tank onto the campus to instil a spirit of nationalism. The then HRD Minister Smriti Irani proposed the installation of 207 feet flag poles in all central universities.[14] These suggestions and proposals, in their deadly sincerity, cannot be dismissed as symbolic or trivial pursuits of the party in power. The debate on the "revival" of Nalanda was suffused by terms which recalled "Indian" educational ideals, and *vidya* as possessing greater moral weight (Pinkney 2014: 135).

If in the period of the national movement a variety of ways of thinking, and not just about nationalism, was celebrated, intellectualism today is being opposed. A different kind of right has been emphasized that pits the army against intellectuals, and amounts to a militarization of the cultural-social ethic. It is a sad day indeed, when we become incapable of appreciating idiomatic or imaginative speech, become averse to the idea that conflictual pasts are a part of our heritage, or strongly oppose the necessity of emplacing the soldier as a protector of borders and boundaries, yes, but not bestowing on him the responsibility of guarding constitutional freedoms.

The public university is moving from being a public good – as it was envisaged in the late nineteenth century – into becoming a private investment and a vast credentialling mechanism. The changes began in the 1980s, under the aegis of global economic transformations, when universities became "public" only in name, as, say, in the United Kingdom and the United States. The effort was to replace them with other undertakings or ventures, introduce fees, and turn them into financialized institutions. Privatization in a financialized era is driven by rankings and ratings: not just basic science is devalued in the process, but also the social sciences and the humanities.

Judith Butler had recently talked, in the context of the university today, of the necessity and difficulty of destruction (Centre for Humanities Research 2016). I would agree that in a society like ours there is much to destroy, but it requires much forethought and planning for it to be "creative destruction", to use those old words of Joseph Schumpeter. What we are witnessing today is a mindless destruction of all that existed, without a clear agenda for what might meaningfully take its place. And we have insufficient appreciation of what has already been achieved: Ananthamurthy in his last work, *Hindutva athava Hind Swaraj* (2014) has rightly reminded us that a person of OBC background becoming Prime Minister is as old as caste itself in India; if a large number of such people of similar backgrounds are today climbing the steps of Parliament, it is not an achievement of the ruling party, but a precious fruit of the legacies of Ambedkar, Nehru and V. P. Singh, and I would add, our public university system.

Let us have the courage to say that at a time of consensus and orthodoxy, the university is obliged to resist, rethink and challenge these orthodoxies. Let us take from the best of our long, very contradictory and conflictual pasts, rather than clichés such as Nalanda. The *kutuhala-shalas* of early India, for instance, were halls and places on the edge of the city where people gathered to discuss things and literally exercise curiosity, as the very word *kutuhala* suggests.[15]

We come from a long tradition of argumentation, of which we have many exemplary exchanges, as between Yajnavalkya and Gargi from *Brihadaranyaka Upanishad*:

> At this point Yajnavalkya told her: "Don't ask too many questions, Gargi, or your head will shatter apart! You are asking too many questions about a deity about whom one should not ask too many questions. So, Gargi, don't ask too many questions!"
>
> (Olivelle 1998: 85)

The word "university" has had many meanings for those who live in the subcontinent: for the first-generation public sector employees of Bharat Electronics Limited, the factory was the university which introduced them to people and ideas from all parts of India for the first time. K Ramaiah speaks of the Dalit Sangarsh Samiti as a "big school, also a university, a real university. The question we need to ask today is what made it a place of real education" (Satyanarayana and

Tharu 2013: 13). In both these definitions, the university is the place that offers the gift of an interval to those who never dreamed of this luxury, allowing the glimpse of a new and unimagined future. It allows questions to be asked, and churns up the known, the comfortable, the commonsensical. The university should prepare us for the unknown, rather than fitting us into an existing world.

We should end here by asking why, just at a time when the poet Sikhamani tells us "Look, the Steel Nibs Are Sprouting", we are responding to the provocations of the public university by calling for its dramatic transformation, even dismantling? What has already been dismantled – with contradictory and unexpected outcomes – for those who, for so long, wielded power? We can do no better than to hear Sikhamani:

> For an untaught lesson
> You demanded our thumbs –
> There sprout nibs of steel
> To write history afresh –
> Then, the people who poured
> Hot metal in our ears
> Would need ladders to climb
> To pluck hairs from our ears!

Notes

* This is a revised version of the K. R. Narayanan Memorial Lecture delivered at the Centre for Research and Education for Social Transformation (CREST), Kozhikode, on November 6, 2016. It has since been published in the *Economic and Political Weekly*, Vol. 52, Issue No. 37, 16 Sep, 2017

I would like to thank Prof D.D. Nampoothiri for inviting me to deliver this lecture, and to the audience for their searching questions. I have been part, since the last two years, of Academics for Creative Reform in Education, a group of teachers from several universities in Delhi, which has been meeting to discuss the predicaments of higher education, and resolutions to it, and some of what I say is an outcome of these discussions and thinking. Academics for Creative Reform in Education may be found at www.facebook.com/groups/acref/ (last accessed on 31 December 2017).

1 *All India Survey of Higher Education* (AISHE), 2016–17 (Delhi: Government of India, MHRD, 2017), pp. 17, 45. As this report has been received only after the article was written, I will only use its data to update what I am arguing rather than attempt an analysis of its implications.
2 This is the title of a recent full-length history of Princeton University (Axtell 2016). These words are attributed to Pope Gregory IX c 1170–1241.

3 This was pointed out in a panel discussion at the Centre for Humanities Research. www.chrflagship.uwc.ac.za/the-university-and-its-worlds-a-panel-discussion-with-achille-mbembe-judith-butler-wendy-brown-and-david-theo-goldberg/, accessed on 10 October 2016.
4 Non-NET fellowships support MPhil and PhD students who do not receive Junior Research Fellowships from the University Grants Commission. NET stands for National Eligibility Test.
5 I am only too aware that private discourse, and even practice, may not reflect, or may even contradict, the public positions that are espoused.
6 Points are given for regional deprivation, to women students, and specified categories of students from defence families.
7 See Section 5.4 entitled "Need to Restrict Political and Other Distractions in University and College Campuses" (MHRD 2016).
8 Madhava Prasad (2011) even describes English as the "peacekeeping force" in a postcolonial, multilingual society like India.
9 V. Sujatha (2015) has suggested an alternative to the Academic Performance Index, which has now led to an industrial scale production of numericals to meet the demand of university administrators for the purpose of appointments and promotions. See also Academics for Creative Reform (2015).
10 The following paragraphs are adapted from the position paper of Academics for Creative Reforms (2015).
11 Therefore, as I am always at pains to explain to my students, the university as an institution is not and should not be the mirror image of the family.
12 As Udaya Kumar (2016) has pointed out, the very idea of the "public" has been distorted by the new emphasis on the self righteous "taxpayer", particularly in the time since Rohith-Kanhaiya.
13 Balavant, alias Bal Apte, intervening in the discussion on the Nalanda University Bill, 2010, echoed Eliot when he said, "Information is relevant if it is knowledge, and knowledge is relevant if it is blessed with wisdom, and all these put together is one word in this country, which is called *vidya*. Vidya is knowledge with wisdom, and we say *sa vidya ya vimukthaya* (that which liberates is knowledge)" (Pinkney 2014: 135).
14 This article was written before the request was made for a tank on the campus by the JNU vice chancellor in July 2017.
15 The reference is from Buddhist texts such as the *Digha Nikaya, I.ix. Potthapada Sutta,* 178–79. They are mentioned in other Buddhist texts as well. It is assumed that *kutuhala-shalas* were known in the time of the Buddha around the mid-first millennium BC. But since the Buddhist texts were written later, probably in the post-Mauryan period, these places and their functions were still remembered, or existed in some form. The cities are likely to have been those of the middle Ganges plain – Vaishali, Shravasti, Rajagriha, etc. Personal communication from Romila Thapar.

References

Academics for Creative Reform in Education. 2015. 'What Is to be Done about Indian Universities? Reflections from Concerned Teachers', *Economic & Political Weekly*, 50(24): 25–9.

Altbach, Philip G. 1970a. 'Student Movements in Historical Perspective: The Asian Case', *Journal of Southeast Asian Studies*, 1(1): 74–84.
———. 1970b. 'The International Student Movement', *Journal of Contemporary History*, 5(1): 156–74.
Ananthamurthy, U. R. 2014. *Hindutva athava Hind Swaraj?* Bengaluru: Abhinava.
Arunima, G. 2017. 'Thought, policies and politics: how may we imagine the public university in India?', *Kronos*, 43(1): 1–20.
Axtell, James. 2016. *Wisdom's Workshop: The Rise of the Modern University*. Princeton, NJ: Princeton University Press.
Bhushan, Sudhanshu. 2016. 'Public University in a Democracy', *Economic & Political Weekly*, 51(17): 35–40.
Birla, Kumaramangalam and Ambani, Mukesh. 2000. *Report on a Policy Frame Work for Reforms in Education*. Special Subject Group on Policy Framework for Private Investment in Education, Health and Rural Development, Prime Minister's Council on Trade and Industry, Government of India.
Calhoun, Craig. 2006. 'The University as a Public Good', *Theses Eleven*, 84(1): 7–43.
Carreau, Dominique G. 1969. 'Towards "Student Power" in France?', *The American Journal of Comparative Law*, 17(3): 359–70.
Centre for Humanities Research. 2016. *The University and Its Worlds: A Panel Discussion with Achin Mbembe, Judith Butler, Wendy Brown and David Theo Goldberg*. University of Western Cape, Republic of South Africa. Available at www.chrflagship.uwc.ac.za/the-university-and-its-worlds-a-panel-discussion-with-achille-mbembe-judith-butler-wendy-brown-and-david-theo-goldberg/ (accessed on 10 October 2016).
Chattopadhyay, Saumen. 2010. 'An Elitist and Flawed Approach Towards Higher Education', *Economic & Political Weekly*, 45(18): 15–17.
Chatterjee, Partha. 2016. 'Freedom of Speech in the University', *Economic & Political Weekly*, 51(11): 35–7.
Chaudhuri, Supriya. 2011. 'What Is to Be Done? Economies of Knowledge', *Theses Eleven*, 105(1): 7–22. Available at http://philpapers.org/rec/CHAWIT-7; http://philpapers.org/rec/CHAWIT-7 (accessed on 17 October 2016).
———. 2016. 'The Crises of the Public University', *Café Dissensus*, 15 September. Available at https://cafedissensus.com/2016 /09/15/the-crisis-of-the-public-university/ (accessed on 17 October 2016).
Datla, Kavita. 2013. *The Language of Secular Islam: Urdu Nationalism and Colonial India*. Honolulu: Hawaii University Press.
Deshpande, Satish. 2016. 'The Public University After Rohith – Kanhaiya', *Economic & Political Weekly*, 51(11): 32–4.
Dhareshwar, Vivek. 1993. 'Caste and the Secular Self', *Journal of Arts and Ideas*, 25–26: 115–26.
Eagleton, Terry. 2015. 'The Slow Death of the University', *Chronicle of Higher Education*, 6 April. Available at www.chronicle.com/article/The-Slow-Death-of-the /228991/ (accessed on 16 October 2016).

Forward Press. 2016. 'Faculty Positions: Another Casteist Fort!', 28 August. Available at www.forwardpress.in/2016/08/faculty-positions-another-casteist-fort/ (accessed on 31 December 2017).

Guha, Ramachandra. 2015. 'In Absentia: Where Are India's Conservative Intellectuals?', *Caravan*, 1 March. Available at www.caravanmagazine.in/reportage/absentia-ramachandra-guha-indian-conservatives (accessed on 31 December 2017).

JNU. nd. 'Admission Policy', Available at https://www.jnu.ac.in/sites/default/files/AdmissionPolicy.pdf (accessed on 10 October 2016).

Kumar, Kanhaiya. 2016. 'We Are of This Country and Love the Soil of India: Full Text of Kanhaiya Kumar's Speech', *Indian Express*, 10 February. Available at http://indianexpress.com/article/opinion/columns/kanhaiya-kumar-speech-jnu-row-is-this-sedition/ (accessed on 9 October 2016).

Kumar, Udaya. 2016. 'The University and Its Outside', *Economic & Political Weekly*, 51(11): 29–31.

Lelyveld, David. 2003. *Aligarh's First Generation: Muslim Solidarity in British India*. New Delhi: Oxford University Press.

Malagatti, Arvind. 2014. *Government Brahmana*. Mysore: Chetana Book House.

MHRD. 2013. *All India Survey on Higher Education, 2011–12 (Provisional)*, Department of Higher Education, Ministry of Human Resource Development, Government of India.

———. 2016. *National Policy on Education 2016: Report of the Committee for Evolution of the New Education Policy*. Ministry of Human Resource Development: Government of India.

———. 2017. *All India Survey of Higher Education* 2016–17. MHRD: Government of India.

Nigam, Aditya. 1986. 'Student Movement and Education Policy', *Social Scientist*, 14(2–3): 79–86.

Newman, John. 1909. 'What Is a University?', *Historical Sketches*, Vol 3, *The Rise and Progress of Universities*, 1856, Longmans, Green and Co. Available at www.newmanreader.org/works/historical/volume3/universities/chapter2.html (accessed on 9 October 2016).

Oakeshott, Michael. The Idea of the University'. Available at www.msudenver.edu/media/content/facultyevaltaskforce/sources/oakeshotttheideaofauniversity.pdf (accessed on 20 October 2016).

Olivelle, Patrick. 1998. 'Brihadaryanaka Upanishad, 3.6.1', in *The Early Upanishads: Annotated Text and Translation* (pp. 29–165). New York, Oxford: Oxford University Press.

Pandey, Gyanendra. 2016. 'Dreaming in English: Challenges of Nationhood and Democracy', *Economic & Political Weekly*, 51(16): 56–62.

Pinkney, Andrea Marion. 2014. 'Looking West to India: Asian Education, Intra-Asian Renaissance, and the Nalanda Revival', *Modern Asian Studies*, 49(1): 111–49.

Prasad, Madhava. 2011. 'The Republic of Babel', in Anjan Ghosh, Tapati Guha Thakurta, and Janaki Nair (eds.) *Theorising the Present: Essays for Partha Chatterjee* (pp. 65–81). New Delhi: Oxford University Press.

Renold, Leah. 2005. *A Hindu Education: Early Years of the Benares Hindu University*. New Delhi: Oxford University Press.

Report of the Committee Appointed to Consider Steps Necessary for the Adequate Representation of Communities in the Public Service. 1919. Bangalore: Government of Mysore.

Satyanarayana, K. and Tharu, Susie.(eds.) 2013. *Steel Nibs Are Sprouting, New Dalit Writing from India: Dossier II, Kannada and Telugu*. New Delhi: Harper Collins.

Seth, Sanjay. 2015. 'Higher Education and the Indian Social Imaginary', *American Historical Review*, Roundtable, October: 1354–67.

Siddalingaiah, D. 2014. *Ooru Keri I: Athma Kathe*. Bangalore: Ankitha Pustaka.

Singh, Dalip. 1991. 'Protest Movements in India', *The Indian Journal of Political Science*, 52(4): 448–57.

Subramanian, Jayashree. 2007. 'Perceiving and Producing Merit: Gender and Doing Science in India', *Indian Journal of Gender Studies*, 14(2): 259–84.

Sujatha, V. 2015. 'The Academic Performance Indicators and Its Follies', *Economic & Political Weekly*, 50(5): 23–5.

UGC.nd. 'University Grants Commission'. Available at www.ugc.ac.in/.

Vernon, James. nd. 'The End of the Public University in England', unpublished paper (accessed on 17 October 2016).

2 Decolonizing the university

Aditya Nigam

> The most important and urgent reform needed in education is to transform it, to endeavour to relate it to the life, needs and aspirations of the people and thereby make it the powerful instrument of social, economic and cultural transformation necessary for the realization of the national goals. *For this purpose, education should be developed so as to increase productivity*, achieve social and national integration, *accelerate the process of modernization and cultivate social, moral and spiritual values.*
>
> – Report of the University Education Commission
> (Dr. S. Radhakrishnan Commission), 1948–9

The draft of the National Education Policy 2016 begins with the above epigraph from the report of the Radhakrishnan Commission on University Education, submitted on the morrow of Independence. There is, in a sense, an unbroken line, despite ups and downs, in the thinking on education – especially university education – that runs through our entire postcolonial history. In between, from the 1980s onwards (the 1986 NEP) and the more recent attempts to think about the problems and direction our universities should take, namely, the reports of the National Knowledge Commission (2008–9) and the Yashpal Committee Report (2009), submitted to the United Progressive Alliance government, the same concerns seem to dominate. There did seem to be an urgency in reforming the university system, especially in the UPA era, but the concern was, once again, with the problem of global integration and rising to the occasion in the context of what was called the emergent 'knowledge economy'. If the orientation of the Radhakrishnan Commission was towards developing education "so as to increase productivity" and accelerating "the process of modernization", the emphasis in the twenty first century had not really changed much insofar as these goals were concerned. What did change was the ethos: an increasingly greater orientation towards the private sector, public-private partnerships and closer alliance with "industry". It is not my intention here to go into a policy critique of these documents, but those interested in pursuing this matter could see the relevant reports themselves, in particular the Knowledge Commission's report entitled *More Quality Ph.Ds*, where the relationship of research with industry has been especially underlined.[1]

In the two concerns that I have highlighted from the Radhakrishnan Commission's quote above, namely, increase in productivity and accelerating the process of modernization, neither of these terms is actually put to any scrutiny. And here I am not talking of any documentary evidence in particular, but of the way thinking of higher education and related policies has unfolded over the decades. "Increasing productivity" (therefore, needs of the economy) and "accelerating modernization", without submitting these two critical terms (i.e. economy and modernization) to any interrogation meant (and continues to mean) that we basically gear our entire higher education and university system to the requirements of certain goals that we have adopted quite unthinkingly. Of course, it is easy to say this today in retrospect. Nonetheless, how can we forget the intellectual labours of a Rabindranath Tagore or a Gandhi in warning us, well in advance, of the perils of equating modernity with the normative ideals of the modern West?

It is true that the entire paraphernalia of the social sciences (and here I confine myself to the social sciences, whose scenario I am more familiar with) bears the birthmarks of Western modernity. So when we set up universities, prepare syllabi and supposedly equip our students to play their role in increasing productivity and accelerating modernization, we are basically training them to produce another replay of the West in our midst. It is not therefore surprising that with that conceptual apparatus and paraphernalia, we are only able to see non-Western lives as always embodying a lack. Once trained in that tradition of social sciences, we can only see our 'modernity' as incomplete, our 'democracy' as immature, our 'secularism' as distorted, our 'development' as arrested or retarded – always in the 'waiting room' of History, to steal Dipesh Chakrabarty's term. We could actually go on expanding the list of such 'lacks': we do not have 'philosophy', we do not have 'history', we do not have 'autobiography', we do not have 'theory' and so on. All these statements may be true but they are largely so because we are trying to judge societies that have experienced 'modernity' in ways very different from the way the West did, where these terms were born. These terms and categories carry with them an entire conceptual universe and a history. What is more, none of them is an innocent descriptive category, for they do not simply contain a history but a whole theory of what it means to be modern, secular, democratic and so on and why they are normatively superior to anything else that went before them. They embody, in other words, an understanding of a whole way of life that sees other ways of being, belonging to other parts of the world, as representing an undesirable past. From that standpoint, we will always remain deficient and always running, ostensibly to 'catch up' but in effect, to stay in the same place.

The crisis of the university in India then, as perhaps in many other universities of the global south, has an added dimension – over and above the largely neoliberalism-induced current crisis – and that has been its structural feature from the very beginning. In a manner of speaking, it was inevitable and unavoidable in the context of the colonial history of modern education in India. It is something that should have been talked about and discussed after Independence but given our collective fascination with the modern, it remained largely uninterrogated till very recently.

In what follows, I will therefore sidestep the question of the current crisis of the university and take this opportunity to talk a bit about a critique that should have been made long ago and which should have enabled us to make a move in a somewhat different direction. Though this is important in itself, I think it is necessary to also spell out what decolonizing the university and decolonizing knowledge might mean today, especially in the context of the current right-wing rhetoric about decolonization. Does decolonizing knowledge mean a rejection of Western knowledge altogether? And what is 'Western knowledge' anyway?

It is necessary at this point to briefly state what I mean by the term 'decolonization'. There have been various moves that talk of the project against the backdrop of the exhaustion of the postcolonial critique of Western intellectual hegemony, notably what has been referred to as the 'decolonial' proposed by Walter Mignolo (Mignolo 2011). If postcolonial studies rendered an invaluable service in providing critiques of different aspects of Western knowledge, decoloniality and other projects like 'epistemologies of the south', seek to move beyond in terms of actually proposing different ways of theorizing. In part, my use of the term resonates with these positions but it also situates itself in the moment of 'decolonization of knowledge' and the 'decolonization of the university' initiated by the movement that began in the University of Cape Town, in South Africa, in March 2015. This movement, known as the 'Rhodes Must Fall' movement, began with the demand for removal of the statue of Cecil Rhodes from the university premises, quickly spread all over South Africa (and even in England), demanding the decolonization of thought, of knowledge and syllabi. However, I move away from the demand for complete rejection of Western knowledge raised within the movement, or by the right-wing in India, which has little understanding about what colonization and Western knowledge mean in the first place. In the next section, I explain why.

Global inheritance of 'Western' knowledge

It is necessary to underline that the decolonization of knowledge does not mean a rejection of Western knowledge and its categories, and their replacement with Sanskrit terms and categories as right-wing proponents of 'decolonization' seem to believe. This is so for the simple reason that such a move leaves the very question of what is 'Western' and what is 'Eastern' untouched and uninterrogated, and simply reproduces the binary that the self-presentation of the modern West puts before us. What we have today under the rubric of Western knowledge is a complex assemblage of ideas and concepts that have much longer histories than what we are made to believe – going back centuries before Europe's Renaissance, to India, China and the Arab world. There is a lot of work that has emerged in recent years, both historical and in the history of philosophy and thought that challenges the commonplace notion that all thought, scientific and philosophical, began properly speaking in Modern Europe. We also know today that Athens and classical Greece actually partook of a geography of thought that had little to do with what we know as Europe today, including Asia Minor, that is Anatolia and parts of the Mediterranean world. But what is even more important to recognize today is the way in which the 'dazzling' rise of the modern West produced the Enlightenment as the true source of light, in relation to which the whole world before it was drowned in darkness. The experience of medieval Christendom with its Crusades and Inquisitions became the template through which the entire past of humanity was rendered 'legible'. Later historians have questioned this notion, to be sure, but the idea that 'modernity' actually began with the Enlightenment (and the Renaissance at best) continues to hold sway, even though we hear occasional references to 'early modernities' in the context of other cultures and societies as well. These references to such 'early modernities' however, remain still particular stories that have done nothing to shake the certainties of the self-presentation of modern Western thought.

The very story of modernity and with it, the idea of 'Western knowledge' therefore, needs to be unpacked as some scholars have been trying to do in recent years. It is beyond the scope of this brief essay to map the details of the picture as it emerges, once we begin to take these new developments into account. The interested reader can of course follow up on some of the references given below. Let a few instances speak for themselves.

John M. Hobson in his *The Eastern Origins of Western Civilization*, cites Francis Bacon who "famously claimed in his *Novum Organum* (1620) that the three most important world discoveries were printing, gunpowder and the compass" and remarks that "strikingly, all three were invented in China" (Hobson 2004: 57). Clearly, without these three discoveries, it is virtually impossible to imagine something like colonialism. What is more, it was the Chinese, who discovered around 1000 AD that the magnetic north and the true north were not the same and that it was "this knowledge that by the fifteenth century, enabled the construction of the most accurate maps then known" (Ibid; 57).

It is no less interesting that colonialism, with its great impulse for calculation and classification, could hardly have made any headway, were it to rely on the awkward alphabet-based Roman numeral system. The great breakthrough in mathematics and the numeral system came with the production of the decimal system and the number zero (*shunya*) by Brahmagupta of Ujjain, in the seventh century. In the early ninth century, the great Arab mathematician, Muhammad ibn Musa al-Khwarizmi, a member of the Bait-al-Hikma (House of Wisdom) set up by the Khalifa Al-Mamun, travelled to India and acquainted himself with Brahmagupta's work as well as of other mathematicians like Aryabhata. It was this system that was later developed and made available to the world by al-Khwarizmi in his book *On Calculation with Hindu Numerals* (Rogers 2008: 18–20; Hobson 2004: 176). This book was lost after the Bait-al-Hikma library was destroyed, following the Mongol invasion in the twelfth century. Its Latin translation, *Algoritmi de Numero Indorum*, survived and this numeral system was adopted by many Arab/Islamic scholars in the tenth century. The idea that zero could enhance the value of a number by a factor of ten, or that any number multiplied by zero yielded zero, was quite incomprehensible to Europeans. Initially it was known mainly in academic circles from around the eleventh century, and it is only around the late fifteenth century that Arab-Hindu numerals begin to be adopted for book-keeping. From the late sixteenth century, it became a more generalized practice in book-keeping.

It is of no less consequence that the astronomical breakthroughs by Ibn al-Shatir of the Maragha school "developed a series of mathematical models which were almost exactly the same as those developed about 150 years later by Copernicus" and he [Copernicus] has been recognized as the most noted follower of the Maragha school (Hobson 2004: 180).

Peter O'Brien notes therefore that

> In their historic awakening at the end of the Middle Ages that ushered in the Renaissance, Reformation, Scientific Revolution and Enlightenment, Europeans borrowed and augmented a vast array of ideas, institutions and practices, particularly from the Islamic, but also from the Indian and Chinese, civilization.
>
> (O'Brien 2011: 18)

The influence of Islamic thinking in the domain of philosophy too is now being acknowledged once again. In a recent essay, Laura Marks has explored the ways in which certain key philosophical ideas of Islamic philosophers like Ibn Sina were adopted by thinkers like Roger Bacon, Thomas Aquinas and Duns Scotus – the last mentioned transmitting it to a contemporary philosopher like Gilles Deleuze (Marks 2012: 57). Late medieval Christian scholastics, argues Marks, acknowledged what they had borrowed from Muslim philosophers, but "later European thinkers disingenuously claimed a direct link between European and Greek thought, disavowing the hundreds of years of Islamic philosophy upon which emerging European thought relied" (Ibid: 52).

Decolonization or 'Swaraj in Ideas'[2]

The point that I am trying to make here then, is not that we should abandon 'Western thought' altogether but that the project of decolonization of thought must reject the self-representation of later European thinkers who sought to erase the longer history of ideas from which they themselves drew, which they undoubtedly developed and enriched. Rejecting that self-representation means that we recognize that in the world of ideas there has always been a long and continuous traffic and ideas cannot be pigeon holed into specific geographic limits.

Ironically, this geographical closure was not just a European gift to societies like ours; early Indian nationalism too was equally guilty of drawing such borders, thus initiating an endless and unproductive quest for 'indigenous' ways of thinking. It was unproductive because it simply led to a resentful retreat into the past, in order to demonstrate that we too had a glorious history of philosophy and thought – a commendable effort that, however, lost all capacity to speak to or theorize the challenges of the present. Where it did, the search for a vibrant Indian thought tradition eventually became a way of making claims to the effect that "we too had our Machiavelli in Kautilya" or we too had a concept of 'state of nature' in the notion of *matsyanyaya*. Such claims remained unperturbed by the fact that Kautilya preceded Machiavelli by fifteen centuries and could not have had the same project as the latter, or that the concept of *matsyanyaya* went back to the Vedas, and had nothing to do with the fiction of 'social contract', for which the fiction of state of nature had been invented. In other words, the search for indigenous traditions did not really break out of the overpowering impact of Western thought, reading its own traditions in the template of Western thought.

The task of intellectual decolonization or what KC Bhattacharya had, in a 1931 lecture, felicitously called 'swaraj in ideas', involved, I want to argue, the capacity to theorize our present, to grasp the challenges produced by the modern condition. That modernity, in its train, had brought in experiences entirely novel in character, actually posed a challenge that went far beyond the frames or the vocabulary that traditional Indian thought could have yielded. And quite apart from the question of cultural and historical specificity, the fact that the modern in our context was the colonial modern, also meant that we could not simply lay hold of philosophical or conceptual categories delivered to us by Western knowledge and use it for our purposes. The challenge was really to take our own experience as the basis of engagement with the categories of thought and frameworks of knowledge received from the West, even as we mined our own intellectual traditions for the resources to do so. However, just as we cannot simply lay hold of Western conceptual categories and deploy them uncritically for our present purposes, so can we not also simply take categories from ancient or medieval Indian thought and deploy them to understand our present. In both cases, additional work needs to be performed – a theoretical labour of sorts – that alone can make them speak to our contemporary concerns.

It should be clear then, that what I am talking about here is 'doing theory' or 'doing philosophy' in a way that may give us a sense of what our present condition is and how might we think about our future. If we turn once more to the two goals identified by the Radhakrishnan Commission, referred to above, it should be immediately clear that both 'increasing productivity' and 'accelerating modernization' relate fundamentally to the way in which 'the economy' and to put it more bluntly, capitalism are to be made to replace our 'archaic' peasant economy. Goals, in short, that are derived straight from the arsenal of Western modernity and its normative standards. It makes no difference to our understanding of our so-called goals that the person heading this Commission on University Education is steeped in Hindu philosophy and would at another level, swear by the great philosophical traditions of India. Cut to 2017, and we now have a regime that cannot cease to talk of the greatness of Hindu tradition, while pushing through ideas like 'smart cities', 'cashless economy' or genetically modified crops, without a moment's reflection on what all this might have to do with our, or any, tradition for that matter. There is not even a make-believe attempt to think afresh the question of other economic and life forms, despite the severe crisis that this model had brought in its train for humanity as such, in the form of high degrees of inequality and an impending ecological crisis that stares us in the face. The two levels – that of exaltation of our great past, and confronting our present challenges – remain as compartmentalized as ever, from Radhakrishnan to the present dispensation. At no point is the 'great thought tradition' ever brought in to bear upon how we might think our present and our future – except as an inauthentic copy of the contemporary West. In purely rhetorical mode though, we can hear political leaders from the present prime minister down, telling the world how our hallowed tradition has 'always been ecologically sensitive'.

What this means is that 'intellectual decolonization', if it is not to remain a mere slogan of the plunderers of thought, must involve serious theoretical labour. It needs to look afresh at the history and experience of the West, not as a model to be imitated but as an experience to be evaluated and critically engaged with. It requires of us that we step back and think, in order to evolve our own understanding of what modernity is and where we want to go. After all, it is no longer evident in these early decades of the twenty-first century that the Western model of economy – capitalism, in short – is either desirable or inevitable. On the contrary, more and more top economists today are coming to the conclusion that concepts like 'growth', especially as measured by the very recent concept, 'GDP', are highly misleading. They are coming to the conclusion that the entire business of the relationship between what we call 'the economy' and the ecology needs to be rethought: no longer can we consider the ecology as mere provider of raw material (natural resources) to the economy whose laws cannot be meddled around with. They are coming around to the idea that it is the economy that is a subset of the larger entity that we call the environment or the ecology. If the economic and political aesthetic of modernity was based on the romance of speed and exponential growth, the early twenty-first century has been witness to a range of movements and initiatives that underline the importance of slowing down – from the slow food movement of Italy (now a global trend) to changing consumer movements that emphasize consumption of locally sourced food with smaller ecological footprints. Considering that Gandhi and Tagore so insistently worked towards an "aesthetic of slowness",[3] largely deriving from a deep engagement with their own tradition, one can only feel sorry that, in 2016, an education policy document in India still underlines "accelerating modernization" and "increasing productivity" as the central "national goal" to which it thinks education should be hitched.

Decolonization of thought and its corollary, the decolonization of the university, would then entail making a radical break with this way of treating education as surrogate to something like 'national development goals'. It would entail the development of our universities as places of developing critical thinking, far more than they have been able to, given the continuing sway of Western knowledge.[4]

Decolonization and the language question

One of the ways in which the continuing colonization of our minds works is through our sole reliance on English as the language of education and thought. Though there have been policies like 'education in mother tongue' at the primary level and the 'three language formula' up to the matriculation or secondary levels, the fact of the matter is that, as we proceed towards more complex disciplinary levels of teaching, both in sciences and the social sciences, our teaching and evaluation tend to become totally dependent on English. One of the reasons has to do perhaps with the position English acquired as a 'neutral' language in the face of entirely wrong-headed effort of the advocates of Hindi to make it a national language. Anxieties about the imposition of Hindi have been quite widespread and many non-Hindi speaking states have preferred a combination of their own mother tongues with English. At the university level – and here I speak from the experience of universities in the Hindi/Urdu region – the problem has remained intractable, primarily because it has been treated as a matter of no consequence so far. My general sense of the situation in Bengal and some other states is that it is not fundamentally different institutionally, though Bengali is certainly far better off more generally.

Thus it happens that in the past seventy years, there has been no effort to address the pedagogic needs of the bulk of students who know only Hindi (for the moment I leave aside Urdu speakers). What this means is that decade after decade, the students, though formally allowed to take their examinations in Hindi, have had no reading materials to refer to. The lectures too are conducted in English. The situation actually starts from the school level, where, except for History, where the state had an investment and therefore key texts were translated by the National Council for Educational Research and Training (NCERT), all other disciplines suffered. As a result, decade after decade, we have been producing students who are ill-equipped to take on the challenge of pursuing research or academics in languages other than English. Research scholars have lately been allowed, say, in Delhi University, to write their PhD theses in Hindi, but those who take that route have had no place to get their research published in journals, for there simply are no journals.[5]

However, my reason for bringing up this mundane sounding issue here is that it is deeply connected with the problem of decolonization of thought. The problem initially presented itself simply as one of translation – of getting English reading materials translated into Hindi and other Indian languages, but soon we realized that this hardly touched the surface of the problem. One could refer profitably here to the experience of bringing out a Hindi version of the journal *Economic and Political Weekly*. This journal, called *Saancha*, was published for about two and a half years in the late 1980s and, though it did help to satisfy a craving for serious research-based material in Hindi, had severe limitations. These limitations were not of its own making but structurally built into the situation: articles could be translated but if one went through references one would realize that practically none of the works referred to was available to Hindi readers.

Some of us who have been writing in Hindi as well as translating have also come to the conclusion long ago that in a thought-world so very different, the very business of finding apposite translated terms is hazardous at best. To take one well-known instance, we all know that when the term 'feudalism' was to be translated into Indian languages, the word '*samant*' and, therefore, *samantvaad* were found to fit the bill, since they referred to a precapitalist system based on land. In reality, this system had nothing remotely to do with feudalism in Europe – it was a system of what Stanley Tambiah has called the 'galactic polity', a circle of small principalities linked to a larger kingdom to which they paid taxes and with whom they formed a larger whole (Tambiah 1973/2013). Soon the term *samantvaad* started referring to European feudalism and even the residual traces of something called *samant/tantra* faded from memory, so much so that a few decades later when Marxist historians asked 'was there feudalism in India?' the term could be made to refer exclusively to European feudalism.

72 Aditya Nigam

The question, '*kya bharat mein samantvaad tha?*' would obviously make no sense to someone who thought in terms of Indian historical-cultural categories. One could similarly take the example of 'secularism' that has often been 'translated' as '*dharma nirapekshata*' in Hindi and some other Indian languages. The fact of the matter is that this term is not a translation of the English word and has little in common with either the separation of Church and State (religion and state) or religion and politics. It was simply made to stand in for the English word, for that was the language of thought, but it really embodied an entirely different thought-universe.

What I am trying to get at here, then, is the fact that languages embody historic-cultural thought-worlds and it makes a world of a difference to what we think and how we think, depending on which language we choose to think in. There can be no swaraj in ideas if English remains our primary language of thought. English is our gateway to world philosophy and world literature and is therefore indispensable, but we can make it our sole or even primary language of thought only at our own peril.

To conclude, then, it may be useful to recall that the project of decolonization demands, first and foremost, an ability to stand on our own feet. It demands that we rapidly overcome the huge gap that separates our sense of our exalted intellectual past and our meek and unquestioning surrender to dominant Western ideas when it comes to facing the challenges of our present. It also demands that we engage in serious intellectual and theoretical labour – the task of decolonization is not a matter of sloganeering, as the right-wing seems to believe; nor is it a matter of beginning once again a futile search for some purely 'Indian ways of thinking'. Decolonization is, above all, opening thought to other traditions, *including but not exclusively* one's own. It is about understanding that in the world of thought, it is not for cow gangs to dictate what can be thought and what cannot.

Notes

1 The Yashpal Committee report too contemplates public-private partnership and more play for private players in higher education but this was apparently, not enough for one member, Kaushik Basu, who submitted a note of dissent where his sole interest was in playing the advocate of the private sector.
2 'Swaraj in Ideas' was the title of Krishna Chandra Bhattacharya's lecture, delivered in October 1931, as part of the Sir Ashutosh Memorial Lecture in Chandernagore.
3 I have made this argument, at length, in relation to Gandhi, based on my reading of *Hind Swaraj* in Nigam 2013.

4 It needs to be underlined today that many of our universities, despite this collective failure, have been vibrant spaces where critical thinking and a culture of questioning have been encouraged. In this, very often it is the role of outstanding teachers that has transformed these institutional spaces into arenas of intellectual inquiry.

5 Only lately has a peer-reviewed research journal been started in Hindi by the Centre for the Study of Developing Societies.

References

Committee to Advise on the Renovation and Rejuvenation of Higher Education (Yashpal Committee). 2009. Report submitted to the Minister of Human Resource Development, March.

Hobson, John M. 2004. *Eastern Origins of Western Civilization*. Cambridge: Cambridge University Press.

Marks, Laura. 2012. 'A Deleuzian *Ijtihad*: Unfolding Deleuze's Islamic Sources Occulted in the Ethnic Cleansing of Spain', in Arun Saldanha and Jason Michael Adams (eds.) *Deleuze and Race*. Edinburgh: Edinburgh University Press.

Mignolo, Walter. 2011. *The Darker Side of Western Modernity: Global Futures, Decolonial Options*. London, Durham: Duke University Press.

National Knowledge Commission. 2008. *More Quality PhDs*. New Delhi, December 2008.

Nigam, Aditya. 2013. 'Towards an Aesthetic of Slowness: Reading *Hind Swaraj* Today', in Ghanshyam Shah (ed.) *Re-Reading Hind Swaraj: Modernity and Subalterns*. New Delhi: Routledge.

O'Brien, Peter. 2011. 'Islamic Civilization and (Western) Modernity', *Comparative Civilizations Review*, 65: 18–32.

Rogers, Elizabeth. 2008. *Islamic Mathematics*, PhD thesis, University of Illinois at Urbana-Champaign. Available at http://new.math.uiuc.edu/im2008/rogers/drafts/IslamicMathematics.pdf (accessed on 15 June 2017).

Tambiah, Stanley. 1973/2013. 'The Galactic Polity in Southeast Asia', *Journal of Ethnographic Theory*, 3(3): 503–34 (Reprint from 1973).

3 The crisis of the public university

Supriya Chaudhuri

In a brief essay – written in the form of a letter – prefaced to a book by his colleague John Higgins at the University of Cape Town, the novelist J. M. Coetzee offered a pessimistic coda to Higgins's powerful appeal for the autonomy of the university and the role of the humanities in fostering 'critical literacy'. As Coetzee noted,

> All over the world, as governments retreat from their traditional duty to foster the common good and reconceive of themselves as mere managers of national economies, universities have been coming under pressure to turn themselves into training schools equipping young people with the skills required by a modern economy.
>
> (Coetzee, in Higgins 2014: xi)

Coetzee's pessimism is founded on two linked perceptions. In the first place, he has no illusions about 'the ideological force driving the assault on the independence of universities in the (broadly conceived) West'. To him, this assault, commencing in the 1980s, appeared cynical and coherent: it was directed at neutralizing sites of agitation and dissent, and preventing the dissemination of ideas that might induce young people to question, rather than accept, the social, political and above all *economic* order. Secondly, he finds that universities have proved reluctant or ill-equipped to protect themselves:

> The fact is that the record of universities, over the past thirty years, in defending themselves against pressure from the state has not been a proud one. Few academics appreciated, from the beginning, the scale of the attack that was being launched on their independence or the ideological passion that drove it. Resistance was weak and ill organised; routed, the professors beat a retreat to

The crisis of the public university 75

their dugouts, from where they have done little besides launching the intermittent satirical barb against the managerial newspeak they are perforce having to acquire.

(ibid.: xiii)

Coetzee's gloom has its origin in a genuine crisis, a global shrinkage, if we might call it that, in the philosophical and critical functions of the academy. As he sees it, the loss of academic autonomy cannot be repaired by reviving certain kinds of intellectual disciplines: it is far too closely linked to political and economic forces that have combined to render the modern university merely the slave of capital. And as a (retired) professor, permanently confined to a metaphorical dugout, I cannot but share his sense of the actual ineffectiveness of rearguard action on our part. Indeed, the only figure in Coetzee's later fiction with whom I feel reluctant sympathy – no doubt because of my own subject position – is the elderly female writer Elizabeth Costello, touring the world to lecture hostile provincial audiences on the lives of animals and the duty of vegetarianism. (By an accident of history, this unpopular subject might receive state patronage in present-day India.) For Coetzee, the threat to the academy is not just from the loss or attenuation of traditional disciplines, but from their substitution by 'skill sets' which are claimed as transferable even without disciplinary foundation – particularly in the humanities. If universities are doomed to extinction, he argues, it is time for philosophy to be taken out of the academy.

Yet the situation in India appears in some respects the reverse of the global picture. Elsewhere, universities are struggling to sustain programmes and departments in a climate of funding cuts, smaller colleges are closing down, students are crippled by debt and unable to make their degrees count, while in India, both Central and State governments periodically announce the creation of new universities and institutes of technology, resolve to increase the gross enrolment ratio, and encourage private and foreign players to enter the market.[1] It might seem, then, that higher education in India is a sector of growth, a site of promise and opportunity, while, worldwide, it is in recession. Of course, such a contrast need not actually negate Coetzee's fears, since these stem not from the physical absence of universities, but rather from a loss of their social and intellectual functions. Unfortunately, even that contrast is more apparent than real.

Even in India, universities – especially public universities – are under threat. Grants did not go up under the 12th Plan; in fact the higher education budget was cut by over 1500 crores in 2015–16 alone. The

University Grants Commission, its existence imperilled by the proposal (still pending) to set up a Higher Education Commission of India that will wield extreme punitive powers, extending to jail terms, is moribund, unable to disburse even sanctioned funds. Both UPA and BJP governments announced new IITs and IIMs, in addition to other populist gestures, including reviving State universities through RUSA, but in fact the promised expenditure of 6% of GDP on education was never reached. The new National Policy on Education document, published in 2016, admits that:

> The earlier National Education Policies of 1968, and 1986 as modified in 1992, had endorsed a norm of 6% of GDP as the minimum expenditure on education. However, this target has never been met. The expenditure by Education Departments of the Centre and States has never risen above 4.3% of the GDP, and is currently around 3.5%.
> (GoI 2016: 24, Section 3.5.3)

Despite the Right to Education Act of 2009, India has the largest population of non-literates in the world. The Gross Enrolment Ratio (of students in higher education) is calculated by different government agencies at lows between 14% and 23%, with glaring regional, caste and community-based disparities. Further, through an imperceptible but momentous shift in the higher education landscape, over 60% of students now study in private institutions (of indifferent merit). Dropout rates among disadvantaged groups remain high, and inclusive education, especially in the private sector, is a myth. Meanwhile, publicly funded institutions – State and Central universities – are stretched to breaking point by the pressure to increase intake while simultaneously achieving high levels of innovation and research to propel them up the global rankings. The NPE reiterates the absurd but sinister proposal to institute an Indian Education Service (IES) under the MHRD, from which all academic appointments will be made, while reputed universities will create 'leadership development centres' offering short-term managerial courses mandated for all future heads of institutions.

Within this depressing scene of negative aspiration, the ground reality is more depressing still. The unrest on public university campuses over the past couple of years, occasioned by issues of gender, caste and political belief, has brought faculty and students into conflict with an apparently repressive administration openly supported by the government. Many of these issues (especially caste) are not new – indeed they remind us of earlier instances treated with equal harshness and indifference by university authorities. Nevertheless, there is a new urgency in the protests, as though faculty and students alike are aware that time is running out, indeed that it may already be too late to voice their anger and despair. And, interestingly, both the protest and the repression draw upon two apparently opposed perceptions of the university, seeing it simultaneously as *closed* and *open*, as a restricted, bounded space governed by its own laws, and as a domain subject to the laws of the state (including the sedition laws). For those within the academy, the idea of the university is in question: is it a free, protected space of enquiry, dissent, *parrhesia* – speaking truth to power from relatively neutral ground – or is it no more than a government department? Public universities are under threat today, though we may not agree on the nature of these threats. Recent events at Delhi's Ramjas College (on 21–2 February 2017) were one reminder among many of the intimidations, attacks, and coercive measures faced by universities in India over several years. But it is worth noting that these violent irruptions, because of their dramatic, open display of hostilities with party lines clearly defined, make for a somewhat reductive analysis of the larger crisis. I do not wish to abdicate the responsibility of taking a stand on those incidents, which I saw then as a fascist attempt, on the part of a politically affiliated student body, to claim the 'nation' as its exclusive property, to prevent the free exchange of views among fellow-citizens, and to use physical violence to muffle dissent. That a muffler was actually used in the near-strangulation of a Delhi University faculty member – a spokesperson for the role of the humanities in public life – appears in retrospect a chilling, almost uncanny, concretization of metaphor. Disappointingly, the most visible muffler-wearer in Delhi, its Chief Minister – though he has minimized this sartorial accessory following corrective throat surgery – saw fit to comment mainly on the role of the police, rather than on larger questions of academic or civic freedom. But I would also like to note that the threat to the public university is more insidious than such dramatic conflicts might suggest, and battle-lines are nowhere so clearly drawn.

All over India, Central and State Governments have made common cause in curtailing intellectual freedom and silencing opinions critical of state power. It was during the UPA regime that a narrowly managerial vision of the modern university began to be projected as a desirable ideal, with several bills brought before Parliament to regulate higher education and transform India into a 'knowledge economy'. The principal means to that end were severe restrictions on the autonomy of all public universities, while opening up the higher education sector to private or foreign players licensed to charge high fees and compete for students and faculty. It seemed as though, after long neglect and apathy, the Central government had just discovered its human resources in higher education, and, backed by a pot of money accumulated through the Education Cess, was determined to bring them under its direct control. But the regime changed before most of the bills could be passed, and the new BJP government initially turned its attention towards 'saffronization' of academic bodies, research councils, and textbooks, together with police measures for the 'protection' and surveillance of university campuses. Still, going by the provisions of the Report of the Committee for Evolution of the New Education Policy (2016), the process of strengthening a central control mechanism has continued unabated. One commitment is reiterated from earlier National Policy on Education manifestos, that of:

> the establishment of a new Central service, the Indian Education Service (IES), which will function as an All India Service; with the officers being on permanent settlement to various state governments, and the MHRD being the cadre controlling authority.
>
> (ibid.: 55, Section 5.5.7)

Not only does this proposal make its intention clear by using the favoured term of a politicized bureaucracy, 'cadre', it directly contravenes the constitutional provision by which the States have equal, if not greater say than the Centre in overseeing education, while it strikes at the root of university autonomy – the power of universities to appoint their own faculty. There are other disturbing indications, moreover, that curricula may also be mandated centrally, and that universities will not have the freedom to frame their own syllabi – though recent pronouncements by the Central Minister for Human Resource Development appear to offer some leeway to 'highly ranked' institutions. All this is in the interest of making nationwide testing of students easier. Meanwhile, far away in the east, the Mamata Banerjee government in West Bengal put through a Higher Education Act (2017) cancelling the administrative autonomy of State universities, with far-reaching interventions in the academic domain. Another recent Act makes mere participation in a rally a ground for possible criminal proceedings. These measures, of course, are notionally directed towards the objective of creating 'world-class' institutions, a pleasing dream for those who do not understand that innovation is linked to intellectual freedom.

If this is the background, the foreground is the site of a vigorous territorial battle, fought partly by political cadre, partly by students, intellectuals and academics of all persuasions, for physical control of university spaces. While this might seem a repetition of past battles, there are some new and disturbing features. Firstly, both within and outside the university, the term 'nation' has been appropriated by the ruling party and its cadre as its exclusive possession, so that all those who hold opposing views can be called 'anti-national'. Though the colonial sedition law was invoked as far back as 2010 against the author Arundhati Roy, the terms *sedition, anti-national, pro-Pakistan*, and possibly *beef-eater*, have regularly figured in the current rhetoric of right-wing ideologues, prone to fascist interventions in what people think, how they behave, and what they eat. If we recall the attacks on writers such as Perumal Murugan, the murders of prominent intellectuals like Narendra Dabholkar (2013), M.M. Kalburgi (2015), and Gauri Lankesh (2017), periodic institution of regimes of coercion and fear on university campuses such as Jadavpur, Hyderabad, and Jawaharlal Nehru University, as well as the lynching of individual Muslims or Dalits by self-appointed cow-protectors, it is to guard against the dangerous illusion of the university as an ivory tower, a 'safe' space where ideas can be freely exchanged irrespective of political realities – like those of Kashmir or of Bastar. The public university in India is an open space, a space of contestation and struggle. With higher education itself in crisis, these struggles are even more tangled in the webs of politics, caste, class and gender. Therefore, Rohith Vemula's death on the campus of Hyderabad Central University, following MHRD-directed action against him, or Najeeb Ahmed's disappearance from Jawaharlal Nehru University, or the arrests of students on sedition charges, or the police action at Jadavpur University, or the Ramjas incidents (sparked off by the desire to interrogate events in Kashmir and Bastar), must be seen as linked phenomena. And we cannot assume that private universities are exempt from the surveillance of the state. A long-drawn out and unpleasant series of consequences followed upon a petition on Kashmir signed by some of Ashoka University's ex-students and current members – Ashoka University being a new-model liberal arts university funded by private capital and charging high fees. In fact while the repercussions of the Kashmir petition issue drew angry responses from some of the faculty and negative reports in the media, Ashoka University dealt, 'in-house', far more efficiently and ruthlessly with the problem than any public university could have done. By contrast, on the public and exposed campuses of our public universities, irruptions of violence bring to light official, state-sanctioned attempts to strangle the university system and make it incapable of producing critical thought. Recent proposals for any kind of creative activity on campus have been met by the immortal line from *Marathon Man*, a film shadowed by the Holocaust: 'Is it safe?' Our answer should be, 'No, it is not safe'. The public university itself is not safe.

In an article written around thirty years ago, the philosopher Jürgen Habermas offered a trenchant critique of what he saw as the idealism inherent in Karl Jaspers's 1923 text, *The Idea of the University*, revised in 1961. As Habermas pointed out, 'the idea of the university' suggests an ideal life-form that can no longer be realistically supposed to exist:

> Even disregarding this extravagant claim to exemplary status, isn't the very premise that a vast and extraordinarily complex structure such as the modem university system be permeated and sustained by a mode of thought shared by all its members, unrealistic in the extreme? Couldn't Jaspers have learned years earlier from Max Weber that the organizational reality into which the functionally specified subsystems of a highly differentiated society imbed themselves rests on wholly different premises? The functional capability of such institutions depends precisely on a detachment of their members' motivations from the goals and functions of the organization. Organizations no longer embody ideas.
>
> (1987: 4)

Can the modern university still claim to be animated by an idea, or ideal? Is there, within functions and specializations, a collective consciousness, a 'shared self-understanding of the university's members'? Habermas is not convinced. Ideas come and go, he says, and it is impossible – even undesirable – that all of the university's members should share a 'normative self-image'. What he hopes for, by contrast (and here we are on familiar Habermasian ground) is that they should share a belief in the communicative or discursive forms of scientific argument that hold learning processes together.

> Even outside the university, scientific learning processes still retain certain features of their roots in the universities. They all live from the stimulating and productive power of discursive disputes that carry the promissory note of generating surprising arguments. The doors stand open, and at any moment a new face can suddenly appear, a new idea can unexpectedly arrive.
>
> (ibid.: 21)

Yet he is anxious to avoid 'stylizing' the work of a 'community of investigators' as something exemplary. 'The egalitarian and universalistic content of their forms of argumentation expresses only the norms of scientific discourse, not those of society as a whole' (ibid.: 22). Despite the caution here, we cannot miss Habermas's faith in the communicative process and the life of argument and reason. How can we associate these processes with the emergence of the modern university in India?

That emergence, from the nineteenth century onwards, was driven by three factors: colonial educational policy, nationalist experimentation, and the patronage system of old and new philanthropy. In this it was perfectly representative of India's own uneasy transition to a 'modernity' whose nature is still in question – based, as it was, on a traumatic loss of the past. The process did in fact produce interventions in the public sphere, though with varying degrees of success. In some cases they were led by charismatic figures whose presence in the university drew it into the urgency of the historical moment. In other cases – such as that of Tagore's Visva Bharati – 'modern' higher education was itself under attack. Subsequent to independence, however, access to state funding and the promulgation of various University Acts tended to erase what was distinctive about each institution, to increase its dependence upon the public exchequer (whether State or Central) and to encourage subservience to bureaucratic control by government. Universities were actively discouraged from raising funds from the public or from other sources (despite having been set up through public donations), forced to maintain fees at a level so low that state subsidy was imperative, and compelled to focus on degree-granting to the exclusion of infrastructure, libraries, research, and social commitments, even direct involvement, of other kinds. Many of these legitimate interests were absorbed by newly founded research institutes and by government departments, or delinked from the state-funded programmes of the university and left to survive on their own.

Still, despite the constraints imposed by an unimaginative bureaucracy, limited funding, decaying infrastructure, and an attenuated research climate, the public universities of India, in the decades after independence, emerged as the first free, democratic and secular space where all classes of Indians could meet and interact. It is true, of course, that there were still monstrous inequalities in access to education at the primary and secondary levels, and literacy rates were low, so only a tiny proportion of the country's population could reach university at all. Yet while differences rapidly multiplied at the school level, and the gap between state and private (or trust-funded) schools instituted itself so permanently that within a generation the aspiring middle-class was sending its children to private schools to receive English-language education rather than in the vernacular, there was no alternative – except for the very rich – to the public university, which received students from both systems, private and state. For all its physical limitations, therefore, the university was a place of excitement, energy, intellectual sophistication, and – perhaps most importantly – direct contact with social reality. My own experience at Presidency College during 1969–72, during the last, bitter flourish of the Naxalite movement, with the idea of higher education itself under attack from Maoist theoreticians, certainly instilled in me an abiding respect for teachers and fellow-students who taught me as much about the life of the mind as they did about the need to put our convictions to test in our daily practice.

All of us will recognize that we are today almost at the limit of that period in the life of the public university in India, a period marked by academic rigidity and inflexibility, bureaucratic narrow-mindedness, student indiscipline, faculty politics, and campus decay, but also a period of democracy by default, as it were – a period when some remarkable achievements were made possible by the simple chemistry of contact, and by a merit-driven (however narrowly merit was defined) academic system. And we can see that that system, those contact zones, have been stretched to impossible limits by the inequalities that have persisted in society at large – between rural and urban, rich and poor, oppressed and privileged, women and men, linguistically empowered or disempowered. Perhaps, if we look back at this history from a later perspective, we will see the Right to Education Act, enacted after such shameful delay in 2009, as the final nail in the coffin of a public education system that should legitimately have answered to the aspirations of those who had newly received education from the state itself. This is a paradox, and for me a deeply painful one. On the one hand, there is the necessary commitment to higher education, at public cost, for the huge mass of learners; on the other, there is the apparent breakdown of the existing system, and the possibly unchecked entry of all kinds of new players (private, corporate, foreign) into a higher education landscape that will soon show exactly those divisions that trouble us with respect to school education. And it is for this reason that I think that the silence of the academy – and by the academy I mean our still dominant public higher education institutions – about the university's role in society must be counted as its worst failure, over and above the systemic defects we can all recognize.

The bureaucratization and impoverishment of the public university was of course a good way of focusing the attention of the faculty on their salaries, students on their degrees, and society on employment.

The crisis of the public university   83

If students and teachers were enlisted for larger social causes, these causes were most often determined by political parties rather than by any independent judgment emanating from within the academic community. I have witnessed no agitations more urgent than those involving pay or arrears. But surely we cannot blame economics, or politics, or bureaucracy, or our other vexations, for a failure that is primarily our own. If our university life gave us nothing else, it gave us, perhaps uniquely, a space of encounter, conflict, socialization, speech. In its extreme state that speech might take the form of *parrhesia*, the will to speak truth to power. Individual plain speaking is not unknown in the Indian academy, but it has seldom emerged as a collective practice. The space of the *parrhesiastes* has been taken over by forms of demagoguery or canvassing that serve the specific interests of political parties. It might seem naïve even to imagine any alternative to this state of affairs, given the subservience of employees to their political masters in the 'subsistence' economy of higher education in India. (Such subservience is of course equally characteristic of the more prosperous educational economies of the West, China or Japan.) Current developments in the higher education sector, putting the All India Council of Technical Education in charge of the technologization of higher education through the creation of Massive Online Open Courses (MOOCS) appear to open up educational opportunities for the disadvantaged millions, but effectively narrow down existing spaces of interaction and debate.

At this point, I would like to return to the critique with which I commenced, J. M. Coetzee's preface to his colleague John Higgins's book on academic freedom in South Africa. It should be noted that both Higgins's book and Coetzee's melancholy preface look specifically at the role of the humanities in ensuring academic freedom and free critical endeavour. Coetzee doubts that the modern university can surmount the challenges to its freedom, in the face of what he describes as a sustained ideological assault, from the 1980s onwards, on all forms of critical thinking – especially those kinds of radicalism that had led, in the 1960s and 1970s, to a 'critique of Western civilisation as a whole'.

> The campaign to rid the academy of what was variously diagnosed as a leftist or anarchist or anti-rational or anti-civilisational malaise has continued without let-up for decades, and has succeeded to such an extent that to conceive of universities any more as seedbeds of agitation and dissent would be laughable.
>
> (Coetzee, in Higgins, op. cit., xii)

In fact, as Coetzee sees it, the modern university has failed lamentably to resist the pressures exerted upon it by the state (and, one might add, by private capital). As a result, a certain phase of 'humanist' culture is now at an end, and no revival of the humanities is possible, simply because there are 'too few people left who really believe in the humanities and in the university built on humanistic grounds, with philosophical, historical and philological studies as its pillars' (ibid.: xiii). Sympathetic though he is to Higgins's dream of revival, he thinks it is unlikely: indeed he feels that if 'critical literacy' is Higgins's goal, it will be suggested by his opponents that this can be achieved simply by foundation courses in critical thinking, without a full-fledged 'humanities' programme.

What Coetzee is saying, in his pessimistic way, goes much further than Higgins. He is suggesting that one needs to cultivate the humanities for their own sake, not for any immediate benefits that such study might bring. In the end, he tells his friend, you will have to say that 'we need free enquiry because freedom of thought is good in itself'. He puts his trust in the life of the mind, as an absolute good. And he cites the example of Polish universities under totalitarian rule, where, if one was not permitted to teach real philosophy, one would let one's students know that the philosophy seminar would be run in one's living room, outside the university. It may be necessary, he says, to take humanities outside the university in order to 'keep humanistic studies alive in a world where universities have redefined themselves out of existence' (ibid.: xv).

Coetzee has never been popular in South Africa, and this last statement may also disconcert us in a country like India, which faces such severe problems in literacy, basic schooling, and access to higher education and employment that the dream of a Socratic academy functioning outside the state-funded system might appear hard to take. Here, too, it may seem wilful and idealistic, even a let-up in the struggle for democratic rights, to discuss the survival of the humanities in a climate where even the Right to Education Act, made law in 2008 after 60 years of shameful delay, has not ensured the access of all children to even the most rudimentary of classrooms. Yet we should remember that it is that very Act that will bring very large numbers of new young learners to our ill-equipped and inadequate universities, and it is all the more necessary, given that reality, to make sure that we understand what the academy has to offer them. For we cannot ignore the fact that the Nehruvian dream of an India empowered by scientific, medical and technological education, a dream that directed our post-Independence investments in these fields, has produced terrible

The crisis of the public university 85

imbalances – from which we are yet to recover. Nor can we assume patronizingly that vocational and technical training will be enough: though such training is vital, and neglected, and requires much more by way of facilities and resources. In fact, this is exactly the time when we need to ask what the place of the humanities is in our universities, and what these humanities are. I suggest that this is all the more important at a time of crisis for the public university, when privately managed higher education is making serious inroads into our economy. According to UGC figures published in 2017, private universities make up 260 out of a total of 377 universities in India, and well over half the undergraduate population is enrolled at privately funded institutes. The balance has shifted, with no major upheaval of the tectonic plates, but with evident consequences in the higher education landscape.

In early January 2014, I attended a conference in Bengaluru, grandly called 'The Future of the Liberal Arts', at which chancellors and presidents of at least six US universities were showcasing their model of a liberal arts curriculum to the Indian academy. Present to receive this gift or commodity were the vice-chancellors of a number of new private universities in India, and much was said there about the 'liberal arts' model as the means of resolving the dichotomy of the humanities and the sciences, and creating well-rounded individuals who could justly enjoy the fruits of India's coming prosperity. Much was said in criticism of early specialization and the failure of the Indian university system as a whole, most of it quite correct. Unfortunately, however, there was virtually no representation from India's vast, if inadequate, public university system, so that the US chancellors probably received quite the wrong impression of the state of play. There were only two representatives from State universities, myself from Jadavpur and an astrophysicist from Presidency University in Kolkata: he spoke in a panel on the sciences, I in one on the humanities, and I think we were united in our sense that the problems within the Indian academy can be addressed only by looking at the foundations of our disciplines and how we understand them, not by simply importing another educational model. We were conscious, too, that the conference was being hosted by the Raman Research Institute, a state-funded research body that exemplifies the split between the university and the research establishment that took place post-independence and helped to further ghettoize general humanities and science teaching. But in view of the fact that new private universities (and it is worth noting their difference from the numerous earlier private universities that sold medical, engineering, or business management courses for high fees) are making a serious bid to take over the 'liberal arts' field, and are in a sense re-inventing the humanities by including them in a mixed undergraduate curriculum, the public university too needs to re-think their place and function.

Since the liberal arts – a term taken from the medieval university, where they were divided into the *trivium* (grammar, logic, rhetoric) and the *quadrivium* (arithmetic, geometry, music and astronomy) – include the sciences in most contemporary definitions, the undergraduate liberal arts curriculum in many US universities, on which these private institutions in India are modelled, holds out the promise of a 'humanities' education in the original Ciceronian sense. Unfortunately, the promise is rarely realized, and there is insufficient evidence to show whether such courses will truly prosper in India. In my view, the Indian public university cannot afford to follow this particular example – or at least not immediately. Rather, it is worth learning from the fact that many public universities and research centres – Central as well as State-funded – have accomplished path-breaking work in interdisciplinary fields, and created new areas of study, courses and working groups. The time seems right to propose, to the Indian academy in general, the pursuit of the 'new humanities'.

The 'new humanities' is a term that has just acquired currency, and is associated with initiatives and working groups located as far apart as MIT and the University of Rome (Roma Tre). At an uninformed level it has been understood as the humanities through digital tools and cultures: thus, simply another name for the digital humanities. Many reactions to such labelling are dismissive, and there is indeed a groundswell of hostility towards the digital humanities generally, particularly in the context of literature, which is my field. On the 2ndof May 2014, Adam Kirsch published a vigorous attack in the journal *New Republic*, titled 'Technology is Taking over English Departments: The False Promise of the Digital Humanities' (Kirsch 2014). Let us leave it to others to deal with these promises, false or otherwise. What I would like to suggest is that the 'new humanities', properly considered, might be a way of rethinking the relation between science, art and philosophy, and allow us to re-define and re-instate the humanities.

The new humanities are nothing if they are not a reconsideration of the relation between human beings and the world. The question of the humanities can be addressed only by looking again at what we mean by 'human', and how we understand this term in relation to other constituents – living and non-living – of our universe. As we all know, the idea of the human and the ideology of humanism have been almost continuously under attack for a couple of centuries, long before

Heidegger's 'Letter on Humanism'. In Western intellectual discourse, it is arguable that the overvaluation of the human that accompanies the Renaissance – and which propels the rediscovery of the classical *studia humanitatis*, or humanities – is accompanied by a painful sense of the limits and contradictions of the human condition. This is evident even in what might be regarded as the most signal achievement of the new philosophy, the 'scientific revolution' of the seventeenth century. On the one hand, mind is separated from matter, human from animal, and animal from machine: on the other, these separations lead to a real loss of confidence in the human subject as such. In *The Open: Man and Animal*, Giorgio Agamben invokes Heidegger's *Letter on Humanism* and its detaching of man's *humanitas* from his *animalitas* in explicitly re-opening the question of man and of 'humanism'. 'In our culture', he writes, 'man has always been thought of as the articulation and conjunction of a body and a soul, of a living thing and a *logos*, of a natural (or animal) element and a supernatural or social or divine element. We must learn instead to think of man as what results from the incongruity of these two elements, and investigate not the metaphysical mystery of conjunction, but rather the practical and political mystery of separation. What is man, if he is always the place – and at the same time, the result – of ceaseless divisions and caesurae?' (Agamben 2002: 16).

Agamben's concern in that philosophical treatise is with the distinction between human and animal (a distinction as important to Descartes as it was to Heidegger). In our post-human condition, we have, I will suggest, gone beyond that distinction as it was classically proposed, so that it makes little sense to speak of the study of the humanities as 'forming us towards being human'. Rather, we are aware that our humanity – such as it is – is a condition of profound dependence on the other constituents of our world, so that we are not human in and for ourselves, but by and for others. So if there is a set of disciplines called the humanities, they should enable us to ask questions about the interdependence of animals, humans and machines, indeed of the connectedness of the entire natural world and our activity within it as agents and as receiving subjects. Historically, the disciplines of human knowledge have emerged through a belief that our skills of language and mathematics – one enabling us to narrate a story, the other enabling us to see a pattern – were all that stood between us and our vulnerability and our mortality, all that enabled us to reflect upon and engage with the processes of time and change.

There was a certain hubris (certainly the ideology of humanism was in its time extremely hubristic) in believing that human beings were therefore separate from the natural or animal world, of which they were in fact part, and that they could use it instrumentally and objectively. To ground the *studia humanitatis* in this notion of *humanitas* was a dangerous and ultimately untenable move, since it claimed for human beings not simply a distinct status, but a moral and intellectual privilege based on the self-love and prejudice of those making the claim. As many have pointed out, European humanism excluded slaves, women, children, people of colour, and many other categories of beings. But the humanities, as a set of academic disciplines that enable us to study the world, its objects, and our relation to it, can, and should, survive the death of humanism. Life for us is not just our life, but the lives of others, of other species and kinds, and it is also dependent, as it has never been to this extent, on technological adjuncts, on a kind of universal prosthetic supplement (particularly in the electronic domain). Traditionally, the humanities have been focused on questions proper to the conduct of life, and these are questions of ethics, of sympathy, of communication, of *how we know* and *what we believe*.

These are universal questions, and the last two belong to the hard sciences as well. In fact, it is from the hard sciences that we learn a certain technique of asking questions and proving answers, which is crucial to the humanities *per se*. On the other hand, the humanities enable us to ask the hard questions about justice and freedom, and to ask them in a way that recognizes the brevity and uncertainty of life. Indeed, we cannot ask these questions in isolation from – say – a mathematical conception of equality, or an economist's notion of freedom. I would like to suggest that our lives today, as individuals, as political beings, as users of technology, as role-players, make it impossible to consider literature, philosophy, the arts, history, sociology (the 'humanities' disciplines) as sealed off into their linguistic or discursive compartments. Rather, to study one is to be touched by all. This is not to suggest that we can achieve, in our university departments, a condition of full interdisciplinarity. Life is short, memory is inadequate, knowledge is imperfect. What I am suggesting, rather, is that older humanities disciplines allow themselves to be transformed from within – as they are already doing to a considerable extent – to acknowledge the relation, say, of philosophy with biology, literature with ethics, and so on.

In J.M. Coetzee's 2003 novel *Elizabeth Costello* (which overlaps with *The Lives of Animals*, published in 1999, and *Slow Man*, published in 2005) an ageing woman writer travels around the world giving talks, not on literature, but on vegetarianism, philosophy, language, sexuality and evil. Deliberately, Coetzee breaks open the format of the novel in order to put questions to society, law, custom and morals. It is as though – like the Polish philosophy lecturers he mentions in his 2014 essay – he is trying to take the subjects that interest him out of the generic straitjacket of the novel and release them into the network of connections, of actions and reactions, that makes up what we think of as the 'human' mind. I would like to think of the new humanities – covering topics ranging from human ecology to statistical probability in plot-construction to censorship, as ways of receiving and processing knowledge, putting facts to question, understanding what things are. The new humanities are impossible without the cooperation of science and technology, but they are – in so far as such divisions can be made – a distinct field of study, in that they offer space for reflecting on the pursuit of life itself and how we can live more attentively, paying more heed to the conditions by which our lives become possible at all.

What has this to do with the public university and the crisis that affects it? Beyond questions of funding and infrastructure, of political compulsions and civil aspirations, the public university has, almost by accident, served as a testing ground for the idea of education *per se*. In India at least, privately funded institutions were from the start driven by a much more instrumental notion of the skills and qualifications required for worldly success. In the public university, by contrast, we witnessed, on the one hand, the projection of higher education as a public good, and, on the other – for many decades – a deadening, self-defeating accumulation of outdated syllabi, meaningless rules, stultifying examinations, and rigid, bureaucratic division of subjects and disciplines. Yet even in these depressing circumstances, it was possible to find space for argument and debate, for questions about what we teach, why we teach, and whom we teach. The fact that we are ultimately funded by ordinary tax-payers to whose ranks we also belong imposes upon us a certain moral responsibility, and perhaps a freedom that can be claimed even if it cannot be ensured. In some ways, our fractured, unequal and impoverished social reality is the only safeguard against 'managerial newspeak' on the one hand, and political slavery on the other. Forced to contend every day with the conflicts and injustices of our social existence, we might want to re-think the public university as *public space*, perhaps the only kind we have. It is a space that does not allow us to think of the life of the mind separately from other life-worlds: it compels us, instead, to understand that the 'idea of the university' is only a place-holder for the still-important function of intellectual labour in a democratic society. I do not want to suggest that such labour is *only*, or in a public university, *primarily*, a form of social engagement. I have myself spent more than half my life in public institutions pursuing recondite ('socially unproductive') kinds of research, and teaching the literature of the past. But by a paradox easily appreciated by others who have done the same, I have felt that it was my task to foster the humanities as a public good, just as education too is a public good. I have felt that it was important to open the door, as Habermas put it, to new faces that might suddenly appear, to cross disciplinary boundaries and think of the interconnectedness of knowledges, just as we are forced to think of ourselves as connected to the world we inhabit. It is in the public university, not in a private institute, that we can claim knowledge, and its dissemination, as a common good: that we can, in effect, give shape to what we might call the knowledge commons. It is on such 'commons' – in the digital realm, in public archives, in public teaching institutions – that the life of our democracy depends.

Note

1 Given India's federal structure, where education is a subject in the Concurrent List, I have chosen to spell 'State' with a capital 'S' where I am referring to the States of the Indian Union, while 'state' in lower case refers to political authority as exercised by government.

References

Agamben, Giorgio. 2002. *The Open: Man and Animal*. (trans.) K. Attell. Stanford: Stanford University Press.

Coetzee, J.M. 2014. 'Preface', in John Higgins (ed.) *Academic Freedom in a Democratic South Africa: Essays and Interviews on Higher Education and the Humanities*. Lewisburg: Bucknell University Press.

Government of India. 2016. *National Policy on Education 2016: Report of the Committee for Evolution of the New Education Policy*. New Delhi: Ministry of Human Resource Development. Available at www.nuepa.org/New/download/NEP2016/ReportNEP.pdf (accessed on 31 May 2017).

Habermas, Jürgen. 1987. 'The Idea of the University: Learning Processes' (trans.) John R. Blazek, *New German Critique*, Special Issue on the Critiques of the Enlightenment, 41(4): 3–22.

Kirsch, Adam. 2014. 'Technology Is Taking Over English Departments: The False Promise of the Digital Humanities', *New Republic*, 2 May. Available at www.newrepublic.com/article/117428/limits-digital-humanities-adam-kirsch (accessed on 23 October 2014).

Part II
'Cultures' of thinking and doing

4 The idea of a university and the invention of culture in colonial/postcolonial India

Mosarrap Hossain Khan

Introduction

In the essay "The University Without Culture?", published a year before his book *The University in Ruins* (1996), Bill Readings persuasively argues about the demise of the university's original social and cultural mission. He contends that the university has been reinvented as an institution of *excellence* in the fast globalizing, 'Americanizing', market-driven modern world. Readings[1] conceptualizes the role and status of the university in the current scenario in three ways:

> Either we seek to defend and restore the social mission of the university by simply *reaffirming* a national cultural identity that has manifestly lost its purchase – the *conservative* position, or we attempt to *reinvent* cultural identity so as to adapt it to the changing circumstances – the *multicultural* position. A third position is to *abandon* the notion that the social mission of the university is ineluctably linked to the project of *realizing a national cultural identity*, which is tantamount to ceasing to think the social articulation of research and teaching in terms of a mission.
>
> (466, my italics)

It is important to note that Readings' formulation is informed exclusively by Western discourses of university education. His Eurocentrism allows him either to 'reaffirm', or 'reinvent' or outright 'abandon' the notion of a national cultural identity. In India, by contrast, the realignment of the idea of a university with the idea of *national culture* is more complex and problematic. Readings' cogitations on the ruin of the modern university, delinked from its original cultural mission, are a useful frame nevertheless for understanding the role and status of universities in India. Although the university appears to have exhausted its socio-cultural mission in the West, as the use of the prefix, 're-', before 'affirm' and 'invent' apparently suggests, the project of fashioning a national culture seems to have just begun in India. For Readings, one of the ways the university in the West could reinvent its cultural identity is by adapting to a *multicultural* position; such a position, however, is not readily available in India as it is yet to *invent* a national culture. However, in the aftermath of the Gujarat Riots (2002), in which more than a thousand Muslims were killed, the question of national culture, a pet project of Hindutva nationalism, has come to dominate the intellectual landscape in India. In *India: A National Culture?* (2003), Geeti Sen demonstrates the difficulty of defining a national culture in India, almost akin to clutching at straws. In a national space fractured along religious divisions, the Nehruvian secular project of nation-building in independent India failed, as Sen writes, to settle the question of a national culture: "We may concede in retrospect that by resisting the influence of both culture and religion in India, secular thinking has not widened in appeal nor grown in its constituency" (n.p.).

This chapter is a brief attempt at understanding the ways in which the idea of the university has evolved in India and the role of the university in inventing an Indian national culture since colonial times. Owing to colonial subjugation, the transplanted modern European university evolved very differently and served a very different function in India than in the West, where the modern university emerged in the eighteenth century in the wake of the Enlightenment. The Enlightenment worldview gestated the modern state and the university was deployed with the practical task of consolidating *national cultures*.[2] Readings argues that, since the 1960s, the university in the West has gone through a transition from being the institution of national culture to the purveyor of global excellence (or 'citizenship' in today's parlance). I will argue that the university in India has been employed to facilitate a reverse process of forging and disseminating a distinct *national culture*. The resurgent Hindu nationalism in the 1990s tried to deploy the university as a space for the invention of a *national culture* in the face of economic liberalization and globalization.[3] In the process of enunciating the present national cultural role of the university in India, this paper will also try to chart the trajectory of the Indian university since the colonial and into the postcolonial times.

Producing clerks and administrators: the utilitarian idea of the university

The Charter Act of 1813 renewed the East India Company's privilege in India for twenty more years and the Company was urged to disseminate education to Indians. A Clause to this effect was introduced in the Parliament by a former Advocate General in Calcutta – Clause 43, passed with a slight modification – which empowered the Governor-General of India to contribute "not less than one lac of rupees" from the territorial revenue of the company for encouraging learning among the natives and for the promotion of knowledge of sciences (Ghosh 2000: 18). The proposed revival, it appears, may have been the outcome of the Orientalist Governor-General of Bengal, Lord Minto's Minute, which endorsed the views of the Orientalists, favouring the promotion of native learning. The Court of Directors of the Company in England sent specific instructions to the Governor-General in India in accordance with the Act of 1813. Despite considering the establishment of public colleges, the Court of Directors' dispatch rejected the idea as incompatible with the native mentality. Instead, the dispatch asked the Governor-General to look into ways to strengthen and modernize indigenous learning.

The next few years saw three major impulses in the field of education in India – the activity of missionaries, who set up schools and colleges to impart education in English; the rise of indigenous elites like Raja Rammohan Roy, who championed the cause of English education in India; the rise of the utilitarians in India in the first half of the nineteenth century, who favoured Western education in India through the medium of English.[4] In the competing and converging ideological space of the early nineteenth century, Lord William Bentinck's appointment as the Governor-General in India in 1828 coincided with the popularity of the utilitarians. His determination to introduce Western education in India through the medium of English language was ably supported by another professed liberal member, Lord Thomas Macaulay, who came to India in 1834 as the Law Member in the Council of the Governor-General of India. In his (in)famous *Minute on Indian Education* (1835), Macaulay advocated the cause of English education in India: "We must at present do our best to form a class who may be interpreters between us and the millions whom we govern; a class of persons, Indians in blood and color, but English in taste, in opinions, in morals, and in intellect" (Ahmad 2007: 470). Macaulay's Minute defined the purpose of English education in India in utilitarian terms – the production of English educated elites, who would help perpetuate British rule in India as clerks and petty administrators. He believed that if the plan of English education was followed up, "there would not be a single idolater among the respectable classes in Bengal thirty years hence; that this would be effected without any efforts to proselytize; without the smallest interference with religious liberty; merely by the natural operation of knowledge and reflection" (Stokes 1959: 46). This attempt at re-imagining native education in purely utilitarian terms was further bolstered by James Mill's previous dispatch in 1824 from the headquarters of the East India Company in London to the Governor-General. He wrote: "We apprehended that the plan of the institutions to the improvement of which our attention was now directed was originally and fundamentally erroneous. The great end should not have been to teach Hindu learning, but *useful* learning" (my emphasis; qtd. in Ghosh 2000: 28). And the only scientific criterion "for judging the content and medium of instruction was that of utility" (Stokes 1959: 57). From the very beginning, Western education in India was, thus, supposed to serve a useful purpose, even though the perceived benefit of such an education was to be the intellectual and moral benefit of the native people.

Charles Wood's dispatch of 1854 enabled the founding of Indian universities in Calcutta, Bombay and Madras in 1857. Wood, like Macaulay, reinforced the view that Western education must be imparted in the Indian universities. For him, the university in India must serve two purposes: "to provide a test of eligibility for government employment and to transmit an alien culture" (Ashby 1966: 63). In his letter to F. J. Halliday, Lieutenant-Governor of Bengal, in 1854, he further discouraged native aspiration for higher education: "I do not see the advantage of rearing up a number of highly educated gentlemen at the expense of the State, whom you cannot employ, and who will naturally become the depositories of discontent" (qtd. in Ashby 1966: 59). From its very inception, the British government delinked the idea of a university from the individual's moral and intellectual development. The university in India was not conceived as an institution with a national cultural mission as was the case in England. In his treatise, *On the Constitution of the Church and the State* (1829), Coleridge writes that the orientation of National Education ought to be Christian in spirit, which "educing, the latent man in all the natives of the soil, *trains them up* to be citizens of the country, the free subjects of the realm" (176). The university system in India, however, treaded cautiously in order not to antagonize the Hindu and Muslim communities by either promoting the culture of a particular community or Christian values. Wood acknowledged "the value of Indian classical literature for historical and antiquarian purposes and the study of Hindu and Muhammadan law. . . [b]ut he declined to bring it within the orbit of university studies" (Ashby 1966: 60). The transition of Western education in India from promoting humanistic values to practical usefulness in the 1850s took the education system back to its

The invention of culture 97

earlier secularist character by divesting "literary studies from the influence of religious culture" (Viswanathan 1989: 144).

Western education in India produced exactly the opposite of what Macaulay had envisioned – the production of civility[5] in the form of docile, reverential Indians. Instead, sixty years after Macaulay's *Minute*, the Englishmen in India complained[6] that Western education was producing a body of raucous, unruly young men in India. The English writer who goes by the name of H.R.J. further complains that "'English education' – and 'English' education has become synonymous with 'liberal' education – is too much valued at its market price. It must be valued for itself, and as a means to a truer and nobler life" (1896: 160). The university in India, thus, could never function as a vehicle of "intellectual and moral enlightenment" (its original mission) and as the purveyor of a national culture. Rather, it promoted an alien, Western education and culture for the sake of producing clerks and petty administrators in the service of the Empire.

Producing citizens: early nationalist ideas of a university in India

Militant nationalism during the first Partition of Bengal (1905) was colonial India's first attempt at conceiving a national education and espousing the cause of that education through the idea of a national university. As a sharp reaction to Lord Curzon's decision to partition Bengal to weaken emergent militant nationalism, the nationalists mooted the idea of an independent national education for producing enlightened Indian citizens. The nationalists favoured the promotion of indigenous education and research in the Indian universities through the medium of a mother tongue. Satish Chandra Mukherjee, the editor of *Dawn* (1897–1913), observed in 1898 how the prevalent system of university education had failed: "From the point of view of *savants*, it is regarded as a failure, since as an examining and not a teaching University, the Indian University has hardly succeeded in drawing to itself a body of learned men who devoted their time and energies wholly to the cause of original research in every department of learning or knowledge" (qtd. in Mukherjee and Mukherjee 1957: 6). Mukherjee's lament foregrounded the avowed instrumental nature of university education, since the Indian universities were committed to producing potential recruits for the British government. Consequently, the university in India became merely a degree-granting authority.

Satish Chandra saw the fruition of his dream in the Bengal National College (1906), which was founded by the nationalists to impart a distinct national education. The Bengal National College had Aurobindo Ghose as its first Principal and Satish Chandra as the Superintendent. Defining the scope of a national university, Ghose wrote that the national education system "will be impregnated with the spirit of self-reliance so as to build up men and not machines – national men, able men, men fit to carve out a career for themselves by their own brain power and resource, fit to meet the shocks of life and breast the waves of adventure. So shall the Indian people cease to sleep and become once more a people of heroes, patriots, originators, so shall it become a nation and no longer a disorganized mass of men" (2003: 11). Whereas Ghose envisages fostering a sense of self-reliance and patriotism through the national university, Bal Gangadhar Tilak, another prominent nationalist and champion of national education, wrote, "religious education will first and foremost engage our attention. Secular education only is not enough to build up character. . . . If there be any religion in the world which advocates toleration of other religious beliefs and instructs one to stick to one's own religion, *it is the religion of the Hindus alone*. Hinduism to the Hindu, Islamism to the Musalmans will be taught in these schools. . . . And it will also be taught there to forgive and forget the differences of other religions" (2003: 13). Tilak conceptualized national education as the originator of a national culture which would integrate elements of both Hindu and Muslim cultures. Tilak's assertion of Hinduism's integrative framework, however, gives his vision of national culture a Hindu core and it sows the seeds of disagreement between the Hindu and Muslim communities. Thus, the kind of *national culture* to be propagated through the Indian national universities during the nationalist movement remained unsolved.

Four years later, reflecting on the failure of National Education, which gradually became synonymous with technical education and was plagued by an unwillingness to discard the British method of imparting useful knowledge, Ghose (1910) foregrounds its flaws: "That the people will not support a mere technical education divorced from that general humanistic training which is essential to national culture, has been sufficiently proved. . . . Unless this movement is carried on, as it was undertaken, as part of a great movement of national resurgence, unless it is made, visibly to all, a nursery of patriotism and a mighty instrument of national culture, it cannot succeed" (388). While the early proponents of a nationalist idea of the university had rightly diagnosed the shortcomings of the colonial Indian universities, they failed to concretely discern the kind of *national culture* to be propagated through the Indian national universities. This crisis of national culture has since been felt in independent India, which I will discuss in the next section of this chapter.

The university and the re-invention of culture in postcolonial India

Reflecting on the importance of universities in India's national life, S. R. Dongerkery writes in 1950:

> The universities have a very important mission to fulfill in India's national life. That is the mission of cultural unity. Sentiment has been the bane of our country. Appeals to narrow loyalties are harmful, especially at the present time when unity is essential for the progress of our country. Disruptive tendencies which, before the declaration of Independence, were kept in check in the desire to present a united front to foreign rule, are now becoming a source of danger. The 'two-nation' theory was responsible for the division of India less than three years ago, and we have not yet got over the effects of partition. While we are trying to eradicate the evils of communalism in all possible ways, new forces of disintegration, more dangerous because they wear the semblance of unity, based on linguistic or regional loyalties, are weakening the bond of national unity. One would, perhaps, meet with as little success in resisting the advancing tide of sentiment based on such loyalties. . . . The only safety lies in clinging fast to the unflattering ideal of *India's cultural unity*, and what better custodians can there be to take charge of this ideal than the Indian Universities?
>
> (36–7)

Dongerkery's anxiety about the possible disintegration of a newly independent nation and his hope in a national cultural unity was to become symptomatic of the Nehruvian vision of India. Jawaharlal Nehru, the first Prime Minister of independent India, envisioned an industrially strong, progressive and rational nation built on the foundations of secularism: a *cultural unity* based on pluralism. Speaking at the Allahabad University in 1947, Nehru had said:

> A University stands for humanism, for tolerance, for reason, for progress, for the adventure of ideas and for the search for truth. It stands for the onward march of the human race towards even higher objectives. If the universities discharge their duty

adequately, then it is well with the nation and the people. But if the temple of learning itself becomes a home of narrow bigotry and petty objectives, how then will the nation prosper or a people grow in stature?

(Indian Opinion, No. 14 Vol. XLVIII, April 7, 1950)

The Nehruvian project of Indian nation-building envisaged a secular composite India and a vague notion of what 'Indian culture' would entail. Partha Chatterjee's compelling study of three nationalist leaders – Bankim Chandra Chatterjee, Mahatma Gandhi, and Jawaharlal Nehru – foregrounds the inherent ambiguity in the conception of Indian nationhood. Bankim's notion of Indian national culture is essentially Hindu, founded on the tenets of the Vedas; Mahatma's idea of modern India was a spiritual one, as opposed to the material culture of the West – the spirituality of Gandhi is implicitly Hindu in orientation as he envisioned India as Ram-*rajya*, based on the idea of the mythic king Rama's rule; Nehru's conception of modern India, however, was grounded on a secular outlook with its inclusive framework for plurality of faith and creed.[7] Nehru's over-dependence on industrialization neglected and repressed the idea of a national culture in a country divided along religious fault lines.

In a resurgent Hindu nation since the 1990s, the idea of the university is being further reconfigured with the purpose of inventing a majoritarian national culture. A good example of this urge is the cover of the *Country Paper* (1998), titled "Higher Education in India: Vision and Action", which was prepared by the then Indian Minister for Human Resource Development and Science & Technology, Dr. Murali Manohar Joshi, for presentation at the UNESCO World Conference on Higher Education in the Twenty-First Century, held in Paris, 5–9 October 1998. The cover of the *Country Paper* bears the following words:

> Juxtaposing the ancient and modern, past and the present, the cover conveys the appreciation that India's ancient civilization had for education at its highest level.
>
> The visual at the top left corner represents our discovery of the "Shunya" – the zero. The lotus at the bottom right corner stands for knowledge and wisdom. The visual at the top right corner is of Nalanda University, a renowned institution of learning, visited by the famous Chinese traveler Hiuen Tsang. The Banaras Hindu University, shown in the bottom left, is a premier educational institution today.

The invention of culture 101

The graphic in the centre, represents the endeavours of modern India to embrace modern knowledge so that *India can contribute to synthesis of science and spirituality which is bound to be the theme of the coming days* (my italics).

(*Country Paper* 1998)

The cover page envisages a *Hindu* spiritual and cultural identity for every Indian, irrespective of his/her ethnic, religious and linguistic identity. This emphasis on an exclusive Hindu past is, to an extent, the result of a sense of dislocation – because the university system in India was imported from England.

The visual of Nalanda University, founded in modern Bihar in India in the fourth century AD, signals to the world that the university system as such is not an alien idea to India; rather, India is the progenitor of one of the oldest universities in the world. In this context, it is interesting to remember that the oldest university in the Indian subcontinent was founded in Takshashila in the sixth century BC. The antiquity of Takshashila is overlooked because of its location in modern Pakistan.[8] For a resurgent Hindutva government in India, the university system becomes a site to proclaim a distinct national cultural identity. This proclamation is starker in the visual of the Banaras Hindu University,[9] which was founded at the height of the Indian freedom movement to impart a distinct Hindu education to Indians. The former HRD Minister's deliberate choice of the Hindu university on the cover page was an explicit statement of the future a Hindutva regime would like to bequeath to the nation. This revisionist perspective of the Indian nation differs from that of the Congress party's seemingly 'secular' position, which espouses a pluralistic and *vague* cultural identity for India. This position again is mired in controversy as the Congress' secular posturing has at its core an implicit Hindu notion of culture. The final paragraph on the cover page envisages a moral leadership for India because of its supposed ability to synthesize science and spirituality. The Indian university is tasked with presiding over the *ruin* of the university system in the world, presumably headed for apocalypse owing to an over-techno-bureaucratization of Western civilization and an individualistic-materialistic culture.

The *Country Paper*, prepared by a Hindu fundamentalist ruling party for the UNESCO Conference, foregrounds the critical role of the university in India in inventing a *national culture*. The growing concern with the lack of a value system in the wake of technocratic globalization invests the university with the task of promoting this *invented national culture*, so that the Indian university produces more than mere techno-bureaucrats for an emerging economic power. The previous Hindu government's vision (which is followed by the present right-wing government as well) offers a counter-discourse to the theorists of the Western universities, who harp on the demise of the social and cultural project of the university in a globalizing, market-driven, post-national world.

Conclusion

To conclude, Readings's diagnosis of postmodern corporatized universities in the West, as one given to the propagation of excellence and accounting at the expense of its original cultural mission, might be true in the European and North American contexts. The Indian scenario is far too complex because the Indian university, sill intertwined with the destiny of the nation, is now being deployed for the propagation of an elusive *national culture*. The national cultural mission of the Indian university has barely begun.

Acknowledgements

My sincere gratitude to Prof. Alexander Dick (University of British Columbia, Canada), who first introduced me to the changing discourses on the idea of the university. I have benefitted immensely from our discussions. I am also grateful to Dr. Samipendra Banerjee (University of Gour Banga, India), who invited me to present some of these ideas in 2011. The comments from the audience have further enriched the chapter.

Notes

1 See Bill Readings, "The University without Culture?" (1995).
2 See Bill Readings, *University in Ruins* (1996); M. J. Hofstetter, *The Romantic Idea of a University* (2001).
3 In a recent article, Dilip Menon advocates the possibility of a similar project in African universities, albeit without the nativist undertone of superiority of a particular African ethnicity and culture. See Menon, "Lessons from India on decolonizing language and thought at universities" (2015).
4 See Suresh Chandra Ghosh, *The History of Education in Modern India 1757–1998* (2000).
5 Production of civility seemed to have been an important motive of western education in India. In order to maintain the existing power relations between the Englishmen and the Western educated native gentlemen, who were derogatorily called 'competition *baboos*', the Indians had to be represented as "un-civil", a poor caricature of the original. See, Anindyo Roy, *Civility and Empire: Literature and Culture in British India, 1822–1922* (2005).

6 See H.R.J., "Indian Universities: Actual and Ideal – III" (1896).
7 See Partha Chatterjee, *Nationalist Thought and the Colonial World: a Derivative Discourse?* (1986)
8 The Rightist Hindu Government came to power in India after the tumultuous Ram Janmabhoomi Movement, which culminated in the demolition of the Babri Mosque in Ayodhya, Uttar Pradesh, India on 6 December, 1992. The Hindu government had consciously harped on the ancient glory of India in an attempt to chart out a distinct national cultural identity.
9 The Banaras Hindu University was set up as a counterpoint to the Aligarh Muslim University. These two universities were the first two denominational universities of colonial India founded on the logic of social reform for the Hindu and Muslim communities.

References

Ahmad, Dohra. 2007. *Rotten English: A Literary Anthology*. New York, London: W. W. Norton & Company.

Ashby, Eric. 1966. *Universities: British, Indian, African, a Study in the Ecology of Higher Education*. London: Weidenfeld and Nicolson.

Chatterjee, Partha. 1986. *Nationalist Thought and the Colonial World: A Derivative Discourse?* United Nations University.

Coleridge, S. T. 1829. *On the Constitution of the Church and the State*. Princeton, NJ: Princeton University Press.

Dongerkery, S. R. 1950. *Universities and National Life*. Hind Kitabs Ltd.

Hofstetter, M. J. 2001. *The Romantic Idea of a University: England and Germany 1770–1850*. London: Palgrave Macmillan.

Ghose, Aurobindo. 1910. 'National Education', *Karmayogin*, 26: 336–40.

———. 2003. 'Editorial Note on the Concept of a National University in the *Bande Mataram* weekly', in Sabyasachi Bhattacharya et al. (eds.) *Educating the Nation: Document on the Discourse of National Education in India, 1880–1920*. Kanishka Publishers.

Ghosh, Suresh Chandra. 2000. *The History of Education in Modern India 1757–1998*. Hyderabad: Orient Longman.

H.R.J. 1896. 'Indian Universities: Actual and Ideal – III', *The Calcutta Review*, July: 139–62.

Joshi, Murali Manohar. 1998. 'Higher Education in India: Vision and Action', *Country Paper*, Presented at UNESCO World Conference on Higher Education in the Twenty-First Century, Paris, October 5–9.

Macaulay, Thomas Babington. 1920 (1835). 'Minute on Indian Education', in H. Sharp (ed.) *Selections from Educational Records, Part I (1781–1839)*. Calcutta: Superintendent Government Printing.

Menon. 2015. 'Lessons from India on Decolonizing Language and Thought at Universities. *The Conversation*, 31 August 2015. Available at https://theconversation.com/lessons-from-india-on-decolonising-language-and-thought-at-universities-46541 (accessed on 19 May2017).

Mukherjee, Haridas and Mukherjee, Uma. 1957. *The Origins of the National Education Movement (1905–1910)*. Jadavpur University Press.

Nehru, Jawaharlal. 1950. *Indian Opinion*, XLVIII(14), April 7.
Readings, Bill. 1995. 'The University with Culture?', *New Literary History*, 26(3): 465–92.
———. 1996. *University in Ruins*. Cambridge, MA: Harvard University Press.
Roy, Anindyo. 2005. *Civility and Empire: Literature and Culture in British India, 1822–1922*. New York: Routledge.
Stokes, Eric. 1959. *The English Utilitarians and India*. Oxford: Oxford University Press.
Tilak, Bal Gangadhar. 2003. 'Tilak's Speech at Barsi in 1908 on National Education for India'. In Sabyasachi Bhattacharya et al. (eds.) *Educating the Nation: Document on the Discourse of National Education in India, 1880–1920*. New Delhi: Kanishka Publishers.
Viswanathan, Gauri. 1989. *Masks of Conquest: Literary Study and British Rule in India*. New York: Columbia University Press.

5 Scientific research productivity in the Indian university sector

Dhruba J. Saikia and Rowena Robinson

Introduction

There are often cries about why Indian universities and institutes do not figure in the top 200 or so of international ranking lists. For example, in the Academic Ranking of World Universities (ARWU),[1] the Indian Institute of Science is in the 301–400 range and none of our prestigious IITs figures in the top 500. In the recently released Times Higher Education World University Rankings[2] for 2016–17, the Indian Institute of Science is in the 201–250 range, IIT Bombay is in the 351–400 range, IIT Delhi, Kanpur and Madras are in the 401–500 range and IIT Kharagpur and IIT Roorkee are in the 501–600 range. The highest-ranked university in either the state or central sector is Jadavpur University, which is placed in the 501–600 range.

Central to these rankings is the quality of research output from our universities and institutes. Although the scientific output from the country has been increasing, even in the select high-quality Nature Index journals,[3] and India ranks 9th in overall scientific output,[4] on the whole, quality remains poor. India ranks 173rd in the average number of citations per paper, which is a notch below Bangladesh. About 35 percent of all publications in the sub-standard 'predatory journals' are by Indians, with 51 percent of these being from Private/Government Colleges, 18 percent from Private Universities/Institutes, 15 percent from State Universities, 11 percent from National Institutes and 3 percent from Central Universities (Seethapathy, Santhosh Kumar and Hareesha 2016). This drive to publish in sub-standard journals has been at least partly aggravated by the University Grants Commission (UGC) norms of measuring academic performance and procedures for listing recognized journals.

There have been several studies of research output of our universities and institutions, a recent one being the research performance of our IITs (Banshal et al. 2017). Banshal et al. have used the Web of Science (WoS) data over a 25-year period (1990–2014) and have done a detailed study of the older as well as newer IITs. In this paper, we use a relatively new database 'Nature Index' launched by the Nature Publishing Group, which considers 68 high-quality scientific journals in select fields, to compare sets of selected institutes and universities. Though we leave out budget/funding considerations, we look at institutions with different institutional structures and no doubt correspondingly different institutional cultures. These have been set up at different points in time, all in the effort to promote advanced research, but the models differ and this is worth analysing a bit more closely. In particular, state and central governments' initiatives in converting historic colleges into new universities or national institutes as well as the recent central government initiative in setting up new science institutions (IISERs) – all in the effort to promote higher learning – deserve some consideration. The study therefore enables us to attempt to draw attention to and make some interesting connections between research productivity and institutional structures and cultures. To begin with, therefore, we look briefly at how science moved from the university sector to institutions outside of it, and what implications this may have had for the growth of research potential and innovative capabilities.

Science in universities and other institutes of higher learning

Some of the most pioneering scientific work in India was done in the early part of the twentieth century by stalwarts such as Jagadish Chandra Bose, Meghnad Saha, Satyendra Nath Bose, Chandrasekhara Venkata Raman and Srinivasa Ramanujan. This era saw many extraordinary Indians whose influence extended far beyond our shores, such as Sarvepalli Radhakrishnan in philosophy, Rabindranath Tagore in literature, B. R. Ambedkar, architect of India's constitution and tireless worker for the uplift of Dalits, Mahatma Gandhi who inspired millions with his message of non-violence, Jawaharlal Nehru who laid the foundations for a modern India based on science and technology, to name just a few. Three Indians were decorated with the Bharat Ratna in the very first year of its inception in 1954, including a scientist, namely Chandrasekhara Venkata Raman, besides the elder statesman Chakravarti Rajagopalachari and the then Vice-President Sarvepalli Radhakrishnan. This was a golden era generating global leaders from India in many different fields, perhaps driven at least partly by the nationalist fervour of the time.

Of the five outstanding men of science mentioned above, Jagadish Chandra Bose was at Presidency College, now Presidency University, where he did his pioneering work on microwaves, Meghnad Saha was at Allahabad University and later became Palit Professor of Physics at Calcutta University, Satyendra Nath Bose was at the Universities of Calcutta and Dhaka, Raman was Palit Professor of Physics at Calcutta University and later Professor and Director at the Indian Institute of Science. What is striking is their location for the most part within university structures. In India, in the post-Independence period, emphasis shifted to the centrally funded laboratories, to usher in a period of rapid growth in science and technology.

Universities were not coupled in any significant way to these national laboratories, and with meagre resources they gradually languished. The sorry state of affairs continues to date with few institutional structures and resources in place to promote excellence in the universities, particularly in the sciences. The state of our universities today is perhaps one of the main reasons for the holding back of Indian science, although there have been significant improvements, particularly with research groups in several universities being part of international collaborative projects. Collaboration, between departments, universities and institutions must certainly be encouraged and facilitated to improve the impact and quality of work done in our universities, and should form an essential component of evaluation of an institution or a university. At the same time, one can be a bit player in many large collaborative researches without contributing at a significant level. Together with the state of our universities is the dearth of persons to think big, take risks and embark on major scientific projects with the courage and freedom to do so. We discuss some aspects of our universities and indicate possible structural and societal reasons for the inability to generate scientific leaders in large numbers.

It is not just that universities lack research or adequate resources; also absent is the kind of pedagogic practices that are the foundation of stimulating curiosity. This is what we highlighted in our response (Saikia and R Robinson 2014a) to Joseph and Robinson (2014), who attribute the holding back of Indian science in post-independence India to a 'stultifying bureaucracy'. Remarkable progress has been made in several areas. Nevertheless, if India is to significantly improve upon its global share of scientific publications and patent applications, an increased support for and emphasis on research in our colleges and universities must be combined with effective teaching-learning processes and robust institutional structures. Millions of students graduate from about 850 universities and 40,000 colleges each year, but there is very little discussion on the quality of classroom teaching, which is critical for generating the leading academics of tomorrow. Teaching is often based on the dictation of notes, with little room or space for inquiry-based learning.

Tutorial sessions, even when they are part of the syllabus, are not used effectively. Laboratories are often badly equipped. There is no effective student feedback mechanism even in several of the leading universities, which may help bring in more accountability in the system. The main purpose of teaching appears to be the examinations, with universities degenerating into degree-doling machines. Upgrading syllabi is often a long and torturous process. There is resistance to change because faculty members are reluctant to learn new things or change the lecture notes they reuse each year, or some may even have their own books prescribed, which deepens their investment in the status quo. Teaching skills are often glossed over while recruiting new faculty members. Unless there is a significant improvement in pedagogic practices and teachers are trained to develop student-centred, inquiry-based learning, enhancing the cognitive and practical competences of students, it would be very difficult to generate the scientific person power to take Indian science rapidly forward.

Joseph and Robinson (2014) refer to bureaucratic hurdles of the state, but what must be pointed out is that, though universities are autonomous organizations and can frame their own objectives and requirements, their individual administrations may be *more* bureaucratic than government departments or funding agencies. University departments are often highly hierarchical, thereby inhibiting the growth of young faculty members who may come up with bright ideas. It was not long ago that, in some universities, heads of departments were appointed till retirement, and Principals of colleges still continue to be appointed for life in some regions. Institutional structures to recognize meritorious research or other academic activity have been typically weak. Promotions of faculty members are often based on years of service; systems of measuring academic performance have severe flaws.

There is little incentive in the system to strive for doing front-line research work. Doctoral theses usually do not require any published work in leading academic journals of the field, thereby seriously questioning the value of such work. Since this work may be of dubious value, academics develop small networks within which by mutual, even unspoken consent, each passes the other's students' theses. In other words, the consequence of such structures and processes is the breeding of a culture of mediocrity, which academics, in fact, develop a stake in defending rather than resisting. To address these varied problems and issues, merely allocating a fraction of the GDP to the university sector is not going to work. Resources are of course important. But without first putting institutional structures in place that promote accountability, professionalism and professionalization of processes, and demand excellence in both teaching and research, funds alone will not meet the objectives. Also, easy access to resources without writing proposals, which are reviewed critically, is usually not conducive to promoting either accountability or good science. Critical and objective reviews may also be a challenge if the peer bodies are small, unless one considers international reviewers.[5]

The University Grants Commission has tried to address the problem of research in the universities by establishing the Inter-University Centres where academics from different universities can come and work and use the facilities for their research. Alternatively to promote science education, the Government of India has also set up a number of institutes of science education and research (IISERs and NISER). Major new projects such as the India-based Neutrino Observatory and LIGO-India have encouraged participation from interested university faculty members. Although all these are important and significant steps, we cannot afford to ignore the vital steps that are first required to rejuvenate our universities.

High-quality research output

The objectives of a leading university must be 'to contribute to society through the pursuit of education, learning and research at the highest international levels of excellence', as outlined in the mission of the University of Cambridge. For Indian universities to be amongst the top 200 or so, the quality of work must be globally competitive, even if one is addressing local issues. Research output in the sciences is usually in the form of scientific papers in peer-reviewed journals, patents and less frequently monographs. To assess high-quality research output from Indian universities and institutions, we focus on the publications in 68 high-quality research journals listed by Nature Index,[6] which provides a proxy for high-quality research output.

These 68 journals have been selected by a panel of active scientists. There appears to be a reasonable consensus that they really represent the upper echelon of journals published in the natural sciences. The list of journals, which is subject to periodic reviews, constitutes merely about 1 percent of the journals listed in the Web of Science (Thomson Reuters), but these account for about 30 percent of the citations in natural science journals. Data are available in Nature Index on an annual basis since 2012; the last year for which data are currently available is 2015. The article output is counted in three different ways as described by Nature Index.

1 "Article count (AC): where a count of one is assigned to an institution or country if one or more authors of the research article are from that institution or country, regardless of how many co-authors there are from outside that institution or country".
2 "Fractional count (FC): that takes into account the percentage of authors from that institution (or country) and the number of affiliated institutions per article. For calculation of the FC, all authors are considered to have contributed equally to the article. The maximum combined FC for any article is 1.0".
3 "Weighted fractional count (WFC): a modified version of FC in which fractional counts for articles from specialist astronomy and astrophysics journals have been down weighted. These journals encompass a much larger proportion of the total publication output of these fields than any other field covered by the Nature Index. The WFC allows ordering of institutions and countries so as not to give undue emphasis to these fields. The weighting is achieved by multiplying the fractional count from these astronomy and astrophysics journals by a factor of 0.2. This down weighting is in proportion to an approximation of the level to which astronomy and astrophysics articles are overrepresented compared to the total publication output of other fields covered by the Nature Index".

A high value of the ratio of AC to FC indicates a large degree of external collaboration, while a small value would indicate very limited collaboration. These measures of course have several caveats such as the size of institutions, the level of funding or even the size of the country in which a particular institution may be located, and may be skewed in favour of universities, which have invested in major international projects, such as CERN, for example.

Using these data, we explore the high-quality scientific research output of

1 Universities which have been established on the foundations of historic colleges such as Cotton, Presidency and Ravenshaw in comparison with the traditional universities of the region;
2 Institutes such as IIT Roorkee and IIEST Shibpur, which have been converted from historic engineering colleges in comparison with other traditional IITs;

3 Newer institutes such as IISERs, NISER, JNCASR in comparison with leading institutes in the country such as IISc and TIFR;
4 A few select well-established universities in different parts of the country.

The faculty strengths in the sciences in these institutions are taken into account. The current strengths as available on the websites (2017 June) rounded to the nearest ten have been assumed to be similar for the period 2012–15 being considered here.[7] This would clearly not be the case especially for recently established universities or institutes which may be in the initial stages of recruitment. It is also relevant to note that we have considered only those Departments, Schools or Centres, which could have contributed to the subject areas of the 68 journals listed by Nature Index, and have counted only the regular faculty members. We have not considered the total budget available for research in each of these institutions as these amounts are not easily available, but it may be worth examining in the future as to which universities/institutes are delivering the best 'value for money'.

Universities on the foundations of historic colleges

With both the central and state governments making moves to convert autonomous or other colleges into universities, it is worth examining how these might perform in the generation of new knowledge and skills, especially in producing high-quality scientific research. Conversion of colleges into universities would help increase the gross enrolment ratio (GER) in higher education, and also possibly infrastructure with increased funding. However, the challenges of putting in place institutional structures that promote academic vibrancy and excellence in all its activities, including high-quality research work, would have to be met while establishing a leading university.

In the context of this discussion, it is worth reflecting on the experiences in recent times of building universities on the foundations of colleges, which have had a rich and distinguished history. Two somewhat different paths were followed: one, termed the 'Presidency model' for conversion of Presidency College, Kolkata (established in 1817), into a university in 2010, and the other termed the 'Cotton model', where the new university, christened as Cotton College State University (CCSU) was created in 2011 with Cotton College, Guwahati (established in 1901) as a constituent college. Recently, Cotton College was upgraded to a university and merged with Cotton College State University to form a unitary structure, christened Cotton University. The conversion of Ravenshaw College, Cuttack (established in 1868), into a university in 2006 is essentially similar to the Presidency model. All three are state-government institutions and required legislation on the part of the respective state governments to bring about these changes. These models were described in an article in *The Telegraph* and are briefly summarized here (Saikia 2014).

One of the challenges in any such conversion is how best to deal with the existing faculty and staff. In the Presidency model, all faculty positions went to the University and the erstwhile College faculty had the option of being considered for the University or transferred to other Government colleges. Of those who preferred to be considered for the University, some were selected while others were not. Presidency University recruited many promising and well-established academics, and earned the status of an Institution of National Eminence from the UGC. Both Presidency and Ravenshaw took the difficult decision to transfer out a number of existing faculty. They have shown a strong commitment to selecting the best candidates, an element critical to the building of a good university. In fact, the Ravenshaw University Act 2005 explicitly states that "the University shall take special measure to facilitate students and teachers from all over India and abroad to join the University and participate in its academic programmes". While Cotton College State University had recruited faculty members and staff directly to the University, all faculty members and staff of both the University and College are now employees of Cotton University vide the Government of Assam Act No. XXII of 2017, which was put into effect on the 1st of June 2017.

Amongst the three universities established on the foundations of historic colleges, publications in the highest levels have varied significantly. While CCSU has made its presence in the list via collaborative projects largely due to one individual, Ravenshaw University does not appear at all, and Presidency University shows evidence of activity at this level gradually building up, with more collaborative work as suggested by the ratio of AC:WFC.

Comparing the newly established universities with a few of the long-standing universities from the northeast and east of India, the Article Count (AC) of the papers shows that Presidency and CCSU do better than long-standing universities of the region supported both by the state governments (Dibrugarh and Utkal Universities) and the central government (Assam University and NEHU). Amongst the universities in the northeast, Gauhati seems to do the best, at least partly due to participation in major collaborative projects, followed by Tezpur University. Calcutta and Jadavpur, two of the leading universities from the eastern part of the country, show a consistent record over this period, with the papers being largely due to individuals or small groups, as indicated by the low values of the ratio AC:WFC, which is approximately 2 for each of the years. Amongst the universities listed in Table 5.1, excluding Ravenshaw, which had no publication, the highest value of article count per year per faculty member is about 0.1 for Calcutta University and Jadavpur University, while the lowest value is 0.005 for NEHU.

What are we to learn from this? While the policy of new recruitments at Presidency holds promise for the future, with the numbers showing signs of catching up with Jadavpur University, it does not seem to have had a similar effect at Ravenshaw University. CCSU's recruitments have been progressing smoothly during most of this period reaching the strength of about 20 in 2016 in the relevant disciplines. During this period, faculty members of Cotton College, which was a constituent college of CCSU, took part in teaching activities. CCSU along with Cotton College, which had about 70 faculty members in the relevant disciplines of which only one was a collaborator in one of the papers listed in Nature Index, together now constitute Cotton University. It would be interesting to examine a few years from now the effects of this unification on the publication of quality papers in the best journals.

Table 5.1 Universities established on the foundations of historic colleges and other major universities of eastern India

University	Faculty strength	2012 AC	2012 WFC	2013 AC	2013 WFC	2014 AC	2014 WFC	2015 AC	2015 WFC
CCSU	20	2	0.03	5	0.10	2	0.05	1	0.02
Presidency	80	–	–	7	1.33	6	0.71	10	0.97
Ravenshaw	40	–	–	–	–	–	–	–	–
Assam	60	–	–	1	0.10	4	1.47	2	0.35
Dibrugarh	60	–	–	1	0.09	–	–	1	1.00
Gauhati	110	17	2.27	11	0.07	10	0.17	15	1.09
NEHU	110	–	–	1	0.25	1	0.20	–	–
Tezpur	60	4	1.72	6	2.44	12	3.40	7	1.17
Calcutta	240	28	13.76	20	8.80	21	10.68	22	10.24
Jadavpur	170	12	4.25	14	7.62	16	8.09	14	8.68
Utkal	40	–	–	–	–	2	0.52	5	0.04

Source: Compiled and tabulated by the authors

Technological institutions on the foundations of historic engineering colleges

IIEST Shibpur and IIT Roorkee have their origins in historic engineering colleges set up in the middle of the nineteenth century to meet the need for these skills in colonial India. IIEST Shibpur has its origins in the Bengal Engineering College, also known as B.E. College, whose history goes back to the nineteenth century. B.E. College was elevated to the status of a "Deemed University" in 1992 and later converted to Bengal Engineering and Science University, Shibpur, in 2004 via an Act of the West Bengal Assembly. The University started M.Sc. programmes in basic sciences in addition to the traditional engineering disciplines. The University was taken over by the Government of India and given the status of an Institute of National Importance via an Act of Parliament in 2014, and renamed as the Indian Institute of Engineering Science and Technology, Shibpur.[8]

The history of Indian Institute of Technology, Roorkee, also goes back to the middle of the nineteenth century.

> The Roorkee College was established in 1847 AD as the First Engineering College in the British Empire. The College was renamed as The Thomason College of Civil Engineering in 1854. It was given the status of University by Act No. IX of 1948 of the United Province (Uttar Pradesh) in recognition of its performance and its potential and keeping in view the needs of post-independent India. Pandit Jawahar Lal Nehru, the first Prime Minister of India, presented the Charter in November 1949 elevating the erstwhile college to the First Engineering University of Independent India.[9]

Table 5.2 Institutes established on the foundations of historic engineering colleges and select IITs

Institutes	Faculty strength	2012 AC	WFC	2013 AC	WFC	2014 AC	WFC	2015 AC	WFC
IIEST Shibpur	50	5	2.73	12	7.43	8	3.86	5	3.75
IIT Roorkee	160	2	0.92	4	3.19	4	1.37	6	2.86
IIT Bombay	250	72	37.00	67	31.15	95	52.74	84	43.18
IIT Guwahati	150	44	10.81	42	13.57	37	14.15	43	20.06
IIT Kanpur	140	39	22.92	47	28.98	55	34.54	47	28.27
IIT Madras	200	48	18.33	41	14.82	44	23.03	38	19.80

Source: Compiled and tabulated by the authors

Its status was changed from the University of Roorkee to Indian Institute of Technology, Roorkee, via an Act of Parliament in 2001, again recognizing it as an Institute of National Importance.

We compare their output in the Nature Index list of journals, using a similar approach as outlined earlier, with a relatively newer IIT (IIT Guwahati established in 1994), and three of the older IITs, namely IIT Bombay (established in 1958) and IIT Kanpur and IIT Madras, both established in 1959. The faculty strengths are again based on departments or centres from which publications in the Nature Index listed journals could be expected. While the research output of IIT Guwahati is comparable to both IIT Kanpur and IIT Madras, it is clear that IIT Roorkee lags behind, although the faculty strengths in the disciplines considered are similar. IIT Bombay, which is usually the leading IIT in the international rankings, has a better publication record than the other older IITs. Although the faculty strength of IIEST is significantly smaller, being close to about a third of the IITs, its research output in the sciences lags behind the traditional IITs, even if one takes account of the smaller faculty strength.

The average value of AC:WFC is about 2 for all these institutions, being marginally higher for IIT Guwahati with a value close to 3, again suggesting that the Actual Counts of research papers have not been boosted by major collaborations. The highest values of papers published per faculty member per year are highest for IIT Kanpur and Bombay with values of 0.34 and 0.32 respectively, with significantly lower values for IIEST and IIT Roorkee. At a first glance, the well-established traditional IITs appear to be doing better than institutes established on the foundations of historic engineering colleges. However, it is important to bear in mind that, in this paper, we are examining only the science output in the Nature Index journals, and this may not be reflective of the Institute as a whole. There is considerable emphasis on technology and pure engineering aspects in these institutions, which is not being examined here. However, the data from Banshal et al. (2017) show that most of the publications listed in the Web of Science are from the disciplines considered here (for example, about 74 percent for both IIT Bombay and IIT Kanpur) rather than core engineering disciplines or Mathematics.

Newer institutes such as IISERs, NISER, JNCASR

The concept of IISERs (Indian Institute of Science Education and Research) had its origins in the 1990s when, noticing the declining number of bright young students taking up research in science, V. G.

Bhide of Pune University and Govind Swarup of TIFR proposed the equivalent of the IITs in the sciences. These institutions were set up by the Ministry of Human Resource Development after an amendment to the National Technology Act. In this paper, we have selected two IISERs, Pune established in 2006 and Thiruvananthapuram (Tvm) established in August 2008; and NISER (National Institute of Science Education and Research), which was established along similar principles by the Department of Atomic Energy at Bhubaneswar in 2006. Along with these, we consider a research institute, JNCASR (Jawaharlal Nehru Centre for Advanced Scientific Research), established in 1989 to mark the birth centenary of Jawaharlal Nehru, and two of the best-known institutes of the country for scientific research, the Indian Institute of Science, established in 1909 with support from Jamsetji Tata and the Maharaja of Mysore, and the Tata Institute of Fundamental Research founded in 1945 by Homi J. Bhabha.

Amongst the science and education research institutes, IISER Pune has shown a marked increase, as well as NISER Bhubaneswar, although the ratio of AC:WFC for IISER Pune is much smaller (average value is 1.62) compared with NISER, where the values range from about 6 to 100. This suggests that the latter's increase has been at least partly due to being in large collaborations. In comparison, the output from IISER Tvm has been significantly lower. While these institutions have strong undergraduate teaching programmes, JNCASR – recognized as a deemed university – promotes interdisciplinary research, and a majority of its students are pursuing the PhD programme, and it also offers an integrated PhD/M.S. programme. It has a steady output of about one paper per faculty member in the Nature-Indexed journals, and a relatively low value of AC:WFC (1.59) suggesting that most of the published work is by small groups.

IISc and TIFR are two of the best-known centres of scientific research in the country. While the average value of AC:WFC is 1.63 for IISc, the corresponding value for TIFR is higher (5.78). This is partly due to large collaborations but also due to Astronomy and Astrophysics being a major activity of the Institute, whose publications are weighted down by 0.2 in the Nature Index while estimating WFC. TIFR and JNCASR faculty on the average publish one paper per year in Nature Index journals; the values for the other institutes listed in Table 5.3 range from about 0.2 (IISER Trivandrum) to about 0.6 (NISER).

A few select well-established universities

In the last set of comparisons, we consider a few select well-established universities, three central and one state supported: University of Delhi

Scientific research productivity 117

Table 5.3 Select national institutes of science

Institutes	Faculty strength	2012 AC	WFC	2013 AC	WFC	2014 AC	WFC	2015 AC	WFC
IISc	290	125	70.88	131	83.63	150	94.06	137	85.45
TIFR	200	214	30.85	247	54.74	201	29.64	228	46.53
IISER Pune	90	4	3.09	28	17.97	24	17.26	58	25.85
IISER Tvm	50	3	1.83	13	4.76	11	7.03	9	6.31
NISER	60	18	0.17	21	2.39	36	5.99	77	7.96
JNCASR	40	43	23.53	40	28.77	43	24.13	37	27.71

Source: Compiled and tabulated by the authors

Table 5.4 A few select well-established universities

Universities	Faculty strength	2012 AC	WFC	2013 AC	WFC	2014 AC	WFC	2015 AC	WFC
Delhi	290	106	16.66	65	7.71	82	10.87	75	10.41
Hyderabad	160	23	14.57	27	19.10	29	20.04	29	20.82
JNU	130	15	10.71	20	13.35	14	8.27	12	6.78
Panjab	170	113	3.00	88	0.86	89	1.44	73	1.60

Source: Compiled and tabulated by the authors

established in 1922, University of Hyderabad in 1974, Jawaharlal Nehru University in 1969, and Panjab University, which was established in 1882 as University of Punjab in Lahore, Pakistan, and now located in Chandigarh (see www.oralhistory.puchd.ac.in for a history of the University). While University of Delhi and Panjab University have higher values of Article Count, this is again at least partly due to being part of large collaborations. The average value of AC:WFC is about 7.4 for Delhi and a huge 62 for Panjab University, while University of Hyderabad and JNU have modest values of 1.5 and 1.6 respectively. Accordingly, the Actual Count of papers per year per faculty member is also higher for Delhi (0.28) and Panjab (0.53) compared with Hyderabad (0.17) and JNU (0.12). This also reflects the different models or paths taken to build up scientific research institutions in the country.

Discussions and concluding remarks

A question we have asked ourselves is: what makes institutions do well in terms of scientific research? While connectivity and collaborations are important to develop expertise and be a part of global science, the number of scientific publications can sometimes be skewed by such collaborations on a large scale when comparing the productivity of different institutions. In these large collaborations it is often difficult to assess the contributions of individual researchers or institutions. Therefore, we now consider only those where the AC:WFC ratio is less than about 6, and discuss those institutions whose Article Count per faculty member per year is at least about 0.2. This list essentially includes the IITs considered here (Bombay, Guwahati, Kanpur and Madras), IISc, TIFR, JNCASR and IISER Pune. These have been established at different periods of time, IISc being the earliest and IISER Pune being the most recent. What distinguishes these institutions are the best possible practices put in place in terms of recruitments and promotions, and being relatively free from the clutches of strong politicized student or staff unions. Typically, these institutes also search out potential faculty without limiting themselves to the pool of applicants who respond to recruitment advertisements, and are more flexible when it comes to allowing faculty leave for conferences, study and research abroad and the like.

Do universities and institutes established on the foundations of historic colleges help foster scientific research at the highest levels, making best use of the available infrastructure and expertise? The answer from this study is rather mixed, with Presidency showing significant improvement, and IIEST Shibpur and IIT Roorkee lagging behind the traditional IITs, including the most recent one considered here, IIT Guwahati. Newly established institutes such as IISER Pune (which has a large proportion of younger faculty) and JNCASR, although the latter does not have undergraduate teaching, are doing well in terms of scientific output at the highest levels considered here. One needs to study this over a slightly longer time scale to examine whether the inertia of practices of historic institutions inhibits the rapid growth of science. One must also bear in mind that this study has taken no account of the level of funding.

Another interesting question to ask oneself is whether the top-heavy universities, measured by the fraction of faculty members at the Professor's level, do better. Senior professors may play an important role in establishing networks of collaboration. Amongst those institutes and universities where at least about 45 percent of the faculty are Professors, the output per faculty per year varies widely with JNCASR and three of the IITs (Kanpur, Bombay and Madras) having values greater than 0.2, NEHU having a value less than 0.01 and Universities of Hyderabad, Calcutta, Jadavpur and JNU having values between about 0.1 and 0.2.

Scientific research productivity 119

In addition to funding, robust institutional structures that promote excellence, and nurturing the young and motivated researcher are important aspects of building up institutions that will generate the scientific leaders of tomorrow. In the context of developing major homegrown projects, one might ask the question: Why don't many more Indians think big? To some extent, it must be admitted that, given the Western dominance in most fields of science, India is often a 'receiver' of research problems and questions and not a 'framer' of them. Be that as it may, why do so few Indians take on these large questions defined by their disciplines? Let us take the example of radio astronomy, which we are both familiar with. Govind Swarup FRS from NCRA, TIFR, who helped put India on the world radio astronomy map, built the Ooty Radio Telescope in the 1960s and 1970s to address whether the universe had a big-bang origin as revealed by radio sources, and the Giant Metrewave Radio Telescope (GMRT) in the 1990s to understand how galaxies formed. GMRT is perhaps the only Indian science facility built indigenously to be used extensively by scientists from across the world. These were pioneering projects attempting to answer the big questions of the day. One may ask, why we as a nation have not generated many more scientists to take on major, perhaps even high-risk, projects. Is risk-aversion within our culture? Or, have our classrooms stymied all initiative as we are treated as mere receptors of information? These are also matters to ponder over and address, as we continue to grapple with the varied issues that affect Indian science.

Meanwhile, the Report of the Subramanian Committee for Evolution of the New Education Policy has been published, titled 'National Policy on Education 2016'.[10] Also, the Government has constituted more recently on the 24th of June 2017 a new Committee for preparing the draft National Education Policy under the Chairpersonship of Dr K Kasturirangan.[11] The latter Committee is to submit its report by 31st December 2017. While the Subramanian Committee notes that the "quality and also quantity of research and innovations emerging out of Institutions of higher education and research leaves much to be desired", its recommendations do not adequately address the requirements for building institutions where teaching and research flourish. The Committee "recommends that over the next decade at least 100 new centres for excellence in the field of higher education need to be established". It says that if "this is successfully accomplished, it will pave the way for India to host major research and innovation initiatives". The importance of institutional structures and culture that promote and nurture excellence, rather than being feudal and strongly hierarchical, as is the case in most of our institutions, and the challenges of getting good faculty members, which has led to about 30 percent of the posts in many of our premier institutes being vacant, are amongst the critical issues which require far greater attention.

The "unity of research and teaching, to uphold the ideal of research without restrictions and to provide a comprehensive education for its students",[12] espoused by the German philosopher Wilhelm von Humboldt, formed the basis of German research universities established in the nineteenth century starting with what is now known as Humboldt-Universitat zu Berlin established over 200 years ago. These institutions have played a critical role in the economic and technological growth of Germany during this period (e.g. Albritton 2009). The above ideals also inspired several leading American universities established in that era, such as the Johns Hopkins University and the University of Chicago amongst many others. The latter established in 1890, was where "William Rainey Harper, the first president, imagined a university that would combine an American-style undergraduate liberal arts college with a German-style graduate research university".[13] President Emeritus Don Michael Randel mentioned in his inaugural speech of 2000: "A number of words and phrases recur through the eleven administrations and 108 years since that first faculty meeting. . . . They speak of the primacy of research, the intimate relationship of research to teaching, and to the amelioration of the condition of humankind, a pioneering spirit, the 'great conversation' among and across traditional disciplines that creates not only new knowledge but whole new fields of knowledge, the 'experimental attitude' and the intellectual freedom that makes this attitude possible" (Randel 2000).

In our context, attempts to delink research and teaching as a policy[14] at any level of higher education may be inadvisable. It is important to fix the shortcomings such as with the API and UGC-recognized list of journals, which have severe flaws, and invest in infrastructure rather than delinking research and teaching. Colleges in more remote locations too could play a vital role in documenting and studying local history, traditional knowledge, and local flora and fauna for example. While the Subramanian Committee notes with justifiable concern that many institutions are producing PhDs "on a commercial basis, which have little real worth or utility", but often merely to fulfil requirements for appointment or promotion, its solution "that a PhD is not necessary for every teaching position in every college" is debatable. In addition to improving access to higher education and the GER, it is equally important not to compromise on the quality of the faculty we select. One must face up to the more challenging and exacting task of

Scientific research productivity 121

putting in place norms which ensure that PhDs and publications are of reasonable quality. The earlier UGC norms of recognizing publications via journals or books having ISSN/ISBN numbers, and its current list of recognized journals where many predatory and sub-standard journals[15] have crept in, have not helped.

As we ponder over ways and means of improving the quality and quantity of research output from our universities, issues of funding are naturally relevant. The World Bank data (World Development Indicators: Science and technology)[16] indicate that during the period 2005–15, India's expenditure on R&D has been 0.63% of GDP, lower than all BRICS nations where values for the other nations range from 0.72% (South Africa) to 2.07% (China). In comparison, the numbers for Germany, Israel, Japan, Korea and the United States are 2.88, 4.27, 3.28, 4.23 and 2.79 percent respectively. The support for social science research has also been minimal and has been diminishing in recent times. The support for education as a percentage of the GDP is also unsatisfactory.[17] The Subramanian Committee notes that the "weighted average of Government spending as percent of GDP for all countries in the world is 4.9%, substantially above that in India", and reiterates that 6% is the minimal level required. The Tapas Majumdar Committee Report of 2005 made a case for about 10% of GDP spending by 2014–15. While increased funding for both education and research are crucial, institutional culture and structures that recognize and nurture a daring of scientific spirit are also vitally important in our university sector to build the institutions of tomorrow that we can be proud of.

Notes

1 www.shanghairanking.com (last accessed on 10 June 2017)
2 www.timeshighereducation.com (last accessed on 10 June 2017)
3 www.natureindex.com (accessed during May and June 2017 for data compilation)
4 www.scimagojr.com (last accessed on 10 June 2017)
5 Some of these points were also discussed in Saikia and Robinson 2014b.
6 **Subjects and journal groups in Nature Index** www.natureindex.com (2017 June):

   Chemistry: *Advanced Materials; Analytical Chemistry; Angewandte Chemie International Edition; Chemical Communications; Chemical Science; Inorganic Chemistry; Journal of the American Chemical Society; Nano Letters; Nature (*only articles classified in this subject area*);Nature Chemical Biology; Nature Chemistry; Nature Communications (*only articles classified in this subject area*);Nature Materials; Nature Nanotechnology; Organic Letters; Proceedings of the National Academy of Sciences of the United States of America (*only articles classified in this subject area); *Science* (only articles classified in this subject area); *The Journal of Physical Chemistry Letters*

Earth and Environmental Sciences: *Earth and Planetary Science Letters; Ecology; Ecology Letters; Geology; Journal of Geophysical Research: Atmospheres; Journal of Geophysical Research: Oceans; Journal of Geophysical Research: Solid Earth; Nature* (only articles classified in this subject area); *Nature Communications* (only articles classified in this subject area); *Nature Geoscience; Proceedings of the National Academy of Sciences of the United States of America*(only articles classified in this subject area); *Science*(only articles classified in this subject area)

Life Sciences: *American Journal of Human Genetics; Cancer Cell; Cell; Cell Host & Microbe; Cell Metabolism; Cell Stem Cell; Current Biology; Developmental Cell; Ecology; Ecology Letters; Genes & Development; Genome Research; Immunity; Journal of Biological Chemistry; Journal of Cell Biology; Journal of Clinical Investigation; Journal of Neuroscience; Molecular Cell; Nature* (only articles classified in this subject area); *Nature Biotechnology; Nature Cell Biology; Nature Chemical Biology; Nature Communications* (only articles classified in this subject area); *Nature Genetics; Nature Immunology; Nature Medicine; Nature Methods; Nature Neuroscience; Nature Structural & Molecular Biology; Neuron; PLOS Biology; Proceedings of the National Academy of Sciences of the United States of America* (only articles classified in this subject area); *Proceedings of the Royal Society B; Science* (only articles classified in this subject area); *The EMBO Journal*

Physical Sciences: *Advanced Materials; Applied Physics Letters; Astronomy & Astrophysics; European Physical Journal C; Journal of High Energy Physics; Monthly Notices of the Royal Astronomical Society; Nano Letters; Nature* (only articles classified in this subject area); *Nature Communications* (only articles classified in this subject area); *Nature Materials; Nature Nanotechnology; Nature Photonics; Nature Physics; Physical Review A; Physical Review B; Physical Review D; Physical Review Letters; Proceedings of the National Academy of Sciences of the United States of America* (only articles classified in this subject area); *Science* (only articles classified in this subject area); *The Astrophysical Journal; The Astrophysical Journal Letters; The Astrophysical Journal Supplement.*

7 Departments/Centres/Schools considered while estimating faculty strengths (in order in which they appear in the text: Cotton College State University: Botany, Chemistry, Environmental Biology and Wildlife Sciences, Geography, Geology, Molecular Biology and Biotechnology, Physics, Zoology; **Presidency University:** Chemistry, Geography, Geology, Life Sciences, Physics; **Ravenshaw University:** Applied Geography, Biotechnology, Botany, Chemistry, Geology, Physics, Zoology; **Assam University:** Biotechnology, Chemistry, Earth Sciences, Ecology and Environmental Sciences, Life Sciences and Bioinformatics, Microbiology, Physics; **Dibrugarh University:** Applied Geology, Centre for Atmospheric Studies, Biotechnology and Bioinformatics, Chemistry, Centre for Studies in Geography, Life Sciences, Physics; **Gauhati University:** Applied Sciences, Bioengineering and Technology, Biotechnology, Botany, Chemistry,

Environment Science, Geography, Geological Science, Physics, Zoology; **NEHU**: Basic Sciences and Social Sciences (only Basic Sciences counted), Biochemistry, Biomedical Engineering, Biotechnology and Bioinformatics, Botany, Chemistry, Environmental Sciences, Geography, Nanotechnology, Physics, Zoology; **Tezpur University**: Chemical Sciences, Environmental Science, Molecular Biology and Biotechnology, Physics (Energy Engineering in the Engineering School not included); **Calcutta University**: Applied Optics and Photonics, Applied Physics, Atmospheric Science, Biochemistry, Biophysics Molecular Biology and Informatics, Biotechnology and Dr B C Guha Centre for Genetic Engineering and Biotechnology, Botany, Chemistry, Chemical Engineering, Chemical Technology, Electronic Science, Environmental Science, Genetics, Genetics and Plant Breeding, Geology, Geography, Marine Sciences, Microbiology, Nanoscience and Engineering, Plant Physiology, Polymer Science and Technology, Physics; Radio Physics and Electronics, S K Mitra Centre for Space Environment; S N Pradhan Centre for Neurosciences, Zoology; **Jadavpur University**: Bioscience and Engineering, Chemistry, Chemical Engineering, Condensed Matter Physics Research Centre, Energy Studies, Environmental Studies, Geography, Geological Sciences, Laser Science and Engineering, Life Science and Biotechnology, Material Science and Technology, Mathematical Biology and Ecology, Metallurgical and Material Engineering, Nuclear and Particle Physics Research Centre, Nuclear Studies and Application, Oceanographic Studies, Physics, Relativity and Cosmology; **Utkal University**: Biotechnology, Botany, Chemistry, Geography, Geology, Physics, Zoology; **IIEST Shibpur**: Chemistry, Earth Sciences, Metallurgy and Materials Engineering, Dr M N Dastur School of Materials Science and Engineering, Physics; **IIT Roorkee**: Biotechnology, Chemical Engineering, Chemistry, Earth Sciences, Metallurgical and Materials Engineering, Physics, Polymer and Process Engineering; **IIT Bombay**: Biosciences and Bioengineering, Chemical Engineering, Chemistry, Earth Sciences, Energy Science and Engineering, Centre for Environmental Science and Engineering, Metallurgical Engineering and Materials Science, Centre for Research in Nanotechnology and Science, Physics; **IIT Guwahati**: Biosciences and Bioengineering; Chemical Engineering, Chemistry, Physics; **IIT Kanpur**: Biological Sciences and Bio-Engineering, Chemical Engineering, Chemistry, Earth Sciences, Materials Science and Engineering, Nanoscience and Soft Nanotechnology Centre, Physics; **IIT Madras**: Biotechnology, Chemical Engineering, Chemistry, Metallurgical and Materials Engineering, Centre for NEMS and Nanophotonics, Physics; **IISc**: Atmospheric and Oceanic Sciences, Biochemistry, Centre for Biosystems Science and Engineering, Centre for Earth Sciences, Chemical Engineering, Divecha Centre for Climate Change, Ecological Sciences, High Energy Physics, Inorganic and Physical Chemistry, Instrumentation and Applied Physics, Materials Engineering, Materials Research Centre, Microbiology and Cell Biology, Molecular Biophysics Unit, Molecular Reproduction, Development and Genetics, Centre for Nanoscience and Engineering, Centre for Neuroscience, Nuclear Magnetic Resonance Research Centre, Organic Chemistry, Physics, Solid State and Structural Chemistry Unit; **TIFR Bombay (including ICTS & NCBS Bangalore, NCRA Pune & TCIS Hyderabad)**: Astronomy and Astrophysics, Biological Sciences, Chemical Sciences, Condensed Matter Physics, High Energy Physics, Nuclear and Atomic

Physics, Theoretical Physics; all faculty from ICTS, NCBS, NCRA and TCIS included); **IISER Pune:** All faculty included barring Mathematics and Humanities and Social Sciences; **IISER Trivandrum:** All faculty included barring Mathematics and Humanities; **NISER:** Biological Sciences, Chemical Sciences, Earth and Planetary Sciences, Physical Sciences; **JNCASR:** All faculty included; **Delhi University:** Biomedical Research, Biophysics, Biochemistry, Botany, Chemistry, Electronics Science, Environmental Studies, Genetics, Geology, Medical Biochemistry, Medical Microbiology, Microbiology, Physics and Astrophysics, Plant Molecular Biology, Zoology; **University of Hyderabad:** Animal Biology, Biotechnology and Bioinformatics, Biochemistry, Centre for Advanced Studies in Electronics Science and Technology (CASEST), Chemistry, Earth and Space Sciences, High Energy Materials Research, Medical Sciences, Neural and Cognitive Sciences, Plant Sciences, Physics, School of Engineering Science and Technology; **Jawaharlal Nehru University:** Schools of Biotechnology, Environmental Sciences, Life Sciences, Physical Sciences, Special Centre for Molecular Medicine, Special Centre for Nanoscience; **Panjab University:** Biochemistry, Biophysics, Biotechnology, Botany, Centre for Biology and Bioinformatics, Centre for Medical Physics, Centre for Nanoscience and Nanotechnology, Centre for Stem Cell and Tissue Engineering, Department cum National Centre for Human Genome Studies and Research, Dr S S Bhatnagar University Institute of Chemical Engineering and Technology, Chemistry, Environment Studies, Geology, Microbial Biotechnology, Microbiology, Physics, Zoology.

8 http://iiests.ac.in (last accessed on 10 June 2017)
9 www.iitr.ac.in (last accessed on 10 June 2017)
10 www.nuepa.org/New/download/NEP2016/ReportNEP.pdf (last accessed on 10 June 2017)
11 http://mhrd.gov.in/sites/upload_files/mhrd/nep/nep/committee.pdf (last accessed on 10 June 2017)
12 www.hu-berlin.de/en/about/humboldt-universitaet-zu-berlin (last accessed on 10 June 2017)
13 http://www-news.uchicago.edu/resources/brief-history.html (last accessed on 10 June 2017)
14 See https://thewire.in/165770/prakash-javadekar-teaching-research, https://thewire.in/166549/teaching-research-javadekar-ugc-api-grants-hoodbhoy/ and https://blogs.timesofindia.indiatimes.com/toi-edit-page/where-javadekar-errs-research-must-be-promoted-for-both-teachers-and-students-from-college-level-itself/ for more details on this (last accessed on 20 November 2017)
15 https://journosdiary.com/2017/09/14/ugc-white-list-predatory-journals/ (last accessed on 20 November 2017)
16 http://wdi.worldbank.org/table/5.13 (last accessed on 10 June 2017)
17 www.thehindu.com/todays-paper/tp-opinion/centres-move-places-education-at-risk/article18464421.ece (last accessed on 10 June 2017)

References

Albritton, F. P. Jr. 2009. 'Humboldt's Unity of Research and Teaching: Influence on the Philosophy and Development of Higher Education in the US', *The FedUni Journal of Higher Education*, 2009: 7–19.

Banshal, K. S., Singh, V. K., Basu, A. and Muhuri, P. K. 2017. 'Research Performance of Indian Institutes of Technology', *Current Science*, 112(5): 923–32.
Joseph, M. and Robinson, A. 2014. 'Policy: Free Indian science', *Nature*, 508: 36–8.
Randel, Don Michael. 2000. 'A University's Lexicon', *University of Chicago Magazine*, 93(2). Available at https://magazine.uchicago.edu/0012/features/speech.html (accessed on 10 June 2017).
Saikia, D. J. 2014. 'Conversion Models', *The Telegraph*, January 14.
Saikia, D. J. and Robinson, R. 2014a. 'Indian Science: Overhaul Teaching', *Nature*, 509: 164.
Saikia, D. J. and Robinson, R. 2014b. 'Debating Higher Education: Areas of Silence and New University Models', *NMML Occasional Paper Perspectives in Indian Development New Series 37*.
Seethapathy, G. S., Santhosh Kumar, J. U. and Hareesha, A. S. 2016. 'India's Scientific Publication in Predatory Journals: Need for Regulating Quality of Indian Science and Education', *Current Science*, 111(11): 1759–64.

6 In search of a scientific public sphere

Shobhit Mahajan

Introduction

A few years ago, a student of mine wanted to clarify some doubts on a particular topic in the theory of relativity with which he was struggling. He was using a textbook that I had co-authored and wanted to ask how to solve a particular problem in the book. He came to my room and showed me his copy of the book – and I was surprised to see that the margins were filled with long notes in Hindi. He told me that he does not understand English and therefore had asked a classmate to translate it into Hindi, which he had then transcribed in the margins.

This story brought home a fact that we have been struggling with for many years now. A large majority of our students are unable to comprehend spoken or written English. And since English is the language of instruction in the sciences in most universities, *ipso facto* they start with a huge disadvantage as regards the subject.

Universities are the locations of teaching, training and research in modern societies. This has not always been the case, as we shall see later. Knowledge is created and distributed and future knowledge workers are trained in them. Universities are also supposed to be arenas of free ranging thought, creativity and debate, which, among other things, leads to new ideas. At least for a century, these characteristics of universities have been almost universally accepted.

Public universities, in addition, have another important role to play. Funded by the state, they are supposed to be free from the pressures of private capital and can use this freedom to explore disciplines and areas of their choice. However, even in the ideal scenario, the public university has an obligation to contribute to society in terms of generation of new ideas and technologies as well as nurturing critical thinking in citizens. It also has an obligation to further whatever goals society has set itself – goals which might go beyond the narrow confines of disciplines and subjects. Universal access is one such goal – 'universal' obviously implying non-discrimination in everything except academic matters. In addition, at various historical junctures, societies might decide to compensate for historical injustices by agreeing to a set of affirmative action programmes. Access thus remains a crucial defining characteristic of a public university.

Research and teaching are the fundamental functions of the university, as we have noted. In this article, we attempt to look at these two strands from the standpoint of the natural sciences in general and physics in particular. We look at teaching and how it has fared with respect to providing access to disadvantaged groups in our society. Access here is defined in its broadest sense, to mean real opportunities for everyone to a high-quality and meaningful education. We then look at research in the natural sciences and explore how it has become more and more specialized in nature, while at the same time becoming more esoteric. The evolution of structures which makes this possible is also explored. The interaction between society at large and scientific workers is also discussed.

Teaching

The Higher Education sector in India has seen a massive growth in the past decade. The Gross Enrolment Ratio (GER) for higher education, defined as the percentage of the population in the relevant age group enrolled in an educational institution, has increased from around 11% in 2006 to more than 23% in 2014. This growth is also evident in the number of higher educational institutions – in 2014, there were 757 universities and more than 37,000 colleges imparting higher education (Gupta and Pushkar 2016; GoI 2014).

One of the consequences of this expansion is the changing demographic and socio-economic profile of university students. The dramatic increase in the number of institutions imparting higher education is of course one major contributor to this. This is simply because of the increase in the number of opportunities for entry for students from varied socio-economic backgrounds. However, a major contributor also seems to be the enhancement of reservations about a decade ago, whereby the Other Backward Classes (OBCs) were included in the reservation ambit for admission to centrally funded institutions of higher learning (GoI 2007). Most states already had some form of reservation for groups other than the Scheduled Castes and Scheduled Tribes.

Interestingly, this had a two-fold impact – it facilitated the entry of socially and economically deprived sections into higher education. But equally importantly, to keep the existing number of unreserved seats constant, it mandated an almost 50% increase in the total number of seats in these institutions (ibid.). Both these factors have resulted in the profile of students changing over the past few years. Hitherto under-represented sections of the society are now being increasingly represented in higher education.

In a survey carried out by us at the University of Delhi, more than 55% of students in the M.Sc. (Physics) class were from non-metropolitan cities (Mahajan 2016). Non-metropolitan cities were defined as those outside of the National Capital Region of Delhi and other metro cities and state capitals. Delhi University has always attracted students from all over the country for various reasons. But what we are seeing is an increasing number of students from small towns and indeed villages. In this cohort, 34% students had their parents still living in villages. This is indeed a radical change from earlier times.

The caste composition of the students broadly reflected the reservation guidelines of the University but not surprisingly, the representation of the socially disadvantaged castes is much higher from the villages than from the metros. This trend is also reflected in the economic composition of the students – more than 75% of the students came from families with an annual income of less than Rs. 5 lakhs and 40% with incomes of less than Rs. 2 lakhs per annum.

It is not just the variables of caste, geography or economics which are defining the relative positions of the students. Educational qualifications too seem to be important – more than 35% of the students had parents who had studied till the twelfth grade or below. These students thus are the first-generation of college goers in their families. This is remarkable since it indicates two things – that increased opportunities are pulling significant numbers up the educational ladder. However, it also implies that this section of students starts with an initial disadvantage compared to their peers from educated families.

The survey is, of course, a small one and is restricted to one course in one university. However, given that the University of Delhi is a premier central university with students from across the country, one can imagine that, if certain trends are observed here, they would possibly be much more pronounced in other universities. Nevertheless, there are certain conclusions that we can draw even from this limited survey.

Firstly, the reservation policy especially for OBCs has been a huge facilitator for many students. This is especially true for the students who belong to educationally and/or economically backward families.

For a long time now, the opponents of caste-based affirmative action policies have been arguing that the beneficiaries of reservations are primarily candidates from economically and educationally well-off families. This has been repeatedly proven false in the case of SC reservations. Thus, for instance, the National Sample Survey (NSS) data for 2011 showed that only around 11% of the SC population, 9% of the ST population and 16% of the OBC population have gone beyond secondary schooling, while almost 29% of the groups not covered by reservations have post-secondary qualifications (GoI 2011). It is clear, then, that caste-based gaps continue to exist in educational status, even after decades of affirmative action policies.

Recently, the rhetoric of the state withdrawing from higher education and encouraging private sector involvement in the field is gaining traction. The higher educational institutions are being asked to raise resources through various means, while the state's allocation is decreasing in real terms. Recently, institutions are also being offered autonomy, which implies not just academic autonomy but more importantly, financial autonomy. Mobilizing of resources from alumni and industry, as well as tuition fee enhancement, are also being suggested (GoI 2016). Alumni contributions have historically never been significant in the Indian context, unlike, say, the research universities in the United States of America. Thus, for instance, Harvard University alone received a contribution of US $ 650 million in 2015 from its alumni (CAE 2016). In India, donations and research funding by industry to universities are miniscule. However, interestingly, on both scores, the IITs seem to fare much better – though nowhere close to the universities abroad.

Given the socio-economic profile of the students that we have seen in the survey sample, it seems fairly obvious that a large number of these students would not have been able to afford the benefit of higher education had it not been for the subsidized public universities. Even a marginal increase in the fees could force a significant number of them to drop out or search for alternatives.

A powerful argument which keeps surfacing is to replace subsidized higher education with a student loan scheme. The draft National Educational Policy also seems to be in favour of an enhanced and more liberal student loan policy. Among its recommendations is a lowering of interest rates, increasing the moratorium period etc., to make loans more attractive. The crux of the argument is that the state should provide free secondary education while tertiary education should be self-financed, though with easy access to educational loans. This, the argument goes, is necessary because of the resource constraints faced by the public exchequer, which should instead concentrate on providing free basic school education. Education loans seem equitable since presumably tertiary education would lead to employment and therefore an enhanced capacity to pay back.

The argument seems powerful and equitable. After all, there is no reason for the state to subsidize higher education while the primary and secondary education sectors are terribly short of funds. Despite fairly large increases in the period 2009–14, government spending on education as a whole (that is on primary, secondary, university and technical education as well as training) was still around 3.8–4.1% of the Gross Domestic Product in 2014. The National Educational Policy 2016 reminds us that

> [t]he earlier National policies of 1968 and 1986/92 had recommended 6% of the GDP as the norm for the national outlay on education. However, the actual expenditure has remained consistently below this level and in recent years has hovered around 3.5%.
> (GoI 2016)

This has had a disastrous impact on education. "Shortfall in the funding has been a major constraint to the complete implementation of some of the programmes designed to further expand school, higher and adult education . . . and maintain a reasonable level of quality". It recommends that "[t]he government will take steps of reaching the long pending goal of raising the investment in the education sector to *at least* 6% of the GDP as a priority" [emphasis added] (ibid.). It stands to reason that increasing the investment in education could in principle obviate the need for increasing the tuition fees and substituting them with education loans.

There are operational and logistical issues in universalizing a student loan scheme. However, there is another shortcoming of the education loan scheme as it is currently operationalized. This is the question of *capacity to pay back* not being commensurate with the expense incurred. Repayment of the education loan is supposed to be correlated to the increase in one's earning capacity, which comes about because of the degree obtained. Thus, for instance, a graduate of a professional or even a highly skilled and in-demand job-oriented course might find it easy to pay back the loan amount because of the employment potential that her education might lead to. On the other hand, it would be difficult for a typical pure science or humanities graduate to pay back the loan. This is because the employment opportunities for such graduates are not in very high paying sectors while the cost of running these courses to the exchequer is substantial. Thus, for instance, in the Department of Physics at the University of Delhi, the expenditure per student is more than 3 lakhs per annum (The total recurring expenditure is close to Rs. 19 crores and there are about 600 students).

On the other hand, the employment prospects of students are financially not very promising. In the case of the Department of Physics and Astrophysics, Delhi University, no data on the employment of its alumni exists. However, informal surveys and interactions with past students seems to indicate that a majority of the M.Sc. students ultimately end up as school teachers in private schools where salaries are much lower than in similar government jobs. It is hard to see how they would be able to repay even a principal amount of 6 lakhs with this kind of employment. The situation for most students of pure sciences and humanities will be similar, with regard to capacity for repayment of a student loan.

Finally, there is the issue of language. This is an extremely important variable which unfortunately almost never enters into any discussion of quality of education or equality of access. As mentioned earlier, even in a premier central university like Delhi University, at the post-graduate level, a majority of the students find it difficult to comprehend spoken or written English. And English being the medium of instruction, this automatically places a large number of them at a fundamental disadvantage compared to their peers from more privileged backgrounds. This linguistic handicap is on top of other handicaps. Indeed, it exacerbates their existing disadvantage of an upbringing which is both intellectually and economically resource-poor.

Interestingly, in the aforementioned survey, more than 85 percent of the students reported having gone to English medium schools and colleges. And, yet, our experience over the years indicates that most of them are unable to comprehend the language. This is obviously an indication of the booming industry of "English medium Public Schools", especially in smaller towns and villages (Nagarajan 2015). It also is indicative of the appalling standards of school education – both state-run as well as private.

The non-availability of good textbooks in an accessible language or the vernacular is another major impediment for the students. The National Translation Mission under the National Knowledge Commission had started an initiative to translate standard textbooks and reference books into Indian languages, but this has not really taken off. In the absence of accessible books and reference material, the learning process suffers.

Opening up higher education to more and more people is in principle an excellent idea. Good education is immensely empowering, both in itself as well as for overcoming historical prejudices. Affirmative action policies are obviously having an impact in getting large numbers of disadvantaged sections into the higher education fold. However, facilitating their entry is only the first step in this process. For the process to be truly meaningful, much more needs to be done. Facilities for language and remedial classes, for instance, must necessarily be provided for those who need them. Maybe, a mentoring scheme could also be introduced.

On a longer time scale, one could also think of generation of high-quality subject material in the vernacular. Here it is not just the State which needs to be taking the initiative – academics need to be sensitive to the importance of such an exercise. Essentially, one needs to recognize that in a deeply unequal society (economically, socially and educationally) such as ours, in order for higher education to be truly open and meaningful for all, one needs to create an appropriate ecosystem for the marginalized.

Research

We now turn to the other defining feature of a university, namely research. Here we talk about scientific research primarily focussing on Physics, though most of the observations would be valid across disciplines. We will explore the increasing nature of specialization in research and try to place it in a historical context. The historical evolution of the nature of scientific research and of its disciplines is important for understanding the trend of specialization. The structures of communication of research, both within and without the scientific community, themselves also play a crucial role in informing this trend.

The modern universities trace their origin to the founding of the first university in Bologna in 1088 CE, and the University of Paris and Oxford University soon thereafter. Before the establishment of these institutions, learning was mostly restricted to monasteries and institutions run by the Church. It is important to note, though, that these universities were essentially guilds of students and masters, organized for the purposes of specialized learning of subjects like law, theology and medicine.

The eleventh century was also the time when the works of Aristotle and others became accessible in Latin. This was because of the translations done during the Golden years of the Abbasid Empire in Baghdad in the ninth and tenth centuries. Aristotle's work in particular had a huge impact on the scholastic environment in Europe. His Physics, Metaphysics and moral philosophy formed an essential component of the curriculum in medieval universities. Apart from Aristotle, the works of Archimedes, Euclid and Ptolemy also became available in Latin during the twelfth century.

These works in natural philosophy and mathematics were expanded and commented upon extensively, and universities became important centres for learning of science. More important than the insights offered by the ancient writers was the slow but steady change in the method – empiricism, reason and logic was on the ascendant.

Two important events profoundly shaped the intellectual climate during the renaissance – the invention of the movable type by Gutenberg and the fall of Constantinople in the fifteenth century. Printing led to the easy reproduction and circulation of texts, while the Byzantine scholars and monks escaping from Constantinople brought with them many Greek texts hitherto unavailable to scholars in Europe. Bacon, Copernicus, Kepler and Galileo, amongst others, laid the foundations of modern science during this time.

The scientific revolution which followed did not just revolutionize science, but brought about a whole new way of thinking. With the scientific revolution, mathematics supplanted Latin as the language of science (Levenson 2015). Religious orthodoxy was increasingly challenged and progress became the ideal. An important development during this period was the birth of scientific societies – voluntary associations of the educated with a shared interest in science. The Royal Society in London and the Academie Royale des Sciences in Paris were both founded in the seventeenth century. These had a profound influence on the growth of scientific knowledge.

The Royal Society was given a Royal Charter in 1663 as the "Royal Society of London for the Improvement of Natural Knowledge". The idea was to be a forum not just to discuss science but also conduct experiments. Thus Robert Hooke, the famous seventeenth-century polymath who was appointed the Curator of Experiments, conducted experiments on gravity as well as microscopy while at the Royal Society.

Scientific societies and academies spread all over Europe during the eighteenth century at both the national and regional-provincial levels, and by the end of the century, there were close to a hundred such societies. The societies, apart from providing a platform for discussing science amongst interested citizens, also played a vital role in advising the state on various technical matters.

Universities continued to grow in Europe as well as the New World, but they focussed on training lawyers and physicians for the most part. The scientific societies complemented the Universities – societies were the locus of knowledge creation, while the Universities were thought to be where it was disseminated. It is noteworthy that even as late as 1836, upon returning from his voyage on the HMS Beagle, Darwin reported his findings not at Oxford or Cambridge, but at the Royal Geological Society.

Another important function of the societies was the popularization of science. Increase in literacy resulted in a hunger for knowledge especially about the developments in science, and weekly lectures by scientists as well as amateurs were very well attended. In addition, the societies started publishing academic journals, like the *Philosophical Transactions of the Royal Society*, with the aim of disseminating new ideas and discoveries amongst other scientists.

The rise of the academic journals was also accompanied by an increasing number of independent periodicals which, unlike the journals published by the societies, included reviews and translations of articles from other languages. These independent periodicals were published more frequently than the academic journals and so new developments in the sciences could be transmitted sooner across the community.

This was a time when knowledge was not differentiated into disciplines, but rather it was encyclopaedic in nature for both amateurs and professionals alike. Disciplines existed but only as a way of ordering knowledge for the purposes of instruction in schools and universities **after** it had been discovered. In a sense, disciplines served an archival function of depositing knowledge. The growth of specialized disciplines as the defining characteristic for professional and occupational roles began only in the nineteenth century (Stichweh 2001).

The categorization of knowledge into disciplines was both in terms of creation and dissemination. Starting with the universities in Germany, higher education came to be divided into separate disciplines and sub-disciplines. This trend of course accelerated in the latter part of the twentieth century. By this time, what we had was not just institutional structures based on these categories (departments and faculties at universities), but also communities of specialists who were much like the scientific communities proposed by Kuhn (Kuhn 1970).

The communities of specialists had their own language and their own channels of communication and there was little by way of any substantive interaction between practitioners of different disciplines. Thus, a physicist working in the area of relativity would ordinarily have little to do with chemists or even mathematicians. The closed communities communicated in the specialized language of their fields and, for the most part, communicated with their peers through academic journals. This trend towards differentiation continued with the growth of sub-disciplines, where even people working in the same discipline could not meaningfully understand the work of someone working in a related sub-discipline.

As far as the sciences go, this hyper-specialization seemed almost inevitable – the tremendous growth in our knowledge about the natural world especially in the twentieth century meant that becoming familiar with all the data, the techniques and the accumulated knowledge as well as the language of the subject required years of training. And even then, it was only possible to be truly familiar with a small part of it. Instruction was and continues to be structured to precisely reinforce this trend – a broad undergraduate training in a subject followed by a narrow specialization in a sub-discipline at the graduate level. The student so trained then goes on to join the ranks of the researchers/teachers. The pressures of publishing to advance her career push her to continue to work in her narrow field of training. The work gets published in academic journals where it is only understood and appreciated by her peers working in the same area. With time, this community grows and on reaching a critical number, a sub-discipline emerges, complete with its own specialized, or rather hyper-specialized journals.

Thus we see that the institutional structures as well as the nature of the disciplines, especially in the natural sciences, ensure that research gets more and more focussed on answering narrow questions. And it is not only that the subject becomes more esoteric but language of discourse among the specialists becomes progressively more arcane.

The situation in India has broadly followed the same contours with regard to growth of disciplines, though with a time lag. The first universities, established in the nineteenth century, were based on the British model and subsequent institutions of higher education have essentially replicated the same. Interestingly though, the location of the intellectual "metropolis" for native knowledge workers shifted to the United States especially after the Second World War.

Though the communication between specialists is mostly through the channels of academic journals, what about the communication of scientific work to the larger society? After all, it could be argued that apart from their work, scientists have some responsibility towards the larger society which supports their academic pursuits. This is as true for researchers in universities as it is for those in research institutes. An essential part of this responsibility is the communication of their work to the larger public. In fact, John Henry Newman, an English theologian who enunciated the core values of a modern university was clear about it. Apart from free speech and free enquiry and intellectual honesty, he believed that universities had a moral obligation to convey the results of research to others. This obligation both demands and explains the unity of research, teaching, publication and other ways of transferring knowledge to the wider world (Pelikan 1992).

As we have seen, in post-renaissance Europe, this was done by scientific societies. It is interesting to note that at the Royal Society, the weekly public lectures delivered by some of the best scientists of their times, were hugely popular. In fact the famous scientist Michael Faraday, who had little formal education, got interested in science by attending these lectures. Faraday of course went on to make seminal contributions to many fields in physics and chemistry and was later the President of the Royal Society.

In India too, the programme of bringing science to a larger audience was taken up by several people. In 1862, Sir Syed Ahmed Khan founded a Translation Society which then evolved into the Scientific Society of Aligarh in 1864. The aim was to promote Western scientific knowledge among the Muslim masses. The Society had a library and a reading room and brought out its own journal. The Mohammedan Literary Society was established in 1863 by Nawab Abdul Latif who worked towards interpreting Western Science in Persian and Urdu. The Society invited several scholars to join in their meetings and demonstrate some of the new inventions of the late nineteenth century. In 1868, the Bihar Scientific Society was set up in Muzaffarpur by Syed Imdad Ali. This society translated many works of science and mathematics into the vernacular, and established many schools. The contrast with the case today, when, as we have seen, no significant translation of standard texts is taking place, is striking.

This was also the time of an intellectual renaissance in Bengal. Mahendralal Sircar, a medical practitioner, established the Indian Association for the Cultivation of Science (IACS) in 1876. From the beginning, Sircar was clear that the object was

> not to establish a technical seminary and thus make his countrymen a nation of artisans and mechanics, but to diffuse among them the ascertained principles of Western Science in the hope that after mastering what has already been discovered by the Europeans, the Hindus might, in course of time, add their own discoveries to those of their fellow brethren of the West.
>
> (Kochhar 1999)

In search of a scientific public sphere 137

Apart from this, the institution aimed to be a place where "lectures on scientific subjects will be systematically delivered". Although Sircar's original aim for the IACS to be a research laboratory failed to materialize, it did provide a forum for delivering popular and college level lectures by eminent Indian scientists who carried out their research at universities and colleges (ibid.). Over the next few decades, eminent scientists including C. V. Raman, J. C. Bose and K. S. Krishnan joined the institute and their public lectures were extremely popular and inspired several people to start similar institutions elsewhere. Ruchi Ram Sharma attended the lectures at IACS in 1885 and went back to Lahore to start the Punjab Science Institute (Das Gupta 2011).

It is interesting to note that, a century and a half ago, when the number of institutions and therefore the number of science workers were small, significant efforts were being made to bring modern science to not just students but also to educated lay audiences. This is in sharp contrast with the situation today – the number of institutions as well as scientists is many times more and yet one does not see any substantial initiatives to popularize science or scientific ideas. Regular public lectures and discussions, writing in the popular press or even writing popular books are things which do not seem to be of much interest to our scientists. With one of the largest scientific and technical human resources, it is amazing that one can hardly point to any popular science book written in India. This is certainly true in English, and I suspect, even truer in the vernaculars.

It is also a sad fact that the incentive structure for scientists discourages anything other than publishing research papers. Career advancement depends solely on the quantity of research publications. This fetish for quantification is best illustrated by the bizarre Academic Performance Index (API) introduced recently by the University Grants Commission, whereby some minimum numbers of points are required for any career advancement for teachers in higher education institutions (UGC 2016). This has given rise to the nefarious industry of fake journals where one can pay to get anything published, just so that one may bag the required number of points (Yadav 2018). In this scheme of things, teaching and engagement with students and the community at large are given little importance.

It is not just that scientists in the universities and research institutes are reluctant to communicate their work to the broader public. They have also not been very forthcoming in producing good quality material for their students. The majority of textual material produced is in the nature of guide books and sub-standard copies of existing texts. Of course, as has been pointed out above, the incentive structure which values research publications over outreach programmes and textbook writing is a major reason for this. However, the reasons are possibly deeper than just the incentives – after all, though the incentive structure might be a reason for junior academics, it cannot be so for well-known, senior academics. They certainly have the freedom to engage in producing high-quality texts for students. In Physics for instance, the number of standard textbooks written in India over the last 70 years has been miniscule.

Globally, a new trend is emerging in the sciences. This is what has been called 'citizen science'. The idea is to use the power of crowd-sourcing and tools of modern technology to carry out tedious yet important tasks in scientific research. These could range from passive tasks, as using the idle computers at night to process telescope data for Search for Extra-terrestrial Intelligence (SETI@home) to data collection of the migration patterns of the Monarch butterfly. A large number of untrained but interested people collect data or analyse data using tools provided by scientists. This data and analysis can then be used by scientists in their work.

A classic example of citizen science is the Galaxy Zoo project initiated by Kevin Schawinski in 2007. Schawinski, an astrophysicist by training, was trying to classify galaxies which had been observed by a robotic telescope in the Sloan Digital Sky Survey. This was an arduous task since there were more than 900,000 galaxies whose images had to be studied and classified. He then decided to involve volunteers to help in this task. The idea was that the volunteers would use certain parameters to classify the images obtained by the telescope into known categories. This project was hugely successful and in less than six months, there were more than 100,000 volunteers working on the data. An important thing to note is that unlike passive projects like SETI@home which used idle time and processing power of the volunteer's computers, Galaxy Zoo was about active participation by citizens and hence immensely popular. It possibly gave the volunteers a sense of creative achievement, which was missing in purely passive projects. With the advent of automation and sophisticated instruments, there is now a deluge of data in many fields of science. And this data needs to be analysed by human beings since even with tremendous progress in Artificial Intelligence, humans are more adept at recognizing patterns. The internet makes it possible for citizens from across the globe to participate in these endeavours and contribute to the advancement of science.

Citizen science has the potential for an enhanced engagement of the general public with science. The process of data collection or analysis, even without detailed knowledge about the discipline or the problem, could increase public interest in science and help demystify science as practised by our scientists today. However, some commentators have pointed out that citizen science, as it is being practised, suffers from a glaring flaw – the professional scientists are basically appropriating the work of a crowd of laypersons without really engaging with them or even acknowledging them. Nevertheless, as scientists tackle very hard, data-intensive problems in their disciplines, citizen science would certainly play an important role.

Conclusion

For more than a century now, universities have been the primary locations of production as well as dissemination of knowledge globally. In our case, all universities have till recently been public universities which have broader goals than simply operating as production and transmission centres of knowledge. These goals include a furthering of social agendas set by the state, which includes increased access to disadvantaged sections of our society.

It could be argued that the interventions that the state has done at the level of entry, to implement this agenda, have been broadly successful. The enrolment has dramatically increased in absolute terms and the enrolment of socio-economically disadvantaged sections has also shown an increase. However, as we have argued, there is a lot more that needs to be done in terms of providing meaningful access to higher education. There are many barriers which need to be overcome for this. Creation of a whole ecosystem for support and nurturing is required.

On the other hand, research in general and specifically in the sciences has become more and more specialized. This trend towards increased specialization has been facilitated by institutional structures as well as structures of communication. The engagement of scientists with society has, over a period of time, become almost non-existent. The tradition of scientists communicating with the public through their writings and lectures has unfortunately died. What we have now are scientists working in their silos – cut off from not only the larger society, but also from their peers who are not working in their sub-disciplines.

In a society in which a majority of the population continues to have little access to good and meaningful education, the role of academicians in general and scientists in particular is a crucial one. Scientists need to engage in the important task of trying to inculcate scientific temper not only in their students, but also in society at large. In these times when superstitions, anti-scientific thinking and anti-rationalism are ascendant, this task is all the more urgent. Unfortunately, there are no indications that our scientists are willing to step out of their comfortable silos and engage in this exercise.

References

Council for Aid to Education. 2016. *Report of Voluntary Support of Education 2015*. Available at http://cae.org/images/uploads/pdf/VSE_2015_Sample_Pages.pdf (accessed on 22 January 2018).

Das Gupta, U. (ed.) 2011. *Science & Modern India: An Institutional History, c. 1784–1947*. New Delhi: Pearson.

Government of India (GoI). 2007. *The Central Educational Institutions (Reservations in Admissions Act) 2006*. New Delhi: Ministry of Human Resource Development. Available at http://indiacode.nic.in/amendmentacts 2012/The%20Central%20Educational%20Institution%20(Reservation% 20in%20Admission)%20Act.pdf (accessed on 16 January 2018).

———. 2011. *National Sample Survey Office (NSSO) Data*. New Delhi: Ministry of Statistics and Programme Implementation. Available at https://data.gov.in (accessed on 31 December 2017).

———. 2014. *AISHE Provisional Report, 2014–15*. New Delhi: Ministry of Human Resource Development. Available at www.aishe.nic.in (accessed on 31 December 2017).

———. 2016. *Some Inputs for Draft National Education Policy 2016*. New Delhi: Ministry of Human Resource Development. Available at http://mhrd.gov.in/sites/upload_files/mhrd/files/nep/Inputs_Draft_NEP_2016.pdf (accessed on 16 January 2018).

Gupta, Madhvi and Pushkar. 2016. 'More Indian Students Will Go to College, But Fewer Will Demand a Better Education', in *The Wire*, June 01. Available at https://thewire.in/39405/more-indian-students-will-go-to-college-but-few-will-demand-a-better-education/ (accessed on 18 January 2018).

Kochhar, R.K. 1999. 'Science in British India', *Indian Journal of History of Science*, 34(4): 317–46.

Kuhn, T. 1970. *The Structure of Scientific Revolutions*. Chicago: University of Chicago Press.

Levenson, Thomas. 2015. *The Hunt for Vulcan: How Albert Einstein Destroyed a Planet and Deciphered the Universe*. London: Head of Zeus.

Mahajan, Shobhit. 2016. 'A Micro Survey of the Socioeconomic Background of Postgraduate Students'. Submitted for publication to *Economic & Political Weekly*.

Nagarajan, Rema. 2015. 'Number of Children Studying in English Doubles in 5 Years', in *The Times of India* (September 28). Available at http://timesofindia.indiatimes.com/india/Number-of-children-studying-in-English-doubles-in-5-years/articleshow/49131447.cms (accessed on 22 January 2018).

Pelikan, J. 1992. *The Idea of the University: A Reexamination*. New Haven: Yale University Press.
Stichweh, R. 2001. 'History of Scientific Disciplines', in N. J. Smelser and P. B. Baltes (eds.) *International Encyclopedia of the Social and Behavioral Sciences* (pp. 13727–31). Oxford: Elsevier Science.
University Grants Commission (UGC). 2016. 'UGC (Minimum Qualifications for Appointment of Teachers and Other Academic Staff in Universities and Colleges and Measures for the Maintenance of Standards in Higher Education) (4th Amendment), Regulations', in *The Gazette of India*. New Delhi. Available at https://ugc.ac.in/pdfnews/3375714_API-4th-Amentment-Regulations-2016.pdf (accessed on 22 January 2018).
Yadav, Shyamlal. 2018. 'Inside India's fake research paper shops: pay, publish, profit', in *The Indian Express* (July 19). Available at https://indianexpress.com/article/india/inside-indias-fake-research-paper-shops-pay-publish-profit-5265402/ (accessed on 19 July 2018).

Part III
Imagining an 'other' university

7 What if the university is a *parrot's training*?

Anup Dhar

> Once upon a time there was a bird. . . . It sang songs, but did not read the scriptures. It flew, it jumped, but did not have the faintest sense of etiquette. The King said, "Such birds! They are of no use at all . . .". He called the minister, and commanded, "Educate it". . . . The scholars held long discussions, the subject being "What is the reason behind the foolishness of this creature?" The conclusion was: much learning could not be stored in the tiny nest that the bird could make with just chips and twigs. So, first of all, it was necessary to build a good cage[1] for it. . . . The goldsmith started building the cage. . . . Some said, "Education indeed!" Others said, "Education or no education, at least the bird has got the cage! . . .". The pundit came to teach the bird. He took a pinch of snuff and said, "A few books won't do". The nephew summoned the scribes. They copied from the books and copied from those copies and made an enormous mound of such things. Whoever saw it, said, "Bravo! Learning is going to overflow!" . . . The King wished to see for himself the lightning speed at which education was proceeding. . . . And he saw it. Very pleasing indeed. The method was so overwhelming compared to the bird that one could hardly notice the bird. . . . There was no corn in the cage, no water either. Only heaps of pages [and Course *Outlines*] had been torn out from heaps of books; and with the tip of a pen, those pages were being stuffed into the bird's mouth. There was no room in the mouth for the bird to squeeze out a cry, let alone a tune. It was really a terribly pleasing sight.
> — Rabindranath Tagore in *The Parrot's Training*

What if Tagore was offered a professorship in (comparative) literature in the University of Calcutta after he was awarded the Nobel Prize? What would Tagore have done? Would he have taken up the position? Or would he have stuck to *Santiniketan* (the "abode of peace")? Why did Tagore in the first instance set up *Santiniketan*? Was it a rejection of the then existing University of Calcutta, set up largely by the British, by the *colonizer*? Was it a rejection of the university (system), a system that trains students and inducts them into capital-logic, the temporal rhythm of industrialism (even if students are being fed on 'critiques of industrialization' in class) and the everyday practice of putting labour-power in the market as commodity?[2] What was wrong with the extant idea of the university that Tagore had to reject it?

Was it simply because the idea of the university was always already coloured with colonizing intentions? Was it because it was an 'alien' plant born in a distant land/soil; the plant-soil metaphor recurs in Tagore's writings (see "Founding of a New Education" [Tagore 2011]) on what he calls his "educational crusade":

> if you want to grow a tree on the sandy soil of a rainless desert, then you not only have to borrow your seed from some distant land, but also the soil itself and the water. Yet, . . . the tree grows up miserably stunted; and even if it does bear fruit, the seeds do not mature. The education that we receive from our universities . . . is for cultivating a hopeless desert, and that not only the mental outlook and the knowledge, but also the whole language must bodily be imported from across the sea. And this makes our education so nebulously *distant* and *unreal*.
>
> (Tagore 2011: 158)

Or were there deeper critiques, critiques beyond education being an alien apparatus? Was it then a rejection of the 'university' as a concept?

Was Tagore setting up in *Santiniketan* the other kind of university,[3] a university that was marking difference with the university imagination itself, a university that was not a university in the classical (European/Western) sense? Tagore argues that the students of the European universities not only have their "human environment of culture", they also acquire their learning "direct from their teachers". We have, on the other hand, "our hard flints, which give us disconnected sparks after toilsome blows; and the noise is a great deal more than the light. These flints are the abstractions of learning; they are solid methods, inflexible and cold" (such methods are like "hard-boiled eggs from which you cannot expect chickens to come out" [Tagore 2011: 151]). "To our misfortune we have, in our own country, all the furniture [i.e. we have the cage] of the European University – except the human teacher" (Tagore 2011: 156) and "like Hanuman of our ancient Epic, who, not knowing which herb might be wanted, had to carry away the whole mountain top", the students, "unable to use the language intelligently, have to carry in their heads the whole of the book by rote" (Tagore 2011: 159).

We [thus] have, instead, merely purveyors of book-lore, in whom the paper god of the bookshop seems to have made himself vocal. And, as a natural result, we find our students to be 'untouchable', even to our Indian professors. These teachers distribute their doles of mental food, gingerly and from a dignified distance, raising walls of notebooks between themselves and their students. This kind of food is neither relished, nor does it give nourishment. It is a famine ration strictly regulated, to save us, not from emancipation, but only from absolute death. . . . Our education to us is like the carriage to a horse; a bondage, the dragging of which merely serves to provide it with food and shelter in the stable of the master (more on the 'Master' and the relationship between 'Master' and 'University' in the next section); the horse has not the same freedom of relationship with the carriage as its owner, and therefore the carriage ever remains for it an imposition of beggarly necessity.
(Tagore 2011: 157)

While Tagore's journey was premised on a critique of the mindless adoption of the European model of the University (Indian universities were like deserts absorbing rain water, and not ponds which contribute in turn to rain clouds), he also had a deeper critique: the critique of university as such. Tagore inaugurated in *Santiniketan*[4] and thereafter in *Sriniketan* (the 'abode of the aesthetic') the perspective of praxis; praxis as the foreclosed of the university imagination – an imagination steeped in and limited to the learning, teaching, writing of the cognitivist sciences; while the classical imagination of the university sharpened largely the cognitive and the intellectual self, Tagore inaugurated in the 'culture of the self' the creative expression and praxis of the affective, the aesthetic, and the ethical; the praxis of being-in-the-world which is "disclosed"; being-with-nature; the praxis of labouring activities in the "average everydayness" of the ashram; the praxis of self- and social transformation. Tagore's turn to *Santiniketan* and *Sriniketan* could be seen as a departure from the classical university imagination and from the kind of cognitivist student subject the university mass-produces; such mass production of cognitive student subjects in turn creates a culture of *turning away* from the masses; more on the history of this turning away in the context of the birth of western philosophy in Plato's dialogues below.

Thus "Tagore, intellectually, was not only outgrowing the discursive liminalities of official nationalism [see Dhar and Chakrabarti 2017: 53–6] but was also formulating his own theories of the nation-building project [we argue in this paper, how Sriniketan could also be seen as his way of nation-building; where building, re-creating, re-constructing the gravel strewn rural everyday emerge as the ideal kind of nation-building] . . . and the hugely important role education and educational institutions should play in that grand exercise. Hence, his attention, for a longish period, became steadfastly focused on his . . . schools, . . . one in Santiniketan and the other in Sriniketan" (Roy 2010: 679). Santiniketan as an institution of [elite] pedagogy and Sriniketan as an institution of grassroots level *transformative social praxis* – praxis that is patient, long term, sustainable and non-violent, praxis that could lead to non-coercive reorganizations of the graph of desire, involving the life, worlds and philosophies as also *lokavidyas* (see Basole 2015) of subaltern bricoleurs – are two path-breaking imaginations of institution building, imaginations fundamentally different from the models of institutions hitherto given in modernity. Santiniketan and Sriniketan would, for Tagore, "ultimately bridge the ever-widening gap between the country and the city; a gap, that originated from the unleashing of forces of 'colonial modernity' by the imperial rulers" (Roy 2010: 679). Especially Sriniketan, which was the site for projects of rural reconstruction (*not* rural development[5]), co-operative movements, agricultural banking, and new methods in agriculture, largely amongst adivasis, etc. Tagore states in the Prospectus (1925) for "A Viswa-Bharati Institute for Rural Reconstruction at Sriniketan":

> The aim of the Institute [founded near the village of Surul] is to train its apprentices [not more than twenty; anyone who has passed matriculation and is seventeen years of age is eligible; the course lasts two years; most of the students are drawn from the cities] as to enable them to not only earn their livelihood but to equip themselves for initiating village welfare and reconstruction work, and to stimulate among villagers . . . the spirit of self-help. It is required, however, that an apprentice should have learnt beforehand the *coordination of brain and hand*.
> (Tagore 2011: 137–9)

The objectives of Sriniketan were: (1) "to bring back life in its completeness into the villages making them self-reliant and self-respectful, acquainted with the cultural tradition of their own country, and competent to make an efficient [and critical] use of the modern resources", (2) "to win the friendship and affection of the villagers and cultivators by taking real interest in all that concerns their life and . . . by making a lively effort to assist them in solving their most pressing problems", (3) "to take the problems of the village and field to the classroom", (4) "to carry the knowledge and experience gained in the classroom and experimental farm [back] to the villages" etc. The coordination between brain and hand, thought and action, theory and practice, however, remained central in Sriniketan.

Lacan meets Tagore at Sriniketan

> When the time comes for our thinkers and intellectuals to take agricultural activities under their responsibility, the schism that at present exists between the hand and the brain . . . will vanish.
>
> (Tagore 2011: 139)

Tagore's critique of the classical university imagination and of the cognitivist perspective (Tagore's writings and Tagore's actions – i.e. Tagore's *turning away* from the kind of *parrot's training* universities impart and the creation of *Santiniketan* for practices of self-transformation through the realization of creative freedom and *Sriniketan* for practices of social transformation through 'rural reconstruction' – stand testimony to such a critique) finds a somewhat surprising ally in Lacan's (2007 [1969–70]) enumeration of the Discourse of the University *on the side* of the Master's Discourse, i.e. on the side of the master-as-oppressor, and of 'reaction'. We were expecting the Discourse of the University to be *on the other side* of the Master's Discourse, to be on the side of the lived experience and discourse of the 'slave'; the university looked to be aligned with the world of the 'slave'; which is also why we feel the need to protect the university; hence the incitement around a protectionist discourse on the university. Does the *existing* university need protection? Or does the university need *re-form*? Does the university need to shed its old habits and re-conceptualize itself anew? Does the university need to exist because the masses are in awe of whatever is going on inside the university? Or would 'legitimacy' among the masses be the ground and cordon of protection; a legitimacy that is born not out of the 'male perspective' ("my seed; my son"), but out of a culture of being-with-Others, a culture of caring connection with the masses? What is or should the university be: the secret theoretical justification for *turning away* or the ground and creation of the "potentiality-for-being-in-the-world"?

What, however, is the Discourse of the University? Lacan, unlike Foucault, talks of only Four Discourses: the Discourse of the University, the Master's Discourse, the Hysteric's Discourse, and the Analyst's Discourse. Discourse is for Lacan the structure of a "fundamental relation" "of one signifier to another" and from this relation emerges what Lacan calls "the subject" (Lacan 2007: 13). And all four discourses revolve around a fundamental impossibility: of education, of mastery, of "inciting of desire", and of analysis. Let us discuss the Discourse of the Master first; all the more because the Discourse of the University, contrary to all expectation, looks to be apposite to and not the opposite of the Master's Discourse. The Discourse of the Master can be seen in the master-slave relation or in authoritarianism where a 'master signifier' standing in for the master/dictator issues orders. In the Discourse of the Master, a master/dictator would speak from the position of agent unaware of its *own* vulnerability. Charlie Chaplin's *Great Dictator* is a representation of the rather tragico-comic relation between the master as actually a vulnerable subject and the master signifier as authoritarian agent; the menacing yet flaccid father or the authoritarian yet vulnerable man in a patriarchal culture is also representative of such a Master's Discourse. Let us now move to the Discourse of the University and its relationship with the Master's Discourse. The Discourse of the University is common to the educational context, where the master signifier is 'unconscious original knowledge' that supports the knowledge that is to be taught in say the classroom context, and the knowledge that is to be taught is addressed to the student-lacking-in-knowledge. The Discourse of the University, according to Lacan, is the secret rationalization of the Master's Discourse; it is the delusional veil of knowledge over the master's lack of discourse. While the Discourse of the University covers the master's lack, the Hysteric's Discourse – according to Lacan – uncovers/unmasks the lack. The Hysteric's Discourse is a kind of subversion of the Master's Discourse through submersion in the Master's Discourse; it is the Discourse which puts to question the Master's Discourse; which shows the limits and the limpness of the Master's Discourse. In the Analyst's Discourse, the analyst becomes the mirror of the analysand's object cause of desire and assists the analysand in her self-arrival at her own 'master signifier' (see Lacan 2007: 41). The Discourse of the Analyst is produced by a twist to the Discourse of the Hysteric, in the same way as Freud developed psychoanalysis by giving an interpretative turn to the discourse of his hysterical patients. The fact that this discourse is the inverse of the Discourse of the Master emphasizes that, for Lacan, the Analyst's Discourse is an essentially subversive practice which undermines

A parrot's training? 151

attempts at domination and mastery. Thus while the political embodying of the Hysteric's Discourse puts to question the Master's Discourse and while the Analyst's Discourse re-conceptualizes the master-slave relation, the Discourse of the University remains on the side of the master. In the ethical embodying of the Analyst's Discourse the would-be-university puts to creative questioning one's own premise of the university. In this discourse one doesn't just protect the university. The extant university serves as a mirror for a future university; which is also the future of the university.

Tagore explored such a creative future in his turning away from the University of Calcutta, i.e. from the colonial apparatus; he would also put to perpetual questioning his own institution/university: Santiniketan, which had made a radical beginning with respect to the work of decolonization in education; it is such a questioning that took him further to the founding of Sriniketan and the turn to praxis (in the form of rural reconstruction). If Santiniketan had addressed the first critique (i.e. *alienation* in colonial educational institutions), Sriniketan had approached the two unequal but interrelated halves of the second critique (i.e. *foreclosure* of praxis in education and *forgetting* of the 'slave's' knowledge-praxis-worldview). In that sense, Sriniketan had problematized an educational experience built around the Master's Discourse; it had instead tried to inaugurate an educational experience attuned to the 'slave' or the 'subaltern's' life-world; hence the turn to the 'rural'; as also to "Heidegger's Hut"[6] (Heidegger's rhetoric of 'hut life' "located him in rigorous contact with existence" [Sharr 2006: 104]) and Socrates in the *haat* (which is about the philosophico-political praxis of being-in-the-polis, being-in-the-marketplace, and not in the private realm of the library [Arendt 2005: 5–39]).[7]

How, however, does the Discourse of the University take shape? Lacan foregrounds the "theft, abduction, stealing slavery of its knowledge, through the maneuvers of the master" in Plato's dialogues. The entire function of the *episteme* as "transmissible knowledge" is borrowed from the techniques of the craftsmen, of the serfs, of women working in households; "It is a matter of extracting the essence of this [community] knowledge in order for it to become the master's knowledge", or "theoretical knowledge" – theoretical knowledge in the emphatic sense that the word "theoria" has in Aristotle, or has in Hegel with respect to "absolute knowledge", and has in 'fieldwork' in the context of the University (Tagore was moving in Sriniketan from 'fieldwork' *on* the 'slave'/'subaltern' to *working in the fields* alongside the 'slave'/'subaltern'). Lacan is also concerned about the "persistence of a master's discourse"; what happens between the classical

152 *Anup Dhar*

and coercive Master's Discourse and that of the modern secular subtle master – the consent generating University – is a modification in the place of knowledge; knowledge becomes theoretical; knowledge becomes cognitive; and the western philosophical tradition "has some responsibility of this transmutation" (Lacan 2007: 31). "Philosophy in its historical function is this *extraction*, of the slave's knowledge [for Lacan, and of the woman's knowledge-praxis for Irigaray 1985], in order to obtain its transmutation into the master's knowledge" (Lacan 2007: 22).

Lacan uncorks the master's discourse, and what one gets is the University Discourse. University Discourse as the "new tyranny of knowledge"; University as the (modern secular) sieve through which we are on the whole, all recruited. The dominant position in the University Discourse is occupied by theoretical and cognitive knowledge. This illustrates the fact that behind all attempts to impart an apparently 'neutral' knowledge, one can see an attempt at mastery (mastery of knowledge, and domination of the Other to whom this knowledge is imparted). The Discourse of the University represents cognitive knowledge, particularly visible in modernity in the form of the hegemony of science and Law; the social sciences which are prompt in their critique of science and Law are, however, not exempt. Here I am reminded of *Women in the Beehive: A Seminar with Jacques Derrida*. While Lacan offers an interesting understanding of the Master's Discourse and the University Discourse as a veil*ing* of the master's lack of Discourse, it is Derrida who offers a more nuanced reading of the University Discourse, in the context of the setting up of women's studies departments in the disciplinary beehive of theoretical and cognitive knowledge – the university:

> Is there in the . . . idea of women's studies something which potentially has the force, if it is possible, to deconstruct the fundamental institutional structure of the university, of the Law of the university? There seem to be two hypotheses, two responses. On one hand, there is the *positive deconstruction*, which consists of saying that one cannot be content with only positive research, but that one must push to the end of the radical question concerning the university Law, and do more than simply institute a department of Women's Studies. That is the *optimistic deconstruction*, the deconstruction which would not submit to the Law. And then there is another deconstruction, perhaps not resigned or fatalist, but more conscious of the Law and of the fact that even the radical questioning, even the radical deconstruction of the institution of

A parrot's training? 153

the university by women's studies would not be able to reproduce the Law in the face of the Law . . . if one were to radically deconstruct the old model of the university in the name of women's studies, it would not be to open a territory without Law. . . . But it would be for a new relation to the Law. It is necessary to establish the departments of Women's Studies which would resemble their brothers and sisters of literature, philosophy, anthropology, etc., but after one had done that, one would already have found the Law again. But at least one would have radically changed the situation. One would have rediscovered the Law. . . . That would be the *pessimistic deconstruction*.

(2003: 192)

(we find ourselves in a similar situation with respect to the setting up of the *Centre for Development Practice* [not 'development studies'] in the university context; see below)

It is difficult to choose between what Derrida calls 'optimistic' and 'pessimistic' deconstruction. It is all the more difficult to imagine a secure path for women's studies or the women's/feminist movement (or for that matter, for the *idea* of development practice; see below). Just like it is difficult to choose a secure path for the future university or the future of the university. In this context, one can gesture towards two broad brush imaginations of the university. The first is a sort of emancipatory movement that is within the tradition of enlightenment and progress, and in some ways very boring, but very secure also, like Tagore's hard-boiled eggs; very necessary but also not so imaginative. The other imagination of the university is more than one more supplement to the beehive; at times it looks a little maverick. It's a way of doing things which can think the *beyond*, or re-think the existing structure. This other imagination of the university is in destructuring structure or in destructuring Discourse, the Master's Discourse; which is why the protection of the extant university is never enough; one needs to *find* (in Tagore for example) and *found* (like Tagore perhaps) in the future another imagination of the University, an imagination that is not strictly cognitive, intellectual or theoretical, an imagination that is (1) singed in praxis and (2) that does not turn away from the slave's know-how (*savoir-faire*) or that which is not just appropriative of the slave's know-how.

The 'university' in that sense is something one cannot (not) give up. The extant imagination of the university requires a rethinking; amidst the protectionist discourse. The problem is that given the attack on the university the protectionist discourse shall prevail as the only counter-hegemonic axis. This in turn may preclude possibilities of rethinking the basic premise and foundation of the university.

Development practice: an idea in search of a home?

> Our *tapovanas*, which were our natural Universities were not abstracted from life[8] . . . and the spiritual education, which the students had, was a part of the spiritual life itself which comprehended all life. . . . Such an institution must group round it all the neighbouring villages and virtually unite them with itself in all its economic endeavours. . . . In a word, it should never be like a meteor – only a stray fragment of a world – but a complete world in itself, self-sustaining, independent, rich with ever renewing life, radiating light across space and time, attracting and maintaining round it a planetary system of dependent bodies, imparting life-breadth to the complete [hu]man, who is intellectual as well as economic, bound by social bonds [not the "greed of profit"] and aspiring towards spiritual freedom.
>
> (Tagore 2011: 160)

The nascent *idea* of Development Practice (*not* Development Studies), which at present has taken the form of an 'immersion'[9] and 'action research'-based M.Phil programme[10] at Ambedkar University, Delhi, tries to make two moves with respect to the discussion above. One, it tries to inaugurate in the "beehive" of the human sciences the foreclosed question of praxis, praxis as the "alluring call to a slave revolt" against university in particular and education in general. Two, it also tries to engage creatively with what Lacan designates as the register of the 'slave', or the register of what could be called the 'subaltern'; engage with the slave's know-how, as also work *with* the slave (and not *on* the slave) for a transformed future. Needless to reiterate, it is difficult to find a home for such an idea – an idea that draws heavily from Tagore's turn to Sriniketan, which in turn is a turn to (transformative) praxis and the rural life-world – in the standard imagination of the university.

The question that thus haunts the idea of Development Practice is not just whether one is political or not, which has now become the paradigmatic caliper in the human sciences. The question is whether one is engaged in transformative praxis. How, however, does one distinguish between 'being political' and 'being engaged in transformative praxis'? How does one distinguish between 'interpreting the world' and 'transforming the world' (questions of transformation, however, require an immediate attention to questions of ethics, justice and even

A parrot's training? 155

well-being)? One way, one demonstrative way, of distinguishing the two would be in terms of the distinction between anti-capitalism and post-capitalism. Anti-capitalism is *Sangharsh*; it is about *questioning* surplus appropriation by non-performers. Post-capitalism is *Nirmaan*; it is about *creating* 'sharing commons'. Universities in their radical imagination have been contexts for anti-capitalist *critique*; could they also become sites for post-capitalist *praxis* (see Gibson-Graham 2006)? Universities in their radical moments have produced critiques of primitive accumulation; could they also become sites for what Tagore called social or rural *reconstruction* (*not* 'rural development'). Needless to reiterate, it is difficult to find a home for transformative praxis in the context of the standard language of the radical/progressive university: *critique*. It is difficult to find a home for, say, praxis in general and post-capitalist praxis in particular in the space of the standard idiom of the university: anti-capitalist critique; as if, the foregrounding of critique, forecloses praxis; the foregrounding of *sangharsh*, forecloses *nirmaan*.

What then is it to find home for (1) transformative praxis and (2) the 'slave's' know-how within the perimeters of the university? One possible way would be to create a ghetto for such knowledge-praxis in one corner of the University, while it is business as usual in the university, while we conduct ourselves like before in the university. These securely secluded places would be given names different from the ones usual discipline-based departments would have; kind of a centre-periphery relation. The other possible way, which is also an impossible way, a very difficult way would be to re-envision the way the university conducts itself or has hitherto conducted itself. Can the university move beyond mere critical knowledge production? Can critical knowing get connected to critical questions around doing/praxis and being/self (the idea of development practice is an attempt to bring questions of knowing,[11] being[12] and doing[13] to critical trialogue). What is it to produce students who are not mere copies of the 'master' but copies of the 'slave's' *forms of life*; who are respectful of the 'slave's' knowledge and praxis; and who do not share in the 'master's' disdain for praxis? Universities usually produce a theory *of* practice; universities pass judgments on practice. What is it to produce a praxis of theory, or a praxis emanating from theory; or theory getting borne in/by/through practice? What is it to *practice* development and not just study and report on processes of development? What is it to *make* a table, rather than *describe* a table? What is it to not just report on transformation, but engender transformation? What is it to engage in transformative social praxis in and *with* the rural, rather than conduct 'village studies' *on* communities? The idea of Development Practice is premised on a critical re-examination of the established idioms of 'social science research' and equally established idioms of 'practice'. It questions the given methodologies of both; and tries to work towards what we call for want of a better phrase 'action research'. Action Research is for us a shorthand for 'action-ing based on sound research findings' as also 'research-ing actions undertaken'. In other words, it is about translating research into practice and taking practice towards research. Thus bridging the historical hyper-separation between research and action[14] (hence 'action research') as also theory and practice (Tagore represented it in the Sriniketan Prospectus as brain and hand). It is to find a third – a third beyond conventional research and conventional (developmental) practice – a third beyond given frameworks of theory and given frameworks of practice.

Put telegraphically, action research is *reflective writing on the reflexive process of righting wrongs* ("righting wrongs" primarily in rural[15] and community contexts; see Spivak 2004: 523–81). But how does one right wrongs? One needs to know, first, what is wrong? Or perhaps, it is not about a first step (i.e. first knowing what is wrong) followed by a second step (i.e. then righting wrongs). The first and second steps work in mutual constitutivity. The process of knowing generates an understanding of righting; the process of righting deepens knowing. In other words, action research is both about knowing and righting, as also righting and writing. It is about knowing what is wrong, but knowing collaboratively. It is about making efforts at righting wrongs, but righting not in a top-down manner, righting with the community as foreground and the researcher as background. It is also about writing on the actual or lived process of righting wrongs, a process lived and experienced by both researcher and community, which is why action research is not research *on* the community, rather research *with* the community.

The inspiration for an idea like development practice – premised on immersion and action research – premised on bringing to trialogue questions of 'knowing'-'being'-'doing' – comes not just from Sriniketan, but also from *phronesis*, a la Heidegger, and *askesis*, a la Foucault (2005). Marx remains a running footnote in this turn to transformative praxis in educational contexts. Marx (2016 [1845]) begins "Theses on Feuerbach" with the question of the "chief defect[s] of all hitherto existing materialism". One of the defects is that in *The Essence of Christianity*, "Practice is conceived and fixed [by Feuerbach] only in its *dirty* Jewish manifestation" (Marx 2016). Why, however, is practice Jewish? Why is practice dirty? Here Marx makes a distinction between the Christian discourse on creation and the Judaic discourse on creation: "'Dirty Jewish' – according to Marshall Berman, is an allusion to the Jewish God of the Old Testament, who had to 'get his hands dirty' while making the world, and is tied up with a symbolic contrast between the Christian God of the Word, and the God of the Deed, symbolizing practical life" (Marx 2016, note 1). Marx is thus foregrounding (Jewish) Deed, i.e. praxis over the (Christian) Word (see Dhar and Chakrabarti 2016: 563–83). It is hence never enough to *teach* Marx in the university; one needs to *be* Marx; one perhaps needs to inaugurate the question of Deed/praxis in the university to be Marx(ian); one needs to *dirty* one's hands; and Tagore, the 'poet' did precisely that in and through Sriniketan; we dirty our hands in Development Practice.

Late Foucault's turn to *askesis* (as against Christian *asceticism*) brings the subject's 'being' into play. It inaugurates the question of self-transformation. It also argues, that knowledge – which is what the university deals with – *could be* transacted, imparted, and received in the university context, *but* 'truth' *cannot* be glimpsed without the long labour of *askesis* (Foucault 2005); i.e. without self-transformation. The standard model of knowledge production in the university, which believes that knowledge can be produced without the researcher being fundamentally touched or transformed by the object of knowledge, is thus put to question by Foucault. Foucault brings truth and self, knowing and being to dialogue and makes one reliant upon the other. Not just reliant. He argues that truth *cannot* be reached without self-transformation (psychoanalytic self-work would be a modern example of Greek *askesis*).

Heidegger's turn to the Aristotelian[16] concept (invoked in Book IV of the *Nichomachean Ethics*) of *phronesis* (as distinct from "sophia" and "episteme"), which is also an overturning of the concept, inaugurates the question of 'doing'; phronesis as pointing to "the possibility of developing a critically self-reflective model of ontological knowledge firmly embedded in the finite world", in life and lived experience (Long 2002, 36); phronesis as being-related to what Heidegger called the "with-which". In one sense, phronesis is practical reason, as distinct from theoretical reason. In another sense, it is reasoning based on concrete action, as distinct from speculative reason. In yet another but related sense, it is reason based on life experiences as distinct from abstract deductions (see Heidegger 1985, 1997).

The idea of development practice – built on and inspired by Tagore's educational crusade at Santiniketan-Sriniketan, especially

Sriniketan – is placed at the cusp of askesis-phronesis-praxis; could this *seedling*, struggling in turn to find home in the standard university imagination, be the germ for a 'future university', or the 'future of/for the university'?

Notes

1 Tagore shows in this piece how much of the education has become a process of constructing cages and less about actual learning; how teachers are increasingly becoming goldsmiths; and how students are learning less, and learning instead and more to abide by the rules and regulations of a caged life-world; how best to live in a cage, how best to lead a caged life; how best to be prepared for what educationist Sujit Sinha calls 'industrialism'; as if, training in the 10:30–4 school schedule is the ground for induction into the industrial schedule.

2 "What we now call a school in this country is really a factory, and the teachers are part of it. At half-past ten in the morning the factory opens with the ringing bell; then, as the teachers start talking, the machines start working. The teachers stop talking at four in the afternoon when the factory closes, and the pupils then go home carrying with them a few pages of machine-made learning. . . . One advantage of factory is that it can make goods exactly to order. Moreover, the goods are easy to label, because there is not much difference between what the different machines turn out" (Tagore, 2011: 112).

3 "[W]hen I sent my appeal to Western people for an International Institution [Viswa-Bharati] in India I made use of the word 'University'. . . . But that word not only has an inner meaning but outer association in minds of those who use it, and that fact tortures my idea into its own rigid shape. It is unfortunate. I should not allow my idea to be pinned to a word like a dead butterfly for a foreign museum. It must be known not by a definition, but by its own life growth. I saved Santiniketan from being trampled into smoothness by the steam roller of your education department. . . . [M]y bird must still retain its freedom of wings and not be turned into a sumptuous nonentity by any controlling agency outside its own living organism" (Tagore, 2011: 125).

4 "Given that the majority of Indians lived in the villages, Tagore found the Santiniketan 'human' landscape with its Hindu, Muslim and Santali villages to be an authentic picture of the social and racial differences of the neglected village. It was an ideal site to give the urban children of his school an education about the 'real' India. . . . His . . . justification was to build an education on the 'firm basis' of the 'life of the people' where the existing colonial mode of education chose deliberately to be ignorant of 'our country's' life (Das Gupta in Tagore, 2011: xxvii–xxviii). Sadler (in Sharr, 2006: xii) shows how the thinking of the Frankfurt school, on the one hand, and of Heidegger's school, on the other, continue to define "two forms of modern truth": "the one discovered, through work in the metropolitan library and urban loft, by the dialectic of ideal and real, the other revealed by an encounter with an uncorrupted ideal at the rural retreat". Tagore opted for the latter form.

A parrot's training? 159

5 "[W]hen the charitably minded city-bred politicians talk of education [or development] for the village folk they mean a little left over in the bottom of their cup after diluting it copiously" (Tagore, 2011: 133); the bhadralok class regard the rural people as chhotolok meaning, "literally small people". "Given such contempt for their own village people, educated Indians prefer to learn about their country's history and society from the Europeans" (Tagore, 2011: 133).

6 In summer 1922, Martin Heidegger (1889–1976) moved into a small cabin built for him high in the Black Forest mountains of southern Germany (fig. 1). Heidegger called this building, approximately six metres by seven, "die Hütte" ("the hut") (see Sharr, 2006).

7 Arendt shows (2005) how "the gulf between philosophy and politics opened historically with the trial . . . and condemnation. . . [and] death of Socrates". This led to Plato's "despair of polis life" or 'life in the polis' or the "philosopher's life in the polis, tied to the polis, to life in the polis, to polis life. It came at a cost, a deadly cost: death; and with the death of Socrates came the death of the philosophic-political praxis of being-in-the-polis".

8 "[T]he thrust of Heidegger's critique is not that previous philosophies had simply failed to grasp life, although that surely happened, but that previous philosophies presuppose life and also the living character of philosophy itself. In essence, their failure to grasp life in and for itself is due to the fact that life is always already present in the background of their philosophy". However, "what is at stake for Heidegger is not whether philosophy can or cannot give us access to life and lived experience [in a radically new, pre-objective, pre-theoretical way], but rather to understand how philosophy itself is lived and situated in life . . . previous attempts to grasp life philosophically failed because philosophy itself had become divorced from life and therefore the attempt to approach life philosophically was an artificial effort to grasp life 'from outside' . . . this required retracing the way in which philosophy becomes alienated from life" (see Bowler, 2008: 2–6 and 116–37). Thus if Heidegger was trying to resituate philosophy in life, Tagore was trying to resituate education in "spiritual life" which in turn "comprehended all life" (Tagore, 2011: 160).

9 The M.Phil Programme in Development Practice (total duration: two years) has a (rural) Immersion component of one year; which is to (1) experience, engage and relate to in a psychoanalytically sensitive manner with adivasi life-worlds (as also Dalit contexts), (2) co-research rigorously with the 'community' on questions, issues, problems relevant to the community (including attention to psycho-biographs of hope, despair and desire), (3) arrive at an action research problematic collaboratively with the community, (4) develop a framework of action-ing the co-researched finding(s), and finally (5) research in a theoretically rigorous manner the action-ing process.

10 The M.Phil programme in Development Practice places the question of (rural) transformation – including transformation of human subjects – at the core of its enquiry, research and practice. The overarching objective of the M.Phil programme is to critically engage with and reflect on existing developmental discourse and practice, usher in psychological-psychoanalytic sensitivity in our work with communities (including an awareness of

160 *Anup Dhar*

questions of 'transference-resistance' in group contexts) and thereby rethink and rework the associated developmental sectoral practices in the rural and forest communities. In a word, the M.Phil programme – through M.Phil dissertations – generates knowledge on transformative social praxis while it engages in, takes part, ushers in, and catalyses transformative social praxis in largely adivasi and partly Dalit contexts. The programme hopes to engender a classroom and field based learning process that brings to dialogue the three hitherto hyper-separated components of 'knowing'-'relating'-'doing' through a one-year long Immersion experience in central India and an 'action research' based pedagogy.

11 The process of knowing in Development Practice involves inculcating a critical-analytical-reflective relationship with the dominant discourses of development. Students come to conceive of 'development' beyond quantitative, top-down and statist approaches. They arrive at a more human-focused, relational or psychologically sensitive understanding of development. It also helps them move from an understanding of "what is wrong" in the rural and in forest societies as also in practices of development to how one can "right the wrongs".

12 The process of 'learning to relate and listen' and 'communicate non-coercively' is engendered in the student. One of the foci of Immersion is on the 'self' of the student, and her experiences of being in close touch with the rural community or the forest society as also the process of being in touch with her own feelings, dreams, hopes and despair. An appreciation of the 'community' as an ever-emergent ever-transforming 'being-in-common' (and not as something given) is also facilitated. One of the other foci of Immersion is on the 'community' and on 'group processes'; it is about building relationships with the rural community/group, and finding community/group voice to arrive at a shared action research agenda emerging out of a dialogue and deliberation on the community's needs/desires.

13 The dimension of 'doing', i.e. transformative social praxis with rural communities in undertaking in and through action research. On the one hand, while we try to make sense of, understand and analyse macro and micro-processes of rural transformation, we also, on the other hand, try to engender/facilitate/catalyse through sustained community participation and collective action processes of 'desirable' (we, hence reflect on and remain reflexive as to 'what is desirable') transformation in rural spaces. We see rural transformation as not a State/government driven affair but a community-driven affair, through a kind of "non-coercive reorganization of community desire". This is also important because bottom-up or grassroots level developmental work in the community is not just about knowing or getting the numbers right, but has much to do with feeling-states; feeling for the Other, as also feeling into one's own Self; including one's nascent identification with (suffering, and why not, the hope, joy, despair of) rural lives. Knowing, relating with community and collective doing thus come to a productive dialogue in the M.Phil action research work with rural communities. The idea is to see what the community/group 'need' is and relate 'my need to know' with the 'community/group need to transform', bringing the two needs to a productive dialogue and a dialectic, to reach a middle ground. In this work 'poor rural women' are not our objects of knowledge, but our co-researchers. They are not

A parrot's training? 161

just 'native tribal/Dalit informants' but 'co-producers of knowledge'. The 'gendered subaltern' thus becomes a colleague, albeit with much difficulty, in our community level research and community guided action.

14 Arendt (2005) foregrounds the "abyss" between thought and action, "an abyss which never since has been closed".

15 Heidegger's Hut: Heidegger's turn to the (rural) 'hut' was not a simple turn to the countryside, as against the city. At stake were two distinct philosophical possibilities. The first philosophico-existential perspective would eschew a concern with the "primordiality of either time or being", with the 'adi' of the *adivasi*, with that which is existing at or from the beginning, with the one who is inhabiting the origin(ary). The second would foreground, even demand it. The idea of the 'hut' comes to the fore within a philosophical project that conceives of time and being in this latter sense.

16 Bowler (2008) argues that while with respect to phronesis if there is a 'turning away' from Aristotle, there is a 'turning to' and an appropriation of Aristotle's conceptualization of praxis in Heidegger's invocation of 'philosophy *as* praxis'.

References

Arendt, H. 2005. *The Promise of Politics*. (ed.) Jerome Kohn. New York: Schocken Books.
Basole, A. (ed.) 2015. *Lokavidya Perspectives: A Philosophy of Political Imagination for the Knowledge Age*. New Delhi: Aakar Books.
Bowler, M. 2008. *Heidegger and Aristotle: Philosophy as Praxis*. New York, London: Continuum.
Dhar, A. and Chakrabarti, A. 2016. 'Marxism as Ascetic: Spiritual as Phronetic', in *Rethinking Marxism*, 29(1).
———— 2017. 'Sriniketan Encounters Ambedkar: Whither the Political?', in *Economic and Political Weekly*, 52(19): 53–56.
Derrida, J. 2003. 'Women in the Beehive', in A. Jardine and P. Smith (eds.) *Men in Feminism* (pp. 189–202). New York and London: Routledge.
Foucault, M. 2005. *The Hermeneutics of the Subject: Lectures at the Collège de France 1981–1982*. (trans.) G. Burchell. London: Palgrave Macmillan.
Gibson-Graham, J. K. 2006. *A Postcapitalist Politics*. Minneapolis: University of Minnesota Press.
Heidegger, M. 1985 [1962]. *Being and Time*. (trans.) J. Macquarrie and E. Robinson. Oxford: Basil Blackwell.
————. 1997. *Plato's Sophist*. Bloomington: Indiana University Press.
Irigaray, L. 1985. *This Sex Which Is Not One*. (trans.) Catherine Porter. New York: Cornell University Press.
Jardine, A. and Smith, P. 2003. *Men in Feminism*. New York, London: Routledge.
Lacan, J. 2007. *The Seminar of Jacques Lacan – The Other Side of Psychoanalysis – Book XVII*. Ed. Jacques-Alain Miller. (trans.) With notes by Russell Grigg. New York, London: W. W. Norton & Company.
Long, C. P. 2002. 'The Ontological Reappropriation of Phronesis', *Continental Philosophy Review*, 35(1): 35–60.

Marx, K. 2016. *Theses on Feuerbach*. (trans.) C. Smith (2002). Marxists Internet Archive. Accessed 7 September. Available at www.marxists.org/archive/marx/works/1845/theses/ (accessed on 31 December 2017).

Roy, D. 2010. 'The Poet as a Polemicist and a Prophet', *Rupkatha Journal on Interdisciplinary Studies in Humanities*, 2(4): 677–682.

Sharr, A. 2006. *Heidegger's Hut*. (Foreword) Simon Sadler. (Prologue) Andrew Benjamin. Cambridge, MA: MIT Press.

Spivak, G. C. 2004. 'Righting Wrongs', *The South Atlantic Quarterly*, 103(2/3): 523–581.

Tagore, R. 2011. *The Oxford India Tagore: Selected Writings on Education and Nationalism*. (ed.) Uma Dasgupta. Oxford: New Delhi.

Tagore, R. *The Parrot's Tale*. (trans.) Palash Baran Pal. Available at www.parabaas.com/translation/database/translations/stories/gRabindranath_parrot.html (accessed on 31 December 2017).

8 Academic freedom and the ownership of knowledge

Lawrence Liang

The assault on academic freedom via the use of speech curbing laws, the rise in the 'structural adjustment' of higher education to make it more professional (a thinly veiled euphemism for making it more market-friendly) and the increased privatization of learning are the common complaints that one hears of the threat to knowledge practices and to the independence of universities as critical spaces. What we do not hear enough of is how the ownership of academic knowledge and the politics of academic publishing are also seriously corroding an ethos of collegiality and knowledge sharing, which was critical in shaping the imagination of the university. Using the example of the recently concluded Delhi University photocopy case,[1] I will argue that what was at stake was more than just a technical question of the scope of copyright or fair dealing exceptions in copyright law. Given that the case was initiated by three respected academic publishers, two of whom are associated with the oldest and most acclaimed universities in the world, the case raised fundamental questions of what a university is and how higher education can be imagined in the time of intellectual property. I will also draw attention, after a discussion of the case itself, to a genealogy of how the language of intellectual property fundamentally redefines academic practices, transforming the idea of academic freedom into a market-driven understanding of freedom.

In 2011, three publishers – Oxford University Press, Cambridge University Press, and Taylor and Francis Routledge – sued Delhi University and a photocopy shop on its premises for unauthorized distribution of course packs to students – claiming $100,000 (6 million rupees) in damages. The shop, Rameshwari Photocopiers, was given space on the campus of the School of Economics following an open tender, with an agreement that it would copy 3000 pages free of cost for the college library in lieu of payment of a licensing fee. The faculty, in turn, could prescribe course material which could be taken from the library (or other sources) by students and submitted to the photocopy shop. The shop would then circulate the combined photocopied materials to the students at a rate of Rs. 0.40 per page. While the initial defendants were Rameshwari photocopy services and Delhi University, subsequently two other associations, Society for Promoting Educational Access and Knowledge ("SPEAK") and Association of Students for Equitable Access to Knowledge ("ASEAK"), consisting of academics and students respectively, impleaded themselves as defendants in the case.

The first decision was given by Justice Endlaw in September 2016, dismissing the petition in its entirety on the grounds that no question of copyright infringement arose as Section 52(1)(i) of Copyright Act 1957 was explicit that reproduction of works in the course of instruction was not an infringement of copyright. On appeal, the division bench (Justices Pradeep Nandrajog and Yogesh Khanna) affirmed in most parts the prior decision on questions of law, but disagreed with Endlaw that no dispute on facts arose and directed that specific reproductions of books could be determined on whether they were for the purposes of instruction.

After the division bench's decision dismissing their appeal, the primary petitioners in the case decided in March 2017 to withdraw their suit and not prefer an appeal. In a joint statement, the three academic publishers (Oxford University Press, Cambridge University Press and Taylor & Francis) acknowledged the importance of course packs for education and stated that rather than continue the legal battle, they would "work closely with academic institutions, teachers and students to understand and address their needs".[2] The Indian Reprographic Rights Organization ("IRRO") decided to continue with an appeal to the Supreme Court, but a division bench of the Supreme Court[3] refused to admit the appeal on the grounds that the original petitioners had withdrawn from the case while IRRO was merely an intervener – thereby bringing an end to a keenly contested case that had galvanized immense public interest and stimulated sharply divided opinions on what constitutes an equitable system of copyright in the sphere of education. With the dust having settled on the immediate case, it is time to take a step back to evaluate the two decisions and to situate their relevance for future disputes about copyright and access to knowledge.

It is pertinent to note that the proceedings in the courts were preceded by innovative activism by a diverse set of players with varied interests in the case. If for the publishers this was an important test case that would determine the scope of the 'educational use' exception in copyright law and establish whether universities are bound to obtain a licence from reprographic societies to create course packs, for academics and students the case entailed the future of equitable access to knowledge. The global interest in the case was also understandable, coming as it did in the wake of a decade of activism around the idea of access to knowledge ("A2K"). In her intellectual genealogy of the A2K movement, Amy Kapczynski argues that the A2K movement fundamentally reframed questions of intellectual property away from the focus on rights management to a larger normative debate on the nature of the knowledge economy and access to ideas, knowledge goods and services (Kapczynski 2008). But even while tracing the rise of the A2K movement, scholars have commented that the A2K community does not really constitute a mass movement, and Gaëlle Krikorian, for instance, maintains that A2K "does not rely on massive street demonstrations as a constitutive means to confront the power structures that it challenges" (Krikorian 2010: 70). The DU photocopy case rebuts this presumption and demonstrates how A2K activism in the global South straddles traditional sites of activism along with demands for legal and policy reform.

In their complaint, the publishers argued that Rameshwari was reproducing and issuing unauthorized copies of their publications for a commercial purpose and that such circulation did not amount to "fair dealing" under Indian law. Unlike US law, where "fair use" involves a process of triangulating among different factors such as the "purpose and character" of the use (e.g., parody or educational use), the substantiality of the reproduction, and the effect on the commercial market for the original, Indian "fair dealing" follows the UK tradition in requiring specific statutory language for exceptions. The case quickly became a litmus test for what constituted fair dealing when it came to photocopying academic materials. The case turned largely on interpretation of two provisions in the Indian Copyright Act. The first is the fairly wide educational exception provided under Section 52(1)(i) which allows for "the reproduction of any work by a teacher or a pupil in the course of instruction, or as a part of questions or answers to questions". The second is Section 52(1)(a), which allows for fair dealing with any work (except computer programmes) for the purposes of private or personal use, including research. The two provisions anchored the university's argument that it was within its rights (and students were, accordingly, within their rights) to photocopy academic texts and articles and to create course packs in the course of instruction.

Because the case dealt with specific instances of copying particular texts,[4] it was relatively easy to determine whether the copying involved a large percentage of the works in question. In most cases, the page counts represented under 10 percent of the work – though in a few, this number climbed to between 20 percent and 30 percent. The overall average was 12.5 percent. If the accepted US "fair use" threshold of 10 percent is used, 11 out of the 19 books fell within the limit. In the absence of statutory guidelines, the question for the Indian court was whether a fair-minded person would consider 12.5 percent of a book to be "substantial". It is worth emphasizing the irrelevance of the counterfactual, in which students actually buy all of the books in the offending course pack – some 17 with a total retail price of around $1700. This is a sum slightly larger than the average per capita GDP in India. The Delhi case was not about getting the students to buy physical copies of the book, so much as creating pressure on the university to impose a reprographic fee for photocopying excerpts as well as clarifying quantitative restrictions on the amount that can be legally copied from a book.[5] The problem with this proposal is that the envisaged licence fee roughly triples the price of photocopying from its current level (40 paisa or around 0.5c) to a rupee per page (currently around 1.5c).

The publishers argued that this is a relatively small amount that will not affect the students – the licence fee, in an often-repeated argument, amounts to around one expensive meal. However, this assumes the perspective of the richest students rather than that of the poorest students who are the real beneficiaries of photocopying. Rather than measuring the fee against imaginary meals, it may be more useful to compare this to the average fees paid at Delhi University. At the Master's level, a student pays approximately $150 (Rs. 10,000) per semester (depending on the college that s/he is enrolled in). At one rupee per page, the cost of photocopying materials just for course packs would amount to around a 10% increase in fees.

The decisions

In September 2016, the Delhi High Court (through a single judge bench) delivered its judgment in the Delhi University photocopying case (Chancellor, Masters and Scholars of the University of Oxford v. Rameshwari Photocopy Services). The single judge bench (Justice Rajiv Endlaw) dismissed the 2012 copyright infringement petition, much to the relief of the students, teachers and photocopiers who had been closely tracking the judgment.

Academic Freedom 167

In his considered and sharply reasoned judgment, Justice Rajiv Sahai Endlaw examined the range of arguments made by both sides and in a stinging observation that gestures to the abuse of copyright for monopolistic purposes which were against public interest, Justice Endlaw held that

> Copyright, specially in literary works, is thus not an inevitable, divine, or natural right that confers on authors the absolute ownership of their creations. It is designed rather to stimulate activity and progress in the arts for the intellectual enrichment of the public. Copyright is intended to increase and not to impede the harvest of knowledge. It is intended to motivate the creative activity of authors and inventors in order to benefit the public.
>
> (2016a: 79–80, Para 80)

This is a very pertinent observation given the 'naturalization' of intellectual property claims in the past two decades. In a clear statement of the philosophical basis of copyright law, Justice Endlaw rejects the populist and uni-dimensional assumption that copyright is about the protection of the property rights of owners. If copyright was always about maintaining a balance between competing ideas of private and public interest, the Delhi High Court has restored to copyright jurisprudence a clear mandate for the future, one which is cognizant that the end goal of technology is the improvement of our lives (material and intellectual) and "no law can be interpreted so as to result in any regression of the evolvement of the human being for the better" (ibid.: 85, Para 87).

By locating it clearly as a creature of legal policy, the judgment lays down the foundation for articulating a jurisprudence of limitations explicitly recognizing that any right that is granted to owners is also limited by exceptions carved out by law. Explicating the relationship between copyright and fair dealing exceptions, Endlaw held that the nature of Section 52 of the Copyright Act is such that any act falling within its scope will not constitute infringement. As we have seen, Sec. 52(1)(i) allows for the "reproduction of any work i) by a teacher or a pupil in the course of instruction; or ii) as part of the questions to be answered in an examination; or iii) in answers to such questions".

The petitioners had argued for a narrow reading of the Section, claiming that at best what the Section allows for is the provision of materials in the course of a lecture and spatially restricted to a classroom. According to the court,

> [t]he crucial question for adjudication is, when does the imparting of instruction begin and when does it end. Whether in the classroom or tutorials only, as suggested by the counsel for the plaintiff or it begins prior to the classroom and ends much after the classroom interface between the teacher and pupil has ended, as contended by the counsels for the defendants.
>
> (ibid.: 66–7, Para 62)

The court, while rejecting this claim, argued that 'instruction' cannot be narrowly understood, and relying on a number of precedents from commercial law, it concluded that the test to be applied by courts should include a temporal understanding of an activity that sees it through a prism of continuity in time as well as in purpose, and this test when applied to copyright would necessitate a wider reading of the word 'instruction'. In Para 72, the court holds that

> 'in the course of instruction' within the meaning of Section 52(1)(i) supra would include reproduction of any work while the process of imparting instruction by the teacher and receiving instruction by the pupil continues i.e. during the entire academic session for which the pupil is under the tutelage of the teacher and that imparting and receiving of instruction is not limited to personal interface between teacher and pupil but is a process commencing from the teacher readying herself/himself for imparting instruction, setting syllabus, prescribing text books, readings and ensuring, whether by interface in classroom/tutorials or otherwise by holding tests from time to time or clarifying doubts of students, that the pupil stands instructed in what he/she has approached the teacher to learn.
>
> (ibid.: 73)

It then locates the question of education within a changing technological environment and argues that "when an action, if onerously done is not an offence, it cannot become an offence when, owing to advancement in technology doing thereof has been simplified" (ibid.: 75, Para 75). To make this point, Justice Endlaw contrasts his own experiences as a law student where photocopying was very limited and studying entailed students copying by hand, scribe-like, pages after pages of books. Photocopiers have just made the task simpler and faster but if

Academic Freedom 169

the act of copying for a particular purpose is itself not illegal, and 'the effect of the action is the same, the difference in the mode of action cannot make a difference so as to make one an offence'.

> In the times when I was studying law, the facility available of photocopying was limited, time consuming and costly. The students then, used to take turns to sit in the library and copy by hand pages after pages of chapters in the books suggested for reading and subsequently either make carbon copies thereof or having the same photocopied. The photocopying machines then in vogue did not permit photocopying of voluminous books without dismembering the same. However with the advancement of technology the voluminous books also can be photocopied and at a very low cost. Thus the students are now not required to spend day after day sitting in the library and copying pages after pages of the relevant chapter of the syllabus books. When the effect of the action is the same, the difference in the mode of action cannot make a difference so as to make one an offence.
>
> (ibid.: 75–6)

While the immediate beneficiaries of the Delhi High Court's judgment in the Delhi University photocopy case were obviously the university, the photocopy shop and the students and academics who filed intervention petitions supporting the right to photocopy, the import of Justice Endlaw's finely reasoned judgment goes well beyond this specific case as well as its impact on access to knowledge in India. The judgment and its treatment of educational exceptions in copyright law are in many ways unprecedented and should serve as a model of how national laws should be interpreted. The judgment has immense consequences beyond India and is a bold articulation of the principles of equitable access to knowledge – and one that deserves to be emulated globally. For a while now, the globalization of copyright norms through international law (Berne convention, TRIPS Agreement) has been accompanied by the globalization of copyright standards that have primarily emerged from the global North. Aggressively pushed by the copyright lobby such as Hollywood, the music industry and the publishing cartels, copyright law has effectively been hijacked by narrow commercial interests (albeit always speaking in the name of authors and creators). Thus even when it came to discussing fair use exceptions and limitations, countries have found themselves constrained by judicial precedents from the US and elsewhere that have defined quantitative restrictions on photocopying.

In a radical move, the Delhi High Court, rejecting the adoption of US standards, concluded that if Indian lawmakers have allowed through statute for the reproduction of a copyrighted work in the course of instruction, they have done so on the basis of a purpose (that is, teaching) and with the conviction that this does not unreasonably prejudice the legitimate interest of the author. Further, this flexibility is provided to it through international law and it is not the place of courts to impose artificial restrictions by way of quantitative limits. Justice Endlaw, while arriving at this conclusion, is acutely aware of the specific needs of countries like India, where libraries and universities have to cope with the needs of thousands of students simultaneously and it would be naïve to expect every student to buy copies of every book. This aspect of the judgment could almost be read as an instructional manual for countries which find themselves straitjacketed under international copyright laws, and yet want to ensure the greatest flexibility in the way they design a system that addresses their specific needs.

The division bench decision

The publishers were understandably less enthusiastic about the judgment than those interested in access to knowledge, and they immediately filed an appeal before a division bench (two judges) of the Delhi High Court. The division bench (Justices Pradeep Nandrajog and Yogesh Khanna) delivered their judgment in December 2016, upholding in substance most parts of Justice Endlaw's orders while making a few distinctions. Aware of the fact that this case is keenly followed by many non-lawyers who may get lost within the thicket of technical legal arguments, the court – towards the end of the judgment – provides a helpful musical analogy which succinctly summarizes the jurisprudential backbone of the judgment.

> 76. A lay person may question as to how a provision in a statute results in an interpretation where a right conferred on a person to use the work of another without any compensation would be just and fair. The question would obviously arise: Is it possible that a provision in a statute partially drowns another provision. This lay person would obviously desire, and perhaps logic would feed the desire, that no provision should be drowned or partially drowned. After all, in the melody of the statute all notes should be heard.
>
> 77. We therefore answer this question, which certainly arises, using the imagery of music. A melody is the outcome of the sounds

created when different instruments, such as a lute, flute, timbale, harp and drums are played in harmony. The notes of the instruments which are loud and resonating have to be controlled so that the sound of the delicate instruments can be heard. But it has to be kept in mind that at proper times the sound of the drums drowns out the sound of all other instruments under a deafening thunder of the brilliant beating of the drums. Thus, it is possible that the melody of a statute may at times require a particular Section, in a limited circumstance, to so outstretch itself that, within the confines of the limited circumstance, another Section or Sections may be muted.

(2016b: 32)

Translated into the Copyright Act, what the judges are making clear is that, if the predominant purpose of the law is to provide exclusive rights to owners of copyright, this right sometimes has to be muted to serve other equally important purposes such as education. In particular, for the true essence of Section 52 to be heard, the judges make a clear argument for the need to mute the 'exclusive rights' presumption of copyright law. They rejected the contention of the publishers and the reprographic rights organizations that the word 'instruction' has to be read narrowly, and the judges referred to the parliamentary debate which led to the enactment of Act No. 27 of 2012 – where the Minister piloting the Bill clearly told the House 'Of course, non-profit libraries should not be charged. Many of these copyrighted materials can be used, should be used and must be used in non-profit libraries' (ibid.: 18, Para 28).

Echoing the policy intentions of the legislature, the judges chose to ignore the technical distinctions sought to be made between education and instruction, and between textbooks and course packs and held that

> The importance of education lies in the fact that education alone is the foundation on which a progressive and prosperous society can be built. Teaching is an essential part of education, at least in the formative years, and perhaps till post-graduate level. It would be difficult for a human to educate herself without somebody: a teacher, helping. It is thus necessary, by whatever nomenclature we may call them, that development of knowledge modules, having the right content, to take care of the needs of the learner is encouraged. We may loosely call them textbooks. We may loosely call them guide books. We may loosely call them reference books. We may loosely call them course packs. So fundamental is education to a society – it warrants the promotion of equitable access

to knowledge to all segments of the society, irrespective of their caste, creed and financial position. Of course, the more indigent the learner, the greater the responsibility to ensure equitable access.

(ibid.: 18–9, Para 30)

They clarify that fairness is an essential aspect of the statute especially when there is an exception being carved out of a person's legal rights. But what is a principle of fairness? In a crucial paragraph, the courts clearly state:

> In the context of teaching and use of copyrighted material, the fairness in the use can be determined on the touchstone of '*extent justified by the purpose*'. In other words, the utilization of the copyrighted work would be a fair use to the extent justified for the purpose of education. It would have no concern with the extent of the material used, both qualitative or quantitative. The reason being, '*to utilise*' means to make or render useful. To put it differently, so much of the copyrighted work can be fairly used which is necessary to effectuate the purpose of the use, i.e. make the learner understand what is intended to be understood.
>
> (ibid.: 19, Para 33)

The significance of this interpretation is that it explicitly rejects the adoption of American standards (the four factor test) into Indian copyright law and grounds the principle of fairness within a philosophy of education, rejecting any claim that there should be either a quantitative or a qualitative restriction imposed. The significance of not laying down any restriction can be best appreciated in light of all the previous discussions in this chapter on the incredible restrictions that students face while accessing learning materials.

The court also rejected the contention of the publishers that Section 52 allows for reproduction of a work, but by making it available through photocopies it is no longer a reproduction but a publication. The court held that publication has an element of profit (for instance, in mass publication) and neither the use of a photocopy machine nor the use of an intermediary (a photocopier) qualifies automatically as publication and the only relevant test is whether copying is "in the course of instruction". The test to see whether copying is "in the course of instruction" involved "considering whether the inclusion of the copyrighted work in the course pack was justified by the purpose of the course pack i.e. for instructional use by the teacher to the class" (ibid.: 25, Para 56), and hence it would be inaccurate to claim that the word reproduction is limited to a single copy.

One crucial difference between Justice Endlaw's judgment and the present one is that, while the former found absolutely no fact that was worthy of being tried since there was no prima facie infringement, in the present judgment the court has held that the specific question of whether the reproduction of full works is in the course of instruction is a matter that can be determined in a trial and has consequently remanded that issue back to a trial judge.

The judgment rightfully rejects the rather ominous attempt by the publishers to lock education within a straitjacket of property, and it is befitting that the appellants who are the university presses of two of the oldest and most prestigious universities should be provided a reminder of what the scope of education is. The significance of this judgment is that while it arose out of a seemingly narrow question of whether the photocopying of course packs was allowed in copyright law, this question could only be answered by returning copyright to its normative foundations in copyright law.

In the wake of the Delhi High Court decision, a number of students and academics created petitions urging the publishers not to appeal against the verdict. Of particular note was an appeal by students at Oxford University to OUP welcoming the decision, which according to them "affirms the right of students to access photocopied copyrighted materials, so long as this is justified by the purpose of educational instruction" ('Open Letter' 2017: 1). The petition further observes that with the increasing privatization of knowledge goods across the world, the cost of education has reached prohibitively expensive levels and even resource-rich universities in developed countries are reeling under the impact of this sharp increase in prices. Citing the instance of Harvard University urging their faculty members to publish in more open access journals, because of the exorbitant cost of subscriptions, the petition hailed the decision as a much-welcomed development, particularly for resource-constrained developing countries such as India.

They reserved their sharpest criticism for collecting societies, arguing the following:

> The history of collecting societies in India has been riddled with instances of mismanagement and malfeasance – and the IRRO itself has come under attack multiple times for its opacity and lack of good governance. This does not lead us to have confidence in the proposed licensing regime. In any case, the IRRO proposal limited the copying to only 15% of a copyrighted work. Much higher proportions have been held to constitute an educational "fair use" even in the world's largest capitalistic economy, namely

the US. Further, when a similar system to the one proposed by the publishers was implemented in Canada, collecting societies ratcheted up their licensing fees to exorbitant levels, causing some universities to walk out of these licensing arrangements. The evidence indicates that the alternative suggested in court will most likely fail to secure the objectives it seeks to achieve.

In the light of these issues, we are truly dismayed that a progressive publisher like OUP would endorse the IRRO as the way forward at this stage. A consideration of the IRRO as a feasible option might be possible in the future, where the institutional malaise that it suffers from is remedied. However, a policy decision as to whether or not to go in this direction is the prerogative of the sovereign republic of India, in much the same way that amending the law to provide for more equitable economic appropriation of the proceedings of publishing might be. As of now, the law is clear, and given the nature of India's stratified educational constraints, we urge you to adhere to it.

(ibid.: 3)

Figure 8.1 Protest in Delhi University, against the copyright case filed by leading publishers

Photo courtesy: Lawrence Liang

Knowledge as/in economy

While the legal case has largely been based on an interpretation of the fair dealing exceptions under the Indian Copyright Act, the case has thrown up a much wider set of issues about the ownership of academic knowledge and its control at the hands of a small set of publishing oligarchies. In a protest organized by students at Delhi University, a large number of academics and authors (including those whose copyright – according to the petition – had been infringed) signed photocopies of their texts and handed them over to the librarian. It also prompted Aditya Nigam to demand the bootlegging of education as one of the ways of fighting against the privatization of academic knowledge by academic publishers.

In a public meeting on the Delhi University photocopy case, Sudhanva Deshpande, an independent publisher, noted that the model of academic publishing had completely transformed in the last decade. If earlier the idea was to produce books which would be bought by students, the first shift was to move away from a low cost high volume model to a high cost low volume model where the main buyers would be institutions such as libraries and research centres rather than individuals (Deshpande 2012). The publishing industry is marked by an opacity which is troubling and while working on the Delhi University case, we received an anonymous email from an insider working with a leading academic press which revealed more damning practices to us (Anonymous 2012).

The gist of the received critique is as follows:

1 Publishing companies have no qualms about violating copyright when it serves their interests. Aspiring – but unqualified – authors in positions of influence at Indian universities routinely get published by leading publishing companies. Some of these books are heavily plagiarized from books by other publishers and even, without attribution, from Wikipedia – which publishers so readily dismiss with contempt – a fact which everyone in the industry chooses to ignore. Publishers publish these manuscripts with minor changes in language to skirt the issue of copyright; this involves re-writing sentences. This is tantamount to copyright violation in spirit, if not in letter.
2 Education boards are corrupted by the influence of sales managers from publishing companies. It is not uncommon for unpublished books, only in the manuscript stage, to appear in the recommended list of university syllabi. It used to be the case that the

syllabus for a course was framed first, and then books matching the syllabus are recommended. These days, the reverse happens – syllabi are framed from the contents of a book by a favoured publisher. What goes in the book is dictated by self-appointed editors at these publishing companies.[6]
3   Publishing companies are concerned with selling their books to the syllabus review committees and not the students. Prices are sometimes kept artificially high for the simple reason that multinational companies do not want to be seen selling their books at the "cheap price-points" of their Indian competitors.

The writer concluded that academic publishing, as it stands, is a fundamentally unethical business. Nowhere is this more evident than in journal publishing, where the publisher collects money from the author for publishing, gets it peer-reviewed for free, and collects more money from the readers. While this may appear to be a problem that particularly plagues the global South, even in the most elite universities in the world there is a recognition of the crisis. The historian and librarian at Harvard University Robert Darnton disclosed that Harvard could not afford the price of electronic journals and the pricing strategy of databases made universities "fiscally unsustainable" and "academically restrictive" (Sample 2012). According to Darnton, "We faculty do the research, write the papers, referee papers by other researchers, serve on editorial boards, all of it for free . . . and then we buy back the results of our labour at outrageous prices". Darnton has since become a champion of open access publishing and made a compelling case for why leading universities which are subsidized by public money ought to ensure that all their academic production should be available in the public domain. Citing Harvard's experiment with open access as a success, Darnton calls it an attempt "to realize an old ideal, a republic of letters in which citizenship extends to everyone" (Darnton 2008).

Darnton's invocation of the idea of academic restrictions invites us to think about what academic freedom may mean in the context of the rise of intellectual property norms governing the sphere of knowledge production, and how we need to rearticulate the radical potential of the university as a space of freedom, not just of thought – but also freedom from property norms that threaten to convert all universities into factories of thought. This is the key question that animates Corynne McSherry's examination of the politics of IP in universities.[7] McSherry turns to the original ideals of a university and locates it within a Kantian ideal, in which what mattered the most in a university education for Kant was the idea of freedom. It is a freedom defined in terms of freedom of thought, and freedom from control, initially from the state and partisan political interests, but she also defines the idea of freedom in the contemporary context as one that needs to be freed from business interests. In his *Conflict of the Faculties* (1794), Kant positioned the university as the embodiment of thought as 'action toward an ideal' – the ideal being the production of a national culture and a reasoning subject to serve as its vehicle. This basic formulation would serve as the template for the creation of the modern university system. For Kant, philosophy, which was the site of pure, rational and disinterested reason, was the necessary grounds on which one had to build the vision of a university, and the production of the autonomous liberal citizen depended in turn on the existence of the university as an autonomous, freely reasoning entity.

According to Kant, only reason can critique reason, so no outside body, including the state, could possibly judge the university. "It is absolutely essential that the learned community at the university also contain a faculty that ... having no commands to give, is free to evaluate everything" (Kant 1979: 27). The university for Kant was a critical site for the creation of the public domain, and he interestingly contrasted this with art, music and literature which for him transformed common resources into privately owned expression, moving from the public to the private and back again. University research, on the other hand, concerned itself with the transformation of the common (e.g. nature) into the specific (e.g. facts about nature).

McSherry traces the development of the Kantian ideal of the university from the German universities through the emergence of the American research university in the nineteenth century, which unites the Germanic principles of reason and autonomy with a commitment to empirical social inquiry drawn from English liberalism. This union was facilitated by the emergence of a new vision of liberal education.

In the post-World War I period, we begin to see the instrumentalizing of the university, with university research being enlisted in war efforts – but that enlistment was still a sporadic one, organized by individual scientists rather than by institutions. But the period does herald a closer relationship between academic science and business, with departments relying on financial aid from business and philanthropic foundations to supplement the meagre financial resources they were allotted. There were significant concerns expressed about what this meant in terms of the rise of instrumental research, and what would happen to the Kantian ideal of 'pure reason' and most scientists tended to decry the turn to utility in their work. It is, however, with the Cold War that we see the greatest integration of the university towards instrumental research, and by now it is widely accepted that many universities act as the laboratory of technical and scientific invention which feeds almost directly into corporate exploitation. A representative example is Yale's licence of the compound d4t to BMS for the manufacture of anti-retroviral drugs which has earned BMS up to 15 billion dollars and Yale received 40 million dollars in royalties.

A citizenship of letters?

What is interesting for me is how the ideals of the university seem to map on to concerns that we see in intellectual property as well. The two institutions share a common epistemic regime, and like the fundamental dualisms upon which they rest (public/private, idea/expression, fact/artefacts, reason/utility), a change in one necessarily results in the reconstitution of the other.

What significance does the expansion of IP as a mindset and as a business model within universities mean for our exploration of the question of Open Access and the academic 'Community'? Lewis Hyde, in his revisiting of Marcel Mauss in the context of knowledge production, cites Jonathan Kind, a geneticist at MIT who remarked that

> [i]n the past, one of the strengths of biomedical science was the free exchange of materials, strains of organisms and information. . . . But now, if you sanction and institutionalize private gain and patenting of micro-organisms, then you don't send out your strains because you don't want them in the public domain. That's already happening now, people are no longer sharing their strains of bacteria and their results as freely as they did in the past.
> (Hyde 2007: 126)

There are two things that seem to be invoked in Kind's observations about the change in the nature of knowledge production, a loss of a spirit of 'collaboration' or 'collegiality', on the one hand, and the threat to a way of doing science which depended on an ethos of generosity.

One of the primary virtues valued within the academic community has been that of academic freedom and collaboration; what does this consist of, and in what ways is it related to the question of openness? David Downing says,

> Collegiality has been historically linked to academic freedom. The implicit premise seemed to be that we had to be 'free' to be

collegial: free to pursue truth and knowledge as liberal subjects seeking our own self-development, and free to manage our own time with respect to the autonomy granted our teaching and research efforts. To this extent, collegiality was a non-contractual but widely shared value of respecting those freedoms among our many different colleagues.

(Downing 2005: 57)

One of the prerequisites of this space of freedom was also a freedom from the constraints of property, since property spoke the language of hostile takings and appropriation. Downing says, a permanent space of non-property was created, a 'knowledge commons' that could legitimate private property in expression and invention – remembering that the (re)creation of a private domain of intangibles was and is justified by the existence of a public domain. Downing traces the shift that has happened in recent times where collegiality becomes standardized as a depoliticized meritocracy and where commoditized knowledge (as intellectual property) and its ownership became the barometer for measuring academic freedom. With the decrease in state funding for research, academics are encouraged to be more 'innovative', to be more 'productive' and to generate more resources for themselves which will assist them to buy time and consequently freedom from the university.

For Downing, this narrow conception of freedom via a negative liberties framework of non-interference and ownership has totally evacuated the idea of academic freedom and collegiality of any radical potential that it has. Produce academic knowledge as intellectual property according to 'our' standards, and you will be rewarded with tenure and promotion, and you will be free. But genuine forms of freedom are not something awarded after the fact of teaching or research. It is the other way around: freedom is actively produced by inquiry, learning, imagination, interaction. Freedom is constitutive of genuine education, not a reward for the good behaviour of educators.

The signposts of our times include the rise of "academic capitalism", the commonplace existence of Intellectual Property Agreements that facilitate technology transfer from university to corporations, and the use of law to grant universities the right to seek patents in the same way as private enterprise. As the public domain shrinks under the increasing pressures of capital, both collegiality and academic freedom, which have historically provided for the defence of a realm of non-property and non-capital, are now being turned around: the discourse of intellectual property and the ownership of knowledge are now being used to "define and defend academic freedom" (McSherry 2001: 35).

According to Corynne McSherry,

> The contest for the meaning of academic freedom is taking place on shifting ground according to novel rules . . . the conflation of property rights and 'academic rights' participates in a set of discourses which offer to replace the hierarchies of the academy with the inequalities of the free market, discourses in which freedom can only be understood to mean 'individual free enterprise'.
>
> (ibid.: 221–3)

Those who have the most academic freedom are those faculty who own the most intellectual property: knowledge workers are subordinated to knowledge owners; "academic freedom is increasingly treated as commensurate with ownership of intellectual property" (ibid.: 2). Downing urges us to resist acceding to these destructive forces and suggests that we reclaim a politics of collegiality – rhetorically and politically – to articulate a new politics of the production of knowledge and ownership. We need to urgently acknowledge that amongst the various terrains of contest over higher education in India, we are increasingly going to see a rise in this American style reward system.

In 2008, for instance, the Indian parliament introduced "The Protection and Utilization of Publicly Funded Intellectual Property Bill, 2008", or what was popularly referred to as the Bah Doyle Act of India. Like its US counterpart, the Indian law was introduced with the presumption that there was a need "to provide incentives for creativity and innovation", to facilitate "commercialisation of intellectual property created out of public-funded research and development", to "increase the responsibility of universities, academic and research institutions to encourage students, faculty and scientists to innovate, to raise royalty income" and to "minimise dependence of universities, academic and research institutions and other recipient organisations for Government funding" (GoI 2008: 8).

If one of the rallying cries of the free software movement was the idea of free as in free speech and not free as in free beer, it is time for us to articulate a radical politics of freedom in academic practice, or free as in academic – and where would one begin, if not with our own knowledge production?

Notes

1 The Chancellor, Masters & Scholars Of The University Of Oxford & Ors. V. Rameshwari Photocopy Services & Anr. The single judge bench decision is available at http://lobis.nic.in/ddir/dhc/RSE/judgement/16-09-2016/RSE16092016S24392012.pdf and the division bench decision is available at https://indiankanoon.org/doc/114459608/ (accessed on 31 December 2017)
2 http://fdslive.oup.com/asiaed/News%20Items%20and%20Images/Joint%20Public%20Statement.pdf (accessed on 31 December 2017)
3 Comprising Justices Ranjan Gogoi and Navin Sinha.
4 Including numerous works on the history of India by Oxford University Press, as well as some more general 'classics' such as Foucault's *The Order of Things*.
5 After the initial hearing, an email from the lawyers representing the publishers was leaked online in which it was clearly asserted that this is a test case to establish stronger enforcement of reprographic rights and fees in India.
6 See also Garga Chatterjee, "Free knowledge versus freedom of the market", available at www.millenniumpost.in/NewsContent.aspx?NID=7803 (accessed on 31 December 2017)
7 Corynne McSherry, *Who Owns Academic Work?: Battling for Control of Intellectual Property*. Harvard University Press, 2001.

References

Anonymous. 2012. 'Academic Publishers – An Insider's perspective', *Kafila*, 19 September. Available at http://kafila.org/2012/09/19/academic-publishers-an-insiders-perspective-anonymous-contributor/ (accessed on 31 December 2017).

The Chancellor, Masters & Scholars of University of Oxford & Ors. v. Rameshwari Photocopy Services & Anr. 2016a. High Court of Delhi Single Judge Bench Judgment, 16 September. Available at http://lobis.nic.in/ddir/dhc/RSE/judgement/16-09-2016/RSE16092016S24392012.pdf (accessed on 31 December 2017).

———. 2016b. High Court of Delhi Division Bench Judgment, 9 December. Available at https://indiankanoon.org/doc/114459608/ (accessed on 31 December 2017).

Chatterjee, Garga. 2012. 'Free Knowledge versus Freedom of the Market', *Millennium Post*, 13 September. Available at www.millenniumpost.in/free-knowledge-versus-freedom-of-the-market-7479?NID=7803 (accessed on 31 December 2017).

Darnton, Robert. 2008. 'The Case for Open Access', *The Harvard Crimson*, 12 February. Available at www.thecrimson.com/article/2008/2/12/the-case-for-open-access-the/ (accessed on 31 December 2017).

Deshpande, Sudhanva. 2012. 'Whose copy, whose right?', *The Hindu*, 19 September. Available at www.thehindu.com/opinion/op-ed/whose-copy-whose-right/article3911970.ece (accessed on 31 December 2017).

Downing, David. 2005. 'Academic Freedom as Intellectual Property: When Collegiality Confronts the Standardization Movement', *Symplokë*, 13(1–2): 56–79.

Government of India (GoI). 2008. *The Protection and Utilisation of Public Funded Intellectual Property Bill*. New Delhi: Ministry of Science and Technology and Earth Sciences.

Hyde, Lewis. 2007. *The Gift: Creativity and the Artist in the Modern World*. New York: Vintage Books.

'Joint Statement by Oxford University Press, Cambridge University Press and Taylor & Francis'. 2017. 9 March. Available at http://fdslive.oup.com/asiaed/News%20Items%20and%20Images/Joint%20Public%20Statement.pdf (accessed on 31 December 2017).

Kant, Immanuel. 1979 (1794). *The Conflict of the Faculties*. (trans.) Mary. J. Gregor. New York: Abaris Books.

Kapczynski, A. 2008. 'Access to Knowledge Mobilization and the New Politics of Intellectual Property', *The Yale Law Journal*, 117(5): 804–85.

Krikorian, Gaëlle. 2010. 'Access to Knowledge as a Field of Activism', in A. Kapczynski and G. Krikorian (eds.) *Access to Knowledge in the Age of Intellectual Property* (pp. 57–95). New York: Zone Books.

McSherry, Corynne. 2001. *Who Owns Academic Work?: Battling for Control of Intellectual Property*. Cambridge, MA, London: Harvard University Press.

'Open Letter to OUP to refrain from appealing in the Delhi University photocopy case'. 2017. Available at https://spicyip.com/wp-content/uploads/2017/01/OUP-Petition.pdf (accessed on 31 December 2017).

Sample, Ian. 2012. 'Harvard University Says It Can't Afford Journal Publishers' Prices', *The Guardian*, 24 April. Available at www.theguardian.com/science/2012/apr/24/harvard-university-journal-publishers-prices (accessed on 31 December 2017).

9 Between disciplines and interdisciplines
The university of *in*-discipline

Debaditya Bhattacharya

> Very concretely, interdisciplinarity is usually the slogan and the practice of the spontaneous ideology of specialists: oscillating between a vague spiritualism and technocratic positivism.
>
> Louis Althusser, 'Philosophy and the Spontaneous Philosophy of the Scientists' (1974)

> I was beginning to understand that 'other' is not simply a matter of imaginative geography but also of discontinuous epistemes.
>
> Gayatri Chakravorty Spivak, 'Foreword', *Other Asias* (2008)

It is not without a certain deliberateness of purpose that I begin this essay on a contrapuntal note, with the two preceding citations framing a crucial debate around the history of the modern university's relationship with 'discipline'. It also needs to be emphasized that I use the word 'discipline' here, in all its etymological fecundity – coming as it does from the Latin root *disciplina*. In its originary sense, *disciplina* refers to both a practice of regimenting the minds and bodies of disciples engaged in the pursuit of wisdom, as well as the carefully segregated bodies of intellectual discourse that are thus institutionalized through limited rights of access and divisions of labour.

This essay begins with an attempt to chart the institutional histories of disciplinarity (in taking off from Simon Schaffer's hypothesis around its intersections with the colonial enterprise). The machineries of docilization – of both the objects of knowledge and the knowing subject – that the 'invention' of the discipline performs will be looked at, before I move into the mistakenly conjoined tales of specialization and interdisciplinarity within the university. Pitted against an unfolding archive of palpable threats against certain fields of interdisciplinary research, and a contradictory move towards co-opting certain others within the logic of global capital, the rest of the chapter will interrogate the ethico-political condition of such work and the 'dangerous' powers of it. I will end by suggesting that the true task of the present-day university consists in a return to the 'outsides' of discipline, as a working towards the 'event' of social justice.

The 'order' of knowledge: science as a system

The idea of the knowledge-'discipline' – with its insistence on definable objects of inquiry, epistemic ascriptions of value and a range of possible pedagogical or research methods – is not innate to the material contexts of the university. In fact, the medieval origins of the university were wedded to an ecclesiastical project of moral instruction and its allied social interests of dominance. As a result, it did not quite subscribe to a disciplinary apparatus of teaching-learning and, instead, assumed the function of a guild-like guardianship over scholastic doctrine as well as forms of *doxa*. The concept of a scientific discipline – mandating regulative norms for the practice of scholarship and its institutional aims or ends – was yet to take root.

Several historians, such as Robert Kohler (1981, 1999), Simon Schaffer (1990, 2013) and Jan Golinski (1998),[1] argue that it was around the late eighteenth and early nineteenth centuries that the transformation of the new research-oriented German university mirrored a distinct move towards the disciplinary re-configuration of science. The medieval conception of the university – emerging from an intuited universality of knowledges, as immanent in the Latin word *universitas* – became the site of convergence between the *artes liberales* (liberal arts) and training for professions. Not surprisingly, it was at the conjunctural cusp of the late Middle Ages and early modernity that we see a conspicuous rise of professional scholarship in the universities of Europe – through an institutionalization of academic studies in law, medicine and theology.[2] Evidence of such nascent disciplinary divisions within early modern practices of scholarship is borne out by a text like Christopher Marlowe's *Doctor Faustus* (1604) – supposed to be historically based on an early-sixteenth-century figure of a university intellectual and alchemist Johann Georg Faust – and allied literary folklore in the *Faust* legend. Marlowe's Faustus is conferred distinction by the University of Wittenberg (an institution famous for its association with the pioneer of the Protestant Reformation in Martin Luther!), and he opens the play by spurning the subjects of his erstwhile study as inadequate measure for the ground of hubristic ambition. His very first soliloquy weighs the relative merits

Between disciplines and interdisciplines 185

of the extant university disciplines – namely, philosophy, medicine, law and theology – and deems each as utterly incommensurate to the humanist vision of 'progress'. He craves for an alternative discipline that made knowledge into an exhibitionist excuse for power, by playing out the aggressions of imperial desire. Rejecting the medieval notion of 'discipline' as limited in both purpose and purview, Faustus declares:

> Philosophy is odious and obscure,
> Both law and physic are for petty wits;
> Divinity is basest of the three,
> Unpleasant, harsh, contemptible and vile:
> 'Tis magic, magic that hath ravished me.
> (Act I Sc. i, ll. 105–9)

While 'philosophy', 'law', 'physic' and 'divinity' are thus pronounced as unworthy disciplines for the Renaissance man, their inherent failures with regard to the project of subject-formation were to be corrected in a hierarchy of knowledge-systems. The fact that there was no system of rules governing the priorities of institutional learning and their exact importance in the life of the student came to be perceived as the root crisis of the humanist experiment. Writing between 1794 and 1799, Immanuel Kant diagnosed a "conflict" between the different disciplinary orders at the university – and consequently, urged for a re-organization of institutional reason according to its epistemic calling. While the 'higher' faculties of professional relevance were conceived by him to be dependent on an ethic of service to the state, the foundational 'lower' faculty of philosophy was to embody the substantive principle of intellectual freedom (Kant 1979 [1799]). It is this philosophical *ground* for the university's pedagogy that now required a disciplinary orientation in the sciences.

The attempted systematization of philosophy *as* science was indeed the basis for a regeneration of the university as tied to the national-allegorical spirit of *Bildung* (general education).[3] There was a felt need to identify and name the epistemological adventures of scientific reason, and in the process organize the labours of the university community into a consciousness of integrative intellectual work. Furthermore, since the modern university – in its promise of national 'progress' – had to produce a class of cognitively enabled citizens adequate to the task of administration and statecraft, the subjects of study had to gain a coherence of their own and delimit their boundaries with respect to specific cognitive-rational capabilities that were to result of them.

Consequently, one discerns in the Kantian attempt to "sketch the architectonic of all cognition issuing from pure reason" (Kant 1996 [1787]: 757) an Enlightenment rationale for knowledge production in the form of disciplinary 'entities'. Kant had already pitched for an internal self-constitution of the sciences in his 1781 edition of *Critique of Pure Reason*, by categorically ascribing to them a near-disciplinary totality despite an otherwise dissembling array of cognitive differentiations:

> Since systematic unity is what first turns common cognition into science, i.e., turns a mere aggregate of cognition into a system, architectonic is the doctrine of what is scientific in our cognition as such; and hence it necessarily belongs to the doctrine of method. . . . What we call science cannot arise technically, i.e., not because of the similarity of the manifold [parts in it] or because of the contingent use of cognition *in concreto* for all sorts of optional external purposes; but it can arise only architectonically, on account of the affinity [of its parts] and the derivation [of these parts] from a single supreme and internal purpose that makes the whole possible in the first place. For the schema of what we call science must contain the whole's outline (*monogramma*) and the whole's division into members in conformity with the idea – i.e., it must contain these *a priori* – and must distinguish this whole from all others securely and according to principles.
>
> (ibid.: 755–6)

The self-governing condition of science as a 'whole' – in accordance with a "single supreme and internal purpose" – was simultaneously the grounds for its distinction from other disciplines. It is this teleological ordering of science as a purposive totality that raises the spectre of a disciplinary ethic in terms of what Kant calls its "final causes".[4] The internal and external motivations for a separation of the scientific from other forms of cognition articulate the desire for an organic composite, which could then become the site for an exercise of critical reason. The centripetal forces at work in this process of negotiating with the sciences as a disciplinary foundation are echoed subsequently in 1790, when the "Critique of Teleological Judgment" maintains:

> Every science is a system in its own right. . . . [W]e must also set to work . . . treating it as a whole and independent building, not as an annex or part of another building, though we may later construct, starting from either building, a passage connecting the one to the other.
>
> (1987 [1790]: 261)

The imagination of the sciences as an "independent" discipline (that Kant alludes to!) was to go hand-in-hand with a necessary amplitude for internal transformations or interventions. The structural aspect of the 'discipline' was thus apprehended as a totality without closure. It is this idea of disciplinarity that was integral to Wilhelm von Humboldt's plan for the establishment of a new University of Berlin. A Prussian diplomat, Humboldt envisioned – along with Friedrich Schleiermacher and Johann Gottlieb Fichte – an "idea of the university" that was at the same time consecrated to an 'idea' of the sciences as a philosophical modality of *knowing*. However, the legislative anchoring of the university in scientific truths was coupled with an in(de)finite commitment to research – insofar as the sciences were deemed to be a discipline in progress.[5] In his treatise "On the Internal and External Organization of the Higher Scientific Institutions in Berlin" (1810), Humboldt clearly comments on the essential unity and perpetual incompletion of the scientific discipline:

> [T]he chief factor remains science. . . . For when the latter stands pure, it is correctly perceived in and of itself and in its totality, even if there are individual deviations. Since these institutions can thus achieve their purpose only if each one, as much as possible, faces the pure idea of science, solitariness and freedom are the predominant principles in their circle. . . . Moreover, it is a peculiarity of the higher scientific institutions that they always treat science as a problem that has still not been fully resolved and therefore remain constantly engaged in research.
>
> (1810: 1–2)

The political economy of discipline

If, as we have seen so far, the rise of the academic discipline at the turn of the nineteenth century coincided with the birth of the new research university, it is important to note that this was also the period of yet another colonial experiment. In 1787, Andrew Bell of the Church of England arrived at Madras and, subsequently, under the aegis of the East India Company, took charge as the superintendent of a school for the orphaned male children of army officers. Having stayed on and observed indigenous schooling practices around the area, Bell devised a system of "mutual tuition and moral discipline"[6] for the students of his asylum. Following the resounding success of his project, Bell's elaborate plan for institutional instruction came to be famously indexed as the "Madras system" (1808, 1823: 1) – a veritable model for further emulation in the schools of England and Scotland.

The documents outlining the exact vision behind Bell's system of tuitions were later published as a collection of papers, titled *An Analysis of the Experiment in Education Made at Egmore, near Madras* (1797). The subtitled description of the volume clarified that the said 'experiment' consisted in

> a System, alike fitted to reduce the expense of Tuition, abridge the labour of the Master, and expedite the progress of the Scholar; and suggesting a Scheme for the better administration of the Poor-laws, by converting Schools for the lower orders of youth into Schools of Industry (see Figure 9.1).

Evidently, this was a system calculated to produce a utilitarian order of benefits – as the use of words 'expense', 'labour' and 'progress' suggest! – but it was not simply to be a material measure of 'profit' that was expected of its eventual unfolding. What lay at the heart of Bell's proposal and its intended outcome was the political economy of discipline, as the governing logic behind models of instruction in educational institutions. By making the latter incumbent on a 'monitorial system'[7] that divided the labours of the classroom into internally organized hierarchical orders of teaching, the more advanced student was ordained as the tutor for those less schooled. In the process, institutional discipline was broken up into differential codes of localized surveillance over student bodies inhabiting the system. Declaredly, the primary agenda for Bell was to abolish the practice of corporal punishment in schools, by making their administration far more amorphous and layered than it ever was. The student was imagined as a subject of disciplinary routines, both by the setting up of an exemplary ideal from among "a jury of peers" (Bell 1807 [1797]: 13) as well as through an incorporation of these local sites of co-optation into a larger machinery of control. As a result, the model worked by using the force of the 'example' as an immediate context for subjectification and then tying it into a distributive order of moral instruction. As Bell remarks about the necessary effectiveness of his system:

> It is the grand boast of this system, not that it thus detects, convicts, and corrects the offender, but that, by the perpetual presence and intervention, as well at play as in School, of our Teachers and Assistants (not to say Tutors) who are tried and approved boys, aided by their (emeriti) predecessors, who acquitted themselves, while in office, with credit and applause, it prevents the offence, and establishes such habits of industry, morality and religion, as have a tendency to form good scholars, good men and good Christians.
>
> (ibid.: 13–4)

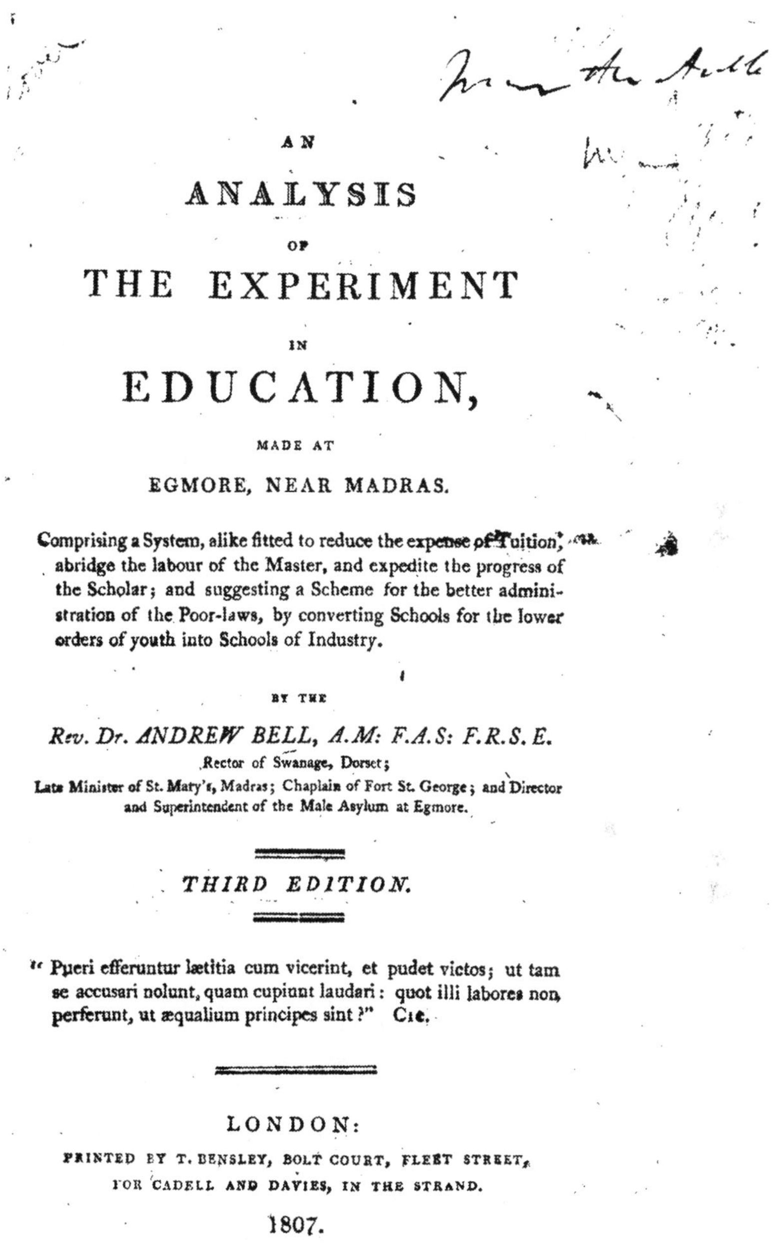

AN
ANALYSIS
OF
THE EXPERIMENT
IN
EDUCATION,

MADE AT

EGMORE, NEAR MADRAS.

Comprising a System, alike fitted to reduce the expense of Tuition, abridge the labour of the Master, and expedite the progress of the Scholar; and suggesting a Scheme for the better administration of the Poor-laws, by converting Schools for the lower orders of youth into Schools of Industry.

BY THE

Rev. Dr. ANDREW BELL, A.M: F.A.S: F.R.S.E.
Rector of Swanage, Dorset;
Late Minister of St. Mary's, Madras; Chaplain of Fort St. George; and Director and Superintendent of the Male Asylum at Egmore.

THIRD EDITION.

" Pueri efferuntur lætitia cum vicerint, et pudet victos; ut tam se accusari nolunt, quam cupiunt laudari: quot illi labores non perferunt, ut æqualium principes sint ?" Cic.

LONDON:
PRINTED BY T. BENSLEY, BOLT COURT, FLEET STREET,
FOR CADELL AND DAVIES, IN THE STRAND.
1807.

Figure 9.1 Cover page of Andrew Bell's publication, detailing the monitorial system of discipline

Source: Google Books digital edition, from Harvard University Library of the Graduate School of Education collection

The "tendency to form good scholars, good men and good Christians" is what animates Jeremy Bentham's inspired efforts at deriving from the Madras system and proposing a panopticon-like arrangement of the educational institution in *Chrestomathia* (1816). Buoyed by the apparent success of Bell's theory of "mutual tuition", Bentham sought to extend the infrastructures of disciplinary surveillance to the "higher branches of learning, for the use of the middling and higher ranks in life".[8] Like his proposed Chrestomathic Day School, Bentham fathomed that even institutions of higher learning could adopt a new design for "intellectual instruction" that would ensure for its beneficiaries "security for admission into, and agreeable intercourse with, good company" (1816: 18). It was to be a disciplining mechanism for the truant body of the student, where the localized and yet impersonal gaze of the machine could potentially transform the aleatory spaces of individual behaviour into socially regulated systems of production.

Bentham's *Chrestomathia*, in its avowing of relations with the "existing great schools, universities and other Didactic institutions" (ibid.: 19), signalled the double senses of a rise of the "disciplinary" regime within universities. That the coming into being of a scientific ethic of self-identification as 'discipline' was to simultaneously mandate a regulative order of membership within its fold is sufficiently foreshadowed by now. The original dualism of meaning implicit in the Latin *disciplina* is borne out by the historical circumstances of a *disciplinary turn* in universities. Alternatively put, the dialectical project of Enlightenment reason did evolve a new imagination of the scientific canon, while its formal organization of knowledge-prerogatives entailed a structural exclusion of the indisciplined, the non-conforming and the non-normative.

The interdisciplinary moment: a return or rupture?

Insofar as the emergence of a scientific discipline paralleled the circumscription of reason as the social norm of modernity and simultaneously provided its institutional contexts of legitimation within universities, when and how did interdisciplinarity appear on the horizon of intellectual discourse? What was the latter's relationship with the disciplinary condition of knowledge production, and how did it challenge both the self-enclosures of value-laden scholarship as well as its penchant for regimenting object-subject interactions in institutional settings? Did the interdiscipline arise out of the same epistemological imperative as specialism?

The intellectual-cognitive stability granted by disciplinary sanctions of knowledge around the period of the Enlightenment was soon to face a dire crisis. By about the 1830s, the philosophical understanding of the sciences started giving way to a culture of specialization and an increasing disconnect with the integrative analytic. The 'natural sciences' inaugurated a fissuring of the erstwhile disciplinary unity posited among myriad forms of scientific reasoning; and before long, the Humboldtian "idea of the university" was confronted by demands for a professional segregation of pedagogical prerogatives, interests and rules/methods of inquiry. The sciences were successively understood as divided in terms of instrumental purpose, and philosophy could no longer bind them under a unified rubric. New departments for studies in natural sciences and human sciences were in the process of being instituted, under utilitarian regimes and their insistence on positivistic outcomes. With systems of higher education being gradually moulded by the economic rationale of production, it was only natural that universities became sites of a proliferating array of disciplines. The scourge of specialism that took over institutional apparatuses and aims of research has often been misread as the moment of origin of the interdiscipline.

Such historical speculation is, however, far from the truth, with regard to both the structural conditions of and material directions in higher education. The logic of specialization is one of heightened disciplinarity, and it is finally about setting up a more insular machinery of the production-consumption of knowledges. In this, specialism prescribes not only a contraction of enclosures around the commons of knowledge, but also through a sustained hierarchy of 'niche' skills necessary for accessing them. Instead of challenging the borders of disciplines and moving between them (as the apparent titular appeal of 'interdisciplinarity' suggests!), a cult of specialization functions on the implicit consensus for a need to further fortify knowledge into discrete units and securitize its limits beyond easy unauthorized permeability. Put differently, specializations are totalitarian self-representations of knowledge, governed by privileges of exegetical access.

As such, the imminence of specialism was underwritten into the birth of the academic discipline and its allied *effects* of ordering subjective investments in knowledge. Writing in the chapter "Natural History of Morals", from *Beyond Good and Evil* (1886), Nietzsche comments on the morality of teleological pursuits of knowledge and its eventual degeneration into the specialist's preoccupation with minutiae:

> That for thousands of years European thinkers thought merely in order to prove something – today, conversely, we suspect every

thinker who "wants to prove something" – that the conclusions that *ought* to be the result of their most rigorous reflection were always settled from the start. . . – this tyranny, this caprice, this rigorous and grandiose stupidity has *educated* the spirit. . . . Consider any morality with this in mind: what there is in it of "nature" teaches hatred of the *laisser aller*, of any all-too-great freedom, and implants the need for limited horizons and the nearest tasks – teaching the *narrowing of our perspective*, and thus in a certain sense stupidity, as a condition of life and growth.

(1966 [1886]: 101–2)

The "need for limited horizons and the nearest tasks" is what Nietzsche subsequently diagnoses as the spiritual condition of the specialist as opposed to the philosopher. As the prototype of the professional scholar, the "new generation" of specialists – Nietzsche alerts – has "inherited in its blood diverse standards and values, [such that] everything is unrest, disturbance, doubt, attempt" (ibid.: 130). This is the disposition of the skeptic, as distinct from the critic – and it revels in a "world of 'modern ideas' that would banish everybody into a corner and 'specialty'" (ibid.: 137). In contrast, the philosophers are ranged against the ideality of their discipline in the present – and are perceived as "disagreeable fools and dangerous question marks, [who] have found their task, their hard, unwanted, inescapable task, . . . in being the bad conscience of their time" (ibid.). Philosophy, for Nietzsche, is the true marker of the 'in[ter]disciplined' as a contradictory insertion into the dominance of the present.

The word 'interdisciplinarity' made its appearance during the inter-War years, and was soon embraced by the climate of technocratic rationalism that employed the sciences at the behest of fascistic agendas around that time. The instrumentalization of the scientific disciplines as directly 'applicable' to political-militaristic designs of dominance brought about a convergence of the desire for maniacal specialism with that of interdisciplinary endeavours. The demands made of intellectual orders at the university to visibly contribute to the project of national resurgence (through a techno-bureaucratic positivism of knowledge-systems) enlisted multiple disciplinary pursuits at the behest of state service. In the process, the state's constant call to scientific innovation and a functionalist pursuit of narrow outcomes ended up misrepresenting the epistemological condition of interdisciplinarity.

It is this technocratization of scientific specialism that Althusser imagines as the ideological aim of interdisciplinarity, and he warns his colleagues at Ecole Normale Superieure against such a brand of round-table eclecticism in 1967. In the first of a series of lectures titled "Philosophy Course for Scientists", Althusser snubs the rising shadow of the interdiscipline as merely a fashion – a 'spontaneous ideology' – among practising specialists of science (1990 [1974]: 73–100). He urges a return to that philosophical function, as consisting in the line of demarcation between the scientific and the ideological. In the process of disavowing the 'slogan of interdisciplinarity', the revisionist Marxist in Althusser goes on to re-assign to philosophy the borderline-conscience of disciplines. Philosophy does become for him the mode of negotiating between epistemic priorities and their disciplinary boundaries – the true mark of the 'interdisciplinary'!

Mixing dread with deference

Having traced interdisciplinarity to a philosophical *figura* of the 'limit', it would suit us well to synoptically survey the current institutional fortunes of interdisciplinary studies through specific case-examples. And there is a strange paradox that one perceives here. Following the revolutionary demands for a restructuring of educational systems in 1968, there has been a distinct move favouring the rise of interdisciplinary interventions within university infrastructures of learning. The embedded prejudices within academic subjects and their departmental fortifications have been challenged both in the cause of alternative epistemologies as well as market demands for innovation and direct public relevance. While the Organisation for Economic Cooperation and Development (OECD) published a report titled *Interdisciplinarity: Problems of Teaching and Research in Universities* (1972) – based on the discussions and recommendations that emerged from a seminar collaboratively hosted by the former's Centre for Educational Research and Innovation (CERI) and the French Ministry of Education in 1970 – the UNESCO's *Quarterly Review of Education* (Vol. XII, No. 3, 1982) went on to maintain in its opening piece:

> It is beyond doubt that in this situation the principle of interdisciplinarity in advanced studies and research is essential if new ground is to be broken and fresh discoveries are to be made.
> (Gozzer 1982: 287)

Despite such clear patterns of consensus among international economic policy forums and advisory bodies, university reformers and scholars in the Euro-American academy recount of the excruciating labours that have gone into setting up departments of women's studies, cultural studies, critical race studies, disability studies, transgender studies or critical legal studies through the 1970s up until now. Tenured faculty positions, research appointments, project sanctions or fellowship grants have been hard to come by in any of these interdisciplinary fields, and have often required years of struggle against state bureaucracies, government agencies of funding and architects of public policy.

Let me now turn to the Indian public university's tryst with interdisciplinary research, in the form of a chronicle of recent developments that have provoked legitimate and widespread alarm.

On 24 March 2017, the administration of Tata Institute of Social Sciences (TISS) – a premier teaching and research institution in Mumbai, deemed as university – issued letters to about 18 faculty members and 17 other research/support personnel contractually appointed in three specific departments of study, informing them of an impending termination of services a week in advance.[9] There were no reasons or charges assigned for this absurd termination order, except for the fact that their respective departments – Centre for Study of Social Exclusion and Inclusive Policy, Advanced Centre for Women's Studies and Nodal Centre of Excellence for Human Rights Education – were all likely to be shut down for lack of any funding commitment from the government. While some amount of irony was of course reserved for what seemed like the eventual destiny of a titularly recognized "nodal centre of excellence", the Director of the Institute issued statements to the press ruing the University Grants Commission's (UGC) prolonged non-response on the question of possible extension of the said programmes.[10] After some amount of public hue and media outcry on the issue (followed by a number of petitions by eminent scholar-activists), the UGC was nudged by the Ministry of Human Resource Development (MHRD) to extend affiliation to these centres for one year, pending further reviews. Barely a couple of weeks prior to this shocking course of events, the Registrar of Jawaharlal Nehru University (JNU) – a university notoriously marked in government annals as the laboratory of 'sedition'! – received a letter signed by the Undersecretary to the UGC, portending a similar fate for its much-acclaimed Centre for the Study of Discrimination and Exclusion (CSDE).[11] Tracing its origins to the concerted efforts of a group of dedicated social scientists way back in 2002, the CSDE was intimated of a decision to discontinue financial support for its teaching-research activities from April 2017 onwards. The same letter, dated March 6, warned the university authorities against any attempt at further communication or negotiation with the UGC. Understandably, faced with massive intellectual censure for such an unconstitutionally threatening form of correspondence, the UGC was subsequently forced to publish a "clarification" on its website deeming the contentious letter as "forged" and its contents untrue.[12]

While the UGC's forced retraction on these two occasions suggests something of sinister proportions, the developments that they signal towards – a defunding and subsequent shutdown of departments of interdisciplinary scholarship aligned to the cause of social justice – bespeak a policy intention that is not without evidence in other universities. It is around the same time that the School of Women's Studies at Jadavpur University and the Centre for Study of Social Exclusion in Manipur University were among a hundred other such departments (across state and centrally funded public universities) confronting identical fortunes for lack of any clear indication from government agencies.[13] While the possibility of an immediate closure of these programmes has been put to rest for another year, the darkening cloud of uncertainty surrounding them has already forced most of the faculty members currently working on an annual contract to explore other job opportunities or potential transfers into allied disciplines. In any case, what the government has managed to do – by carefully manufacturing a climate of deliberate confusion and controversial media reporting – is a wilful emptying out of these departments by both faculty and students in the not so distant future.

Opened between 2002 and 2007, most of these infrastructures of interdisciplinary research in the social sciences derived their vision from the Tenth Five-Year-Plan (2002–2007) drafted by the Planning Commission – which issued guidelines for the study of structural exclusions and sustained persecutions on the basis of class, caste, gender and religion. The centres thus instituted were subsequently incorporated into the Eleventh and Twelfth Plans, with pre-ordained budgetary allocations for their sustenance and deemed renewable on a plan-to-plan basis after every five years. While the extent of financial assistance was limited to one-time non-recurring establishment grants till the Eleventh Plan, a lot of reform struggles and policy consultations went into finally securing faculty positions and an annual recurring grant for research/support staff appointments as part of the Twelfth Five-Year Plan (2012–2017).[14] The Yash Pal Committee Report (2009), with its thrust on overcoming disciplinary boundaries to forge ties with a "community of participant citizens" (2009: 18) and its underlining of the need for disbursal of "block grants against a plan" (ibid.: 42), contributed to a relative funding-stability in the functioning of these interdisciplinary programmes.

The Modi government, soon after its coming to power in 2014, declared the abolition of the Planning Commission and claimed to embark on a route of infrastructural overhaul for development sectors. In this, it allowed a lapsing of state-regulated agendas for 'planned growth' after the exhaustion of the Twelfth Plan on March 31, 2017. Along with that announcement came crumbling the existing areas of planned expenditure – one of the casualties of which happened to be the university centres for interdisciplinary teaching and research. With the government's purported macroeconomic shift from state-regulated planning to outcome-based policy (reflected in the establishment of NITI Aayog), the obvious implication was a systematic desiccation of state funding or subsidies for non-profit-making public goods like higher education. However, this was in no way the first assault on the existence of these departments. Way back in 2013, during the previous government's tenure – and soon after the Twelfth Plan Guidelines mandated the UGC's commitment to complete financial assistance under the Scheme for establishment of Centres for Study of Social Exclusion and Inclusive Policy (CSSEIP) – the UGC sent notices to 32 such centres threatening withdrawal of the scheme. The timely intervention of the National Commission of Scheduled Castes (NCSC) prevented a materialization of the move.[15]

What is glaringly evident from the above sequence of onslaughts is that the interdisciplinary centres for social justice research in Indian universities have long been awaiting the final axe-stroke of a neoliberal amputation. Yet, paradoxically enough, it is these same governments that have gone to absurd lengths in violating and restructuring national education policies in order to introduce interdisciplinary curriculum within universities. The recently imposed metric of standardization across public universities in the country – the Choice Based Credit System (CBCS) – reworks an already discredited curricular pattern from the Delhi University's Four Year Undergraduate Programme (FYUP) "so that students depending upon their interests and aims can choose interdisciplinary, intra-disciplinary and skill-based courses" (*Minimum Course Curriculum Document*, UGC 2015: 2). Animated by an exalted rationale of upgrading higher educational institutions existing within diverse local contexts to a single template of 'global standards', the CBCS proposes a common minimum course structure with little amplitude of institutional autonomy despite all kinds of infrastructural constraints. The latter comprises a substantial interdisciplinary component in Ability Enhancement Compulsory Courses (AECC) that "provide value-based and/or skill-based knowledge" (ibid.: 6).

A few questions would better be posed at this point. Why has interdisciplinarity generated such a contradictory set of responses from those in positions of political-bureaucratic privilege and economic power? How has the epistemological condition of the interdiscipline played itself out, in order to merit these oppositional narratives of simultaneous celebration and censure? Inasmuch as the interdisciplinary turn within academic departments has been successfully co-opted by neoliberal policy directions in educational reform, how might its socially transformative potential be realized? Can interdisciplinarity challenge our commonsense-ordering of the world and, in that, become the means for an ontological restructuring of the university space?

Agendas behind the euphoria

In the "Introduction" to a collection of essays and research findings titled *Interdisciplinarity: Reconfigurations of the Social and Natural Sciences* (2013), Andrew Barry and Georgina Born explain the nexus of concerns that underlies the "emergence and prominence of the contemporary discourse on interdisciplinarity" (2) thus:

> Two inflections of the discourse on interdisciplinarity are particularly apparent. The first portrays interdisciplinarity as offering new techniques for accountability, or even as itself an index of knowledge practices that are accountable to society. The second lays emphasis on the capacity of interdisciplinarity to assist in forging closer relations between scientific research and the requirements of the economy through fostering innovation.
>
> (ibid.: 3)

It is this twin logic of accountability and innovation as the necessary forces governing a global economy of knowledge production that has come to dominate governmental demands for interdisciplinary research within universities. In this, there is an attempt to make knowledge-investments directly incumbent on their potential for real-world 'application' and revenue-generation (Nowotny 2001). Interdisciplinarity, within the governmental instantiations of it, is shaped by a policy that believes in deregulating the disciplinary ownership of knowledge outcomes – such that it may eventually devolve into marketable/auctionable currencies of 'skill' and 'competence' at the behest of transnational capital. The state-sanctioned projects of interdisciplinarising higher education curriculum, through 'add-on' insertions of skill-based training and real-life problem-solving approaches, are precisely geared towards this purpose of reconfiguring knowledge as purchasable capital. With greater ascriptions of employability-as-'value' within interdisciplinary programmes, comes an allied demand of a greater 'price' that one has to pay for attaining the desired ends. This 'higher price for better higher education' argument is then rationalized as the cost of more efficient infrastructures of integrated learning (involving internships, industrial collaborations and hands-on experience), thus providing impetus to an effective privatization of public universities.

The functionalist imagination of public accountability that animates much of the state's commitment to interdisciplinarity consists in peddling a return to broad-based cognitive training as the proper task of the university. The interdiscipline here is made to represent a patchwork of divergent disciplines, such that a simplified rhetoric of education's relationship with a 'diversity of social needs/demands' may seem as the grounds for its justification. Both the earlier-discussed models of CBCS and FYUP – in its enabling of 'choice' in the student's pursuit of disconnected disciplines, simplified as 'skills' and 'abilities' – use a similar ideological vision.

What results of this preferred agenda of inter-curricular training within universities – where, as the *Minimum Course Curriculum Document* of CBCS attests, a student may opt for "unique combinations" in studying "[f]or example, Physics with Economics" (2015: 3), etc. – is a set of two related possibilities. First, the mechanical juxtaposition of unrelated disciplines not only involves an inordinate dilution of the elective subsidiary papers into pre-programmed skill sets or mere cognitive literacies, but it also defeats the inherent political basis of interdisciplinarity. The political nature and organization of knowledge via the categorical imperatives of disciplinary wisdom are left untouched and unquestioned. Crucially enough, the process of interrogating the assumptions that go on to make a discipline is abandoned through such a model of interdisciplinary studies, now in universal currency. Second and more importantly, the attempted depoliticization of knowledge protocols through a forceful welding of multiple disciplines also performs a further regimentation of learning into competitive-performance codes of efficiency and employability.[16] As a result, the student subject is re-inserted within relations of social and material production – and thus to the very disciplinary impulse within formal-institutional education. Interdisciplinarity is made to play out its very antithesis, in that it neither translates into a practice of critical inquiry nor a challenge to the disciplinary matrix of relations that churns out fit agents of production.

While the instrumental appropriation of interdisciplinary studies for the production of a cognitively enabled corporate workforce has of course failed its purpose, there are other problems that plague its avowed re-politicization within departments of development studies or cultural studies or area studies. While apparently seeking to investigate the political erasures of a dominant historical imagination, such fields of inquiry have often gone on to normalize economic-social-territorial inequities through Enlightenment categories of 'nature', 'culture' and 'civilization'. The developmentalist analyses of economic inequity have often paraded as a cultural apology for the inevitability of globalization, while the field of area studies has continued to work with imperial conceptions of sovereignty in the nation-state. Even departments like women's studies or queer studies – Wendy Brown suggests in "The Impossibility of Women's Studies" (2005 [1997]: 116–35) – have given in to fetishistic essentialisms about identity, which have then assumed oppression and liberation outside of their structural contexts of subjectification. Visions of interdisciplinarity that do not recognize the intersections of identity – and merely perform a questioning of reified discursive types of the 'woman', 'queer', 'black', 'masculinity', etc. – only end up re-erecting undifferentiated hegemonies that scarcely allow difference.[17]

Siting the 'event' of social justice

If the history of interdisciplinary scholarship has been so fraught with political failures, strategic erasures and reactionary appropriations, why – one cannot but ask at this point! – must structures of power attempt to foreclose its institutional forms of practice? In other words, how does interdisciplinarity become a threat to the disciplinary *status quo*, if it has been subsumed so well and on so many pretexts by the normative order of reason?

The answers to these, I suggest, lie in the possibilities thrown open by the relationship between a practice of interdisciplinarity and the 'event' of social justice. The interdiscipline, in its insistence on a principle of *non*-belonging to the legislative order of disciplined truths,[18] can singularly become the site of emergence of social justice. It demonstrates in and through its forms of practice that justice is not a legislated insertion of redistributive good will into the existing social order, not is it a matter of policy-driven goals pertaining to a formal equality of opportunity. Social justice – as the practice of interdisciplinarity teaches us – is essentially and prior to everything else, a question of imagining the 'outside' to social relations. It is in making the 'other' imaginable without a condition, and apart from the hermeneutic closures of a social situation. The work of social justice requires an act of moving out, a secessionist breaking out from the certainties of knowledge in and as the social.

By calling into doubt the disciplinary circumscription of reason, the interdiscipline resides in a permanent condition of immigrancy. And it is this vantage-position of non-coincidence – the state of being non-identical and non-extensive with the frontiers of any one *subject*-field – that makes possible not only an unsparing questioning of the objects of knowledge, but also the structures of intelligibility and interpretive competence that construct such objects as worthy targets of inquiry. Put simply, if the workings of the social formation are indisputably regarded as the object of social scientific research, it is an interdisciplinary study of social exclusion that opens up an apprehension of how 'society' gets configured as *commonsense* for the beneficiaries of historical privilege.

In its necessary relationship with social justice, the order of the interdisciplinary becomes – in a Foucauldian strain – a study of "alethurgic forms" (2011: 3), that is, the forms of *production* of truth. In his lectures on *parrhesia* at College de France, Foucault clarified that an analysis of truth-telling must take for its object not the ways in which discourses are pronounced as true, but the processes through which the subject identifies himself and is identified by others as the teller of 'true' discourses. He calls this an *analytic* of alethurgy – a study of the conditions of intelligibility that create the objects and subjects of truth.[19] It is only through interdisciplinary scholarship that such an analytic may be realized. Simon O'Sullivan makes a persuasive case for this, in the anthology on *Interdisciplinarity and Social Justice* (2010), when he reads Deleuze and Guattari into the politics of the interdisciplinary project:

> Such a project involves less an object of study – indeed objects might themselves strategically disappear in such a project. Even less does it involve a reading, an interpretation of objects (that is, it has no clearly defined, fixed, subject either). Instead it involves a *pragmatics*, the creation of 'psychic tools' with which to reorder our 'selves' and our world.
> (Parker and Samantrai 2010: 84)

If taking the first provisional step towards an ethics of social justice consists in an imaginative *intuition* (not interpretation!) of *otherness* – despite its immediate absence within infrastructures of intellectual labour – interdisciplinarity is most certainly the site for that preparation. Those very centres for social scientific studies that are now labouring under a threat of closure have come to embody what Alain Badiou calls "eventual sites".[20] According to Badiou, the 'event' announces the incalculable advent of 'truth' outside of relations and numbers. It is a rupture within the organized totality of order, the immanent arrival of one that cannot be re-presented.

> As an un-founded multiple, as self-belonging, undivided signature of itself, the event can only be indicated beyond the situation, despite it being necessary to wager that it has manifested itself therein.
>
> (Badiou 2005 [1988]: 197)

Social justice is the *name* of that 'event' – one that can only be "indicated beyond the situation" of determinate presences. The move towards it therefore calls for a "rupturing with the order" (ibid.: xii) that supports the situation as materially apprehensible 'reality'; it is a call to an imaginative training for democracy – as Gayatri Spivak calls it[21] – through the practice of interdisciplinarity. As an unimpeachable site for the 'event' of social justice, the interdiscipline is the accurate setting for an "un-founded multiple", a "self-belonging", the non-mathematizable *advent*(ure) of the *other*.

The university must, by default and on principle, become the consecrated space for this call to social justice in a singular commitment to the interdisciplinary. Because such a practice of scholarship is the *only* condition of possibility of the university's self-critique. It is by studying the embedded invisibility of social discrimination or heteronormativity or, say, the regional imbalances of growth within the classroom that one finally comes to confront the potent nexus of class-caste-gender-racial solidarities that make up the 'idea of the university' and its hermeneutic communities of self-representation. The interdiscipline is what forces the university space to re-examine its own ontologies against its long-abandoned and now-deferred ideal of 'social justice', evidenced only in tokenistic instances of state welfarism. It is the only condition which enables the university to transgress its own image in the liberal 'idea', and thus become the *dangerous ground* for democracy.

It is no wonder that an ethico-political practice of interdisciplinarity must be feared as an insurrectionary force, and departments that profess or perform this *task* of social critique be ticked off into a policy-driven state of crisis. Because the interdiscipline alone can potentially return the university to a necessary future of *in-discipline* – that is, its power of an ontological interruption, a moment of radically rethinking itself.

Notes

1 For an exhaustive discussion, also refer to the 'Introduction: Problems in the Emergence of New Disciplines' in Gerard Lemaine, Roy Macleod, M.J. Mulkay, Peter Weingart, eds. *Perspectives on the Emergence of Scientific Disciplines*, Hague: Mouton, 1976, pp. 1–26
2 See Julie Thompson Klein (1990) and Joe Moran (2002: 4–5)
3 For a detailed analysis on the place of '*bildung*' in the imagination of the modern German university, refer to David Sorkin (1983: 55–74)
4 In distinguishing between blind efficient causes (mechanical in nature) and final causes (purposive in nature) with regard to the organization of nature by a supersensible principle, Kant maintains: "It goes without saying that this principle [for judging nature teleologically] holds only for reflective but not for determinative judgment, that it is regulative and not constitutive. It only serves us as a guide that allows us to consider natural things in terms of a new law-governed order by referring them to an already given basis [a purpose] as that which determines them. Thus we expand natural science [*Naturkunde*] in terms of a different principle, that of final causes, yet without detracting from the principle of mechanism in the causality of nature" (1987 [1790]: 259). It is here that one discerns the teleological principle in natural science anticipating its self-organization into a disciplinary system of reason.
5 Humboldt, in his treatise on the 'internal' and 'external' forms of organizing university life in Berlin, categorically emphasizes: "[W]hen it comes to the internal organization of the higher scientific institutions, everything depends on preserving the principle of seeing science as something that has not been and can never be entirely found, and to constantly pursue it as such. As soon as one ceases to seek true science, or imagines that it does not need to be created out of the depth of the spirit, but could be externally strung together by collecting things, everything is irretrievably and eternally lost; lost to science, which, if this is continued for a long time, takes flight and leaves behind the language like an empty shell, and lost to the state. For only the science that comes from the inside and can be implanted into the inside also reshapes the character, and the state" (1810: 2).
6 Refer to the title of Rev. Andrew Bell's *Manual of Instructions for Conducting Schools through the agency of the Scholars Themselves* (1823).
7 Bell recommends in the concluding sections: "This experiment, having been made in a charity school, is, in a peculiar manner, adapted to the education of the lower orders of youth. . . . In many schools, monitors (for it signifies not what name is given them) have of old been employed for such offices, or for purposes of discipline: and it is my humble opinion, that the system itself may be adopted, with great advantage, in schools of every description, where youth can be found, who, for the sake of their own improvement, or in consequence of the general law of the school, or for their own free education, or any other perquisite or motive, would engage themselves as teachers" (1807 [1797]: 82).

Between disciplines and interdisciplines 203

8 Refer to the subtitle of Bentham (1816).
9 See Chari (2017), available at https://scroll.in/article/832881/35staffatm umbaistissarefiredbecauseofugcfundingambiguity, detailing exact particulars of the termination order (last accessed on 31 December 2017)
10 A *Hindustan Times* report by Qazi dated March 28, 2017 (available at www.hindustantimes.com/mumbainews/studentsaskforclarityafter tissannouncesclosureofthreecentres/story last accessed on 31 December 2017) cited the Director of the Institute as saying: " 'Since we depend on government grants to pay for these professors, we have informed them that no grants have come our way in a while and if the same is not cleared by March 31, we might have to discontinue some courses, and eventually contracts of some teachers', . . . He added that in the meantime, the institute is constantly in touch with UGC authorities for updates on this front. 'I am doing everything in my power to avoid such a situation. However we thought it was only fair to make teachers aware of the situation', he said".
11 The national edition of *Hindustan Times* reported on March 21, 2017 (accessible at www.hindustantimes.com/opinion/noticetojnussocial exclusioncentreforgedsaysugcistheremoretoit/story, last accessed on 31 December 2017): "On March 15, the Jawaharlal Nehru University registrar received a letter – No. F-24–1/2017/ (CU) dated March 6 – regarding the closure of the schemes for the study of social exclusion and inclusive policy (CSDE). It stated that the University Grants Commission (UGC) will not provide financial support to the university's centre for study of social exclusion after the end of the 12th five-year plan and no communication whatsoever would be 'entertained or solicited by UGC' on the issue. But on March 16, after a news report in *The Telegraph*, the UGC did an about-turn: It said that the notification sent to JNU was 'blatantly false' and 'based on a forged letter'".
12 Refer to 'Clarification by UGC', dated March 18, 2017 and available at http://pib.nic.in/newsite/erelease.aspx?relid=159507 (last accessed on 31 December 2017). See also KumKum Dasgupta (2017).
13 For detailed discussion on the disparate contexts of UGC's actions in this regard, refer to reports by Priyanka Dasgupta published in the Kolkata edition of *The Times of India* (March 31, 2017, and accessible at http://timesofindia.indiatimes.com/city/kolkata/juschoolofwomensstudies staffersbraceforuncertainfuture/articleshow/57926340.cms) and Ramakrishnan in *The New Indian Express* (March 17, 2017, and accessible at www.newindianexpress.com/states/tamilnadu/2017/mar/17/allforana mejnucentreonugcfundexclusionlist1582297.html) (last accessed on 31 December 2017).
14 See Section 5 of 'XII Plan Guidelines For Establishment of Centres in Universities for Study of Social Exclusion and Inclusive Policy' (2012: 3).
15 For reference, see report by Mukul, published in *The Times of India* (dated June 4, 2013 and accessible at http://timesofindia.indiatimes.com/ home/education/news/UGCfacesflakforwithdrawingschemefor32CentresforStudyofSocialExclusion last accessed on 31 December 2017)
16 Disapproving of the OECD-approach to 'interdisciplinarity', as consisting in a systematic implosion of 'considerations of politics and social justice' within utilitarian agendas of 'social need', Joe Parker and Ranu Samantrai contend in the "Introduction" to their book: "[Such prerogatives] define interdisciplinarity as the attempt to synthesize existing disciplinary

concepts with the goal of achieving a unity of knowledge for a nonspecialized general education. This apolitical, holistic approach to interdisciplinarity, which we would term multidisciplinarity, is found across the board in the academy from the humanities to science research centres to professional associations. . . . [It] largely disregards the social and intellectual challenges to academic orthodoxy and the politics that were the breeding ground for interdisciplinary programs. . . [and] advocates an interdisciplinarity that rejects narrow specialization in favour of an integrative blend of disciplines on the grounds that social needs are best served by the latter's general education approach" (2010: 3).

17 Brown insightfully diagnoses the eclipse of intellectual nuance in the political anxieties of 'women's studies' in her essay (originally published in a 1997 special edition of *Differences: A Journal of Feminist Cultural Studies*). She persuasively makes a case about the discursive overdeterminations of identity (within women's studies departments and curricula) that go on to disregard the complexities/non-coincidences underlying systems of social production of subjectivity, and finally urges: "[A]s feminism has for many become irreversibly connected to the project of multicultural, postcolonial and queer analysis, terms such as "multiplicity", "intersections", "crossroads", "borderlands", "hybridity", and "fracturing" have emerged to acknowledge – without fully explaining or theorizing – the complex workings of power that converge at the site of identity. The currency of these terms suggest the limitations of existing theories of both power and history for articulating the making of subjects, and especially gendered subjects. For this work of articulation, I would argue that we need a combination of, on the one hand, analyses of subject-producing power accounted through careful histories, psychoanalysis, political economy, and cultural, political, and legal discourse analysis, and, on the other, genealogies of particular modalities of subjection that presume neither coherence in the formations of particular kinds of subjects nor equivalence between different formations. In other words, what is needed is the practice of a historiography quite different from that expressed by notions of cause and effect, accumulation, origin, or various intersecting lines of development, a historiography that emphasizes instead contingent developments, formations that may be at odds with or convergent with each other, and trajectories of power that vary in weight for different kinds of subjects. The work I am describing involves serious and difficult research, arduous thought, and complex theoretical formulations – it will not be conducive to easy polemics or slogans in battle. And it will add up neither to a unified and coherent notion of gender nor to a firm foundation for women's studies. But it might allow us to take those powerful founding and sustaining impulses of women's studies – to challenge the seamless histories, theories, literatures, and sciences featuring and reproducing a Humanism starring only Man – and harness them for another generation or two of productive, insurrectionary work" (2005: 131).

18 As Roland Barthes emphatically put it: "Interdisciplinary studies, of which we hear so much, do not merely confront already constituted disciplines (none of which, as a matter of fact, consents to leave off). In order to do interdisciplinary work, it is not enough to take a 'subject' (a theme) and to arrange two or three sciences around it. Interdisciplinary study consists in creating a new object, which belongs to no one" (1989 [1972]: 72).

19 Elaborating on the study of 'alethurgic forms', Foucault says in his first lecture on February 1, 1984: "Rather than analyzing the forms by which a discourse is recognized as true, this would involve analyzing the form in which, in his act of telling the truth, the individual constitutes himself and is constituted by others as a subject of a discourse of truth, the form in which he presents himself to himself and to others as someone who tells the truth, the form of the subject telling the truth. In contrast with the study of epistemological structures, the analysis of this domain could be called the study of "alethurgic" forms. . . . Etymologically, alethurgy would be the production of truth, the act by which truth is manifested. . . . On the basis of what discursive practices was the speaking, laboring, and living subject constituted as a possible object of knowledge (*savoir*)?" (2011: 3)

20 Much like the non-combinatory logic of the interdiscipline, Badiou terms as 'eventual site' an "entirely abnormal multiple; that is, a multiple such that none of its elements are presented in the situation. The site, itself, is presented, but 'beneath' it nothing from which it is composed is presented. As such, the site is not a part of the situation. I will also say of such a multiple that it is on the edge of the void, or foundational. . . . Just 'beneath' this multiple – if we consider the multiples from which it is composed – there is nothing, because none of its terms are themselves counted-as-one. . . . The border effect in which this multiple touches upon the void originates in its consistency (its one-multiple) being composed solely from what, with respect to the situation, in-consists. . . . One could call it a primal-one of the situation; a multiple 'admitted' into the count without having to result from 'previous' counts. It is in this sense that one can say that in regard to structure, it is an undecomposable term. . . . Since they are on the edge of the void, . . . they interrupt questioning according to combinatory origin" (2005 [1988]: 175).

21 Refer to the "Foreword" of Spivak's *An Aesthetic Education in the Era of Globalization*: "Training for the habit of the ethical can only be worked at through attending to the systemic task of epistemological engagement" (2012: 9).

References

Althusser, Louis. 1974. 'Philosophy and the Spontaneous Philosophy of the Scientists', in Gregory Elliot (ed.) (1990) *Philosophy and the Spontaneous Philosophy of the Scientists and Other Essays* (trans.) James H. Kavanagh (pp. 69–165). London, New York: Verso.

Apostel L., Berger G., Briggs A. and Michaud G. (eds.) 1972. *Interdisciplinarity: Problems of Teaching and Research in Universities*. Paris: OECD.

Badiou, Alain. 2005 [1988]. *Being and Event*. (trans.) Oliver Feltham. London, New York: Continuum.

Barry, Andrew and Born, Georgina. 2013. 'Introduction', in A. Barry and G. Born (eds.) *Interdisciplinarity: Reconfigurations of the Social and Natural Sciences* (pp. 1–56). London, New York: Routledge.

Barthes, Roland. 1989 [1972]. 'Research: The Young', in R. Barthes (ed.) *The Rustle of Language* (trans.) Richard Howard (pp. 69–75). Berkeley, Los Angeles: University of California Press.

Bell, Andrew. 1807 [1797]. *An Analysis of the Experiment in Education Made at Egmore Near Madras*, 3rd ed. London: Cadell and Davis.
———. 1808. *The Madras School, or Elements of Tuition*. London: Cadell and Davis.
———. 1823. *Mutual Tuition and Moral Discipline; or, Manual of Instructions for Conducting Schools*, 7th ed. London: G. Roake.
Bentham, Jeremy. 1843 [1816]. 'Chrestomathia', in John Bowring (ed.) *The Works of Jeremy Bentham*, Volume 8 (pp. 8–240). Edinburgh: William Tait.
Brown, Wendy. 2005 [1997]. 'The Impossibility of Women's Studies', in W. Brown (ed.) *Edgework: Critical Essays on Knowledge and Politics* (pp. 116–35). Princeton, NJ, Oxford: Princeton University Press.
Chari, Mridula. 2017. '35 Staff at Mumbai's TISS Are Fired Because of UGC Funding Ambiguity', *Scroll.in*. Available at https://scroll.in/article/832881/35staffatmumbaistissarefiredbecauseofugcfundingambiguity (accessed on 31 December 2017).
'Clarification by UGC'. 2017. Press Information Bureau. Available at http://pib.nic.in/newsite/erelease.aspx?relid=159507 (accessed on 31 December 2017).
Dasgupta, KumKum. 2017. 'Notice to JNU's Social Exclusion Centre Forged, Says UGC. Is There More to It?', *Hindustan Times*. Available at www.hindustantimes.com/opinion/noticetojnussocialexclusioncentreforgedsaysugcistheremoretoit/story (accessed on 31 December 2017).
Dasgupta, Priyanka. 2017. 'JU School of Women's Studies Staffers Brace for Uncertain Future', *The Times of India*. Available at http://timesofindia.indiatimes.com/city/kolkata/juschoolofwomensstudiesstaffersbraceforuncertainfuture/articleshow/57926340.cms (accessed on 31 December 2017).
Foucault, Michel. 2011. *The Courage of the Truth (The Government of Self and Others II)*. (ed.) Frederic Gros (trans.) Graham Burchell. Basingstoke: Palgrave Macmillan.
Golinski, Jan. 1998. *Making Natural Knowledge: Constructivism and the History of Science*. Cambridge: Cambridge University Press.
Gozzer, Giovanni. 1982. 'Interdisciplinarity: A Concept Still Unclear', *Prospects: UNESCO Quarterly Review of Education*, 12(3): 281–92.
Humboldt, Wilhelm von. 1810. 'On the Internal and External Organisation of the Higher Scientific Institutions in Berlin', in Andreas Flitner and Klaus Giel (eds.) (1982) *Works* (in German), Volume 4: *Writings on Politics and Education* (trans.) Thomas Dunlap (pp. 253–65). Darmstadt: Wissenschaftliche Buchgesellschaft. Available at germanhistorydocs.ghi-dc.org/sub_document.cfu?document_id=3642 (accessed on 31 December 2017)
Kant, Immanuel. 1979 [1799]. *The Conflict of the Faculties*. (trans.) Mary J. Gregor. New York: Abaris Books.
———. 1987 [1790]. *Critique of Judgment* (trans.) Werner S. Pluhar. Indianapolis, Cambridge: Hackett Publishing.
———. 1996 [1787]. *Critique of Pure Reason* (trans.) Werner S. Pluhar. Indianapolis, Cambridge: Hackett Publishing.

Klein, Julie Thompson. 1990. *Interdisciplinarity: History, Theory, Practice*. Detroit, MI: Wayne State University Press.
Kohler, Robert. 1981. 'Discipline History', in W. F. Bynum, E. J. Browne and R. Porter (eds.) *Dictionary of the History of Science* (p. 104). London: Palgrave Macmillan.
———. 1999. 'The Constructivists' Toolkit', *Isis*, 90: 329–31.
Lemaine, Gerard, Macleod, Roy, Mulkay, M. J. and Weingart, Peter. (eds.) 1976. *Perspectives on the Emergence of Scientific Disciplines*. The Hague: Mouton.
Marlowe, Christopher. 1965 [1604]. *The Tragical History of the Life and Death of Doctor Faustus*. (ed.) John D. Jump. London, New York: Routledge.
Minimum Course Curriculum for Undergraduate Courses Under Choice Based Credit System (2015). New Delhi: UGC.
Moran, Joe. 2002. *Interdisciplinarity*. London, New York: Routledge.
Mukul, Akshaya. 2013. 'UGC Faces Flak for Withdrawing Scheme for 32 Centres for Study of Social Exclusion and Inclusive Policies', *The Times of India*. Available at http://timesofindia.indiatimes.com/home/education/news/UGCfacesflakforwithdrawingschemefor32CentresforStudyofSocialExclusion (accessed on 31 December 2017).
Nietzsche, Freidrich. 1966 [1886]. *Beyond Good and Evil: Prelude to a Philosophy of the Future*. (trans.) Walter Kaufmann. New York: Vintage Books.
Nowotny, H., Scott, P. and Gibbons, M. 2001. *Re-Thinking Science: Knowledge and the Public in an Age of Uncertainty*. Cambridge: Polity Press.
O'Sullivan, Simon. 2010. 'Cultural Studies as Rhizome – Rhizomes in Cultural Studies', in Joe Parker and Ranu Samantrai (eds.) *Interdisciplinarity and Social Justice* (pp. 81–93). Albany: State University of New York Press.
Parker, Joe and Samantrai, Ranu. 2010. *Interdisciplinarity and Social Justice*. Albany: State University of New York Press.
Qazi, Musab. 2017. 'TISS Announces Closure of 3 Centres: Students Demand Answers', *Hindustan Times*. Available at www.hindustantimes.com/mumbainews/studentsaskforclarityaftertissannouncesclosureofthreecentres/story (accessed on 31 December 2017).
Ramakrishnan, Sushmitha. 2017. 'All for a name? JNU centre on UGC fund exclusion list', *The New Indian Express*. Available at www.newindianexpress.com/states/tamilnadu/2017/mar/17/allforanamejnucentreonugcfundexclusionlist1582297.html (accessed on 31 December 2017).
The Report of the Committee to Advise on Renovation and Rejuvenation of Higher Education. 2009. New Delhi: Ministry of Human Resource Development (MHRD), GoI.
Schaffer, Simon. 1990. 'States of Mind: Enlightenment and Natural Philosophy', in G. S. Rousseau (ed.) *Languages of Psyche: Mind and Body in Enlightenment Thought* (pp. 233–90). Los Angeles: University of California Press.
———. 2013. 'How Disciplines Look', in Andrew Barry and Georgina Born (eds.) *Interdisciplinarity: Reconfigurations of the Social and Natural Sciences* (pp. 57–81). London, New York: Routledge.

Sorkin, David. 1983. 'Wilhelm von Humboldt: The Theory and Practice of Self-Formation (*Bildung*)', *Journal of the History of Ideas*, 44: 55–74.

Spivak, Gayatri Chakravorty. 2008. *Other Asias*. Oxford: Blackwell Publishing.

———. 2012. *An Aesthetic Education in the Era of Globalization*. Cambridge, MA: Harvard University Press

XII Plan Guidelines for Establishment of Centres in Universities for Study of Social Exclusion and Inclusive Policy. 2012. New Delhi: UGC.

Part IV
Drafting manifestos for change

10 The commoditization of education

Prabhat Patnaik

I

One of the most striking features of the current Indian scenario is the commoditization of education, which means not only that the labour power of those who are the products of the education system becomes a commodity, but that the education itself that goes into the production of this commodity becomes a commodity. The education system becomes, in other words, a process for the production of a commodity (the labour power of those who receive education) by means of a commodity (the education they receive).

The question immediately arises: those who receive education have always sought employment, i.e. joined the labour market to sell their labour power. Their labour power, in other words, has always been a commodity. What difference does it make if the education that goes into the formation of this labour power itself now commands a price, instead of being provided virtually *gratis*? In other words, what difference does the commoditization of education make to the pre-existing situation? If anything, some may argue, it only streamlines the production of the final commodity, namely the labour power of the educated, apart from saving tax-payers' money, used up in providing education *gratis* to persons who use it to build their careers, for other more worthwhile purposes. So, why should one make a fuss over the commoditization of education?

The answer lies in the meaning of the term "commodity". *Not everything that is supplied for exchange ipso facto constitutes a commodity.* Karl Kautsky in his book *The Economic Doctrines of Karl Marx*, written in 1887 (and revised in 1903), at a time when he was the outstanding exponent of Marxism after Frederick Engels, makes an extremely important point about what constitutes a commodity – namely, that for the seller of the commodity it does not provide any use value, in the sense of satisfaction or utility, but constitutes exclusively an exchange value, i.e. command over a certain sum of money. (This perception of the "commodity" incidentally strikes at the very root of bourgeois economics, according to which everything exchanged in the market is supposed to be a source of "utility" for *both* the buyer and the seller.)

One can extend Kautsky's definition to say that, for the seller of a commodity, who thus perceives it only as an exchange value, the *input* used in its production also does not constitute any source of "satisfaction" or "utility". A steel manufacturer, for instance, does not derive any personal pleasure or satisfaction from the pig iron that goes into steel making; he looks at it entirely in terms of the money paid for it relative to its appropriateness for steel making, i.e. entirely in terms of how much of surplus in the form of money it will enable him to command in the market from the sale of the final product, steel.

When this stage is not reached, as, for instance, in the *jajmani* system in traditional India, we may at best have preliminary forms of commodity production, or imperfect and rudimentary commodity production, but not authentic commodity production. When we talk of commoditization of education, therefore, we are really talking about the conversion of education into an authentic commodity, where those who receive this input look upon it not as a source of pleasure, or of learning, or of cultivation of the mind, but exclusively in terms of the amount of money it can help the recipient to command in the market. Education is getting commoditized in India today in the sense that it is being seen, as pig iron in the above example, entirely in terms of the amount of exchange value that it will enable its recipient to command as a consequence of its being used as an input. And its supplier correspondingly attempts to provide this commodity called education, which is perfected to act as such an input, at a price that fetches him the maximum profit.

Now, this commoditization of education also means that the labour power which the "educated" sell on the market is getting refined too into an authentic commodity from the somewhat loose form it may have had earlier (of which being occasionally absent with impunity, some flexibility in the duration of the periods of break for tiffin or toilet etc. are examples). This authentic commoditization is the direct result of the hegemony of international finance capital, of the fact that the "educated" now sell their labour-power in a market dominated by international capital which sets the "norm". Little wonder then that our neoliberal rulers get so exercised over whether Indian universities figure in the top 100 of the world, according to some metropolitan agency. These ranking agencies, like the credit rating agencies, provide information to international capital about the quality of the labour power of the "educated" that they would be purchasing; and our

The commoditization of education 213

neoliberal rulers, keen to convert the country into an entity for provisioning the needs of international capital, get dismayed if the quality of its labour-power is "downgraded" (exactly the way they get dismayed when its credit rating gets "downgraded"). Needless to say, the neoliberal rulers are keen to expedite the process of commoditization of education to cater to the needs of international capital.

The question may be immediately asked: what is wrong with the commoditization of education? There are five obvious and immediate problems with it, all of which ultimately add up to the fact that it perpetuates, and dialectically accentuates, human unfreedom. The first and the most obvious is that education as a means of introduction to the grandeur of ideas is replaced by education as a means of money-making, *and this latter obsession is something that the recipients of education are coerced into internalizing by the immanent logic of commodity production.* This internalizing, however, is a loss not only at a personal level for those who so internalize, but also at the social level.

Secondly, a commodity by its very nature is a finished, packaged thing; indeed the more finished and packaged it is, the better it is supposed to be. Commoditized education therefore entails handing over packaged things called "learning" to the students, which necessarily precludes their asking any questions, being critical, engaging with the received ideas, and hence being creative and original. Commoditized education in short destroys creativity and originality. And the rot begins from school itself. When middle class parents (whose children are the only ones likely to be finishing schooling, even after seventy years of independence), express deep anguish that their child has obtained "only 98 percent" marks and not 100 percent, and when to prevent such a dire consequence they engage tutors to cram the maximum possible amount of "learning" into their children, we already have a concept of "education" as getting hold of a package and delivering it as completely as possible in the examination hall.

Illustrating what Marx had called the "fetishism of commodities", commoditized education which begins as an input into the production of the labour power of the educated, thus *turns human beings themselves into an input* (like transport) which carries a package called "education" from the classroom and the tutorial room to the examination hall; and the more undamaged, the less interfered with, the delivered package happens to be, the greater the reward for the delivery medium.

The third obvious problem with commoditized education is its total dissociation from any social sensitivity. Such education, in short, is intrinsically incapable of playing any social role, of creating in the minds of those receiving education any concern for the "human condition" in general, or any awareness of the lives of fellow human beings. The role of education in "nation-building", in inculcating in the minds of the young the values underlying the Indian Constitution itself, namely democracy, secularism, social and economic equality, gender equality and the transcendence of the caste-system, gets undermined.

This is not to suggest of course that all educated people in India have actually become devoid of these values; just that the education system itself ceases progressively to be the source of such values (and to the extent that capsules called "values" are dished out at the behest of some well-meaning minister as part of the curriculum, they also become mere lifeless things to be swallowed and regurgitated, if necessary, at examinations). If a person who presided over the 2002 pogrom against the Muslims in Gujarat can be acceptable, reportedly, to large numbers of professionals, who would be considered the most educated section in India, then that certainly says something about the current direction of our education system.

The fourth obvious problem with the commoditization of education is that even this commodity becomes available only to a few. It excludes the bulk of the people from access to it, and hence undermines substantive, as opposed to merely formal, equality of opportunity.[1] Substantive equality of opportunity can be said to prevail when the representation of various social groups within any selected set, say of doctors or academics or engineers or civil servants, is roughly in the same proportion as their representation in total population. To achieve substantial equality, therefore, affirmative action, like reservation in educational institutions and in jobs, for particular social groups for a certain period, becomes necessary. While this may superficially appear to be a violation of *formal* equality of opportunity, it is actually a means of achieving *substantive* equality of opportunity. Not that it can ever succeed in genuinely achieving substantive equality of opportunity, for that is not possible within the capitalist system with its perennial reserve army of labour and its inherent tendency towards inequality of income and wealth; but affirmative action does constitute an ameliorative step. And commoditized education entails a negation, even in principle, of the need for substantive equality of opportunity, since only those who can afford it, get to buy this commodity.

A facile argument is sometimes put forward against this position by government spokesmen who claim that as long as credit-finance is made available to anyone who is good enough to pursue education, there is no violation of equality of opportunity. This argument, however, is a facile one, both because not everybody in society is considered equally "creditworthy" by the financial system, and also because the ability to bear the risk of educating oneself through borrowed money, in an economy where there is no guarantee of employment, is non-existent as far as the poor are concerned. And if a State could guarantee full employment (in which case large-scale credit-financed education could be a conceivable option), then that State would not let education get commoditized in the first place.

Indeed the fifth obvious argument against the commoditization of education consists in the fact that the withdrawal of the State from funding education entails a worsening of "dualism" within the education system, between a few elite institutions and the vast numbers of underfunded, understaffed and poorly furnished institutions located in peripheral regions. This is already happening in India to an alarming extent: the contrast between the well-funded private educational institutions that are coming up, say around the nation's capital, on the one hand, and the miserably staffed, miserably housed, miserably funded provincial universities on the other, could not be greater.

We have, in short, two very distinct concepts of education in our context: one sees education as an activity which is entrusted by society to some people, who are funded by it, because the outcome of their labours in terms of advancing the frontiers of knowledge, cogitating over ways of removing the fault lines in society, generating social sensitivity among students, and producing what, following Antonio Gramsci, one might call the "organic intellectuals of the people", is considered essential for the progress of society and for the freedom of the human beings who constitute it. The other sees education as a package bought and sold in the market, which some people who can afford to pay for it, buy in order to enhance their money-making capacity. We are in this country in the process of making a transition from the first concept, which, notwithstanding the fact that it was never actually realized, at least informed the thinking on education, including even official thinking, to the second concept.

The people of the country will be ill-served by this transition. In the absence of a group of "organic intellectuals of the people", they would be forced either to reconcile themselves silently to the burden of their unfreedom, or to express themselves through sporadic bursts of unproductive anger – which would provoke retaliation on the part of the State that can only accentuate their unfreedom – or to fall prey to the inflammatory rhetoric of fascist upstarts that would push them towards mutual animosity and self-destruction. The recent ascendancy of communal-fascism in the country is *inter alia* a manifestation of this transition that is occurring in the sphere of education.

II

Commoditization of education and communal-fascism

Communal-fascism, like all fascism, invokes a specific type of nationalism as its ideological weapon. I use the term "specific type" advisedly: there is a pervasive tendency to see "nationalism" as one homogeneous category, which in my view is erroneous.[2] The "nationalism" that informed the anti-colonial struggles in countries like India in recent times and the "nationalism" that emerged in Europe after the Westphalian Peace Treaties in the seventeenth century are by no means identical. The latter kind of nationalism, which I would call "aggrandizing nationalism" was characterized by three crucial features, which were absent from the former. First, it always located an "enemy within", such as the Catholics in Northern Europe, the Protestants in Southern Europe, and the Jews everywhere. Secondly, it was imperialist from the very beginning, sanctioning a drive for territory, including above all "economic territory", all over the world. And thirdly, it put the "nation" above the "people"; the "people" were supposed to make sacrifices for the "nation" without expecting anything in return. This latter kind of nationalism, "aggrandizing nationalism", was taken over, according to Rudolf Hilferding, the eminent Marxist theorist and author of *Das Finanzkapital*, by finance capital when it emerged in the late nineteenth century, to constitute its core ideological prop. It reached its apogee under fascism in the thirties and hence created a revulsion in Left and liberal circles against itself. This revulsion persists to this day, and erroneously takes the form of opposing *all* nationalism, as if *all* nationalism is of the "aggrandizing" sort, which the anti-colonial nationalism, inclusive and secular by the very circumstances of its birth, was not.

The point of communal-fascism is that it performs a sleight-of-hand. It promotes an "aggrandizing nationalism", complete with all the three features described above, while pretending that it is no different from the anti-colonial nationalism of the freedom struggle, and claiming for it the prestige that such anti-colonial nationalism had enjoyed among the people. But in lieu of the anti-colonial struggle's idea of a "nation" whose *raison d'être* consists in bringing about an improvement in the lives of the people, "aggrandizing nationalism" demands sacrifices from the people for an entity called the "nation" which remains completely metaphysical. And since this latter "nationalism" cannot confront metropolitan capital, but, rather, on the contrary, promotes the interests of such capital and of the domestic corporate-financial oligarchy that has become closely integrated with it, it talks not of *economic* nationalism but of *cultural* nationalism. The invoking of such "nationalism" therefore amounts to demanding an endorsement from the people for a mix of neoliberal economic policies and a dominance of *Hindutva*. The realization of such a demand, however, requires a subservience of the educated segments of the population, a destruction of reason on their part, so that the metaphysical concept of the "nation" can be filled with whatever pebbles the *Hindutva* forces choose to fill it with: eating beef is "anti-national", keeping *karwachauth* is "national", *saraswativandana* is "national", vegetarianism is "national", speaking up for civil rights in Kashmir is "anti-national", criticizing the Modi government is "anti-national", and so on. The term "nationalism" in short, by being detached from the people and elevated above them, becomes an empty box which can be filled by any content in accordance with the whims of the communal-fascists.

For this to be acceptable, however, the scope for rational discourse in society must be eliminated. To a certain extent this can be achieved through terror, not just of the State but also of vigilante groups, who invade people's privacy and take the law into their own hands. But these methods are insufficient. A cultivation of social insensitivity among the educated, their immersion in a world of self-absorbed money-making – in short, precisely the kind of effect that commoditization of education produces – becomes necessary. *Commoditization of education and the growth of communal-fascism go hand in hand*. International finance capital finds a worthy ally in the communal-fascist elements, which rally people around a particular concept of nationalism, according to which national interests are best served not by contesting but by attracting international capital, and promoting a "cultural nationalism" that is synonymous with *Hindutva*.

It is not surprising that the communal-fascists at the helm of the central government are all for commoditizing and privatizing education, especially higher education; for inviting foreign universities to set up campuses here, so that the output of such institutions is more easily marketable internationally; for eliminating politics from campuses so that the students "concentrate on their studies", i.e. become exclusively pre-occupied with absorbing the capsules called "education" that are dished out to them; for introducing "discipline" into student life so that they do not ask too many questions; and for destroying such institutions in the country where students still are in the habit of critical thinking.

Let me dwell briefly on this last point. I mentioned earlier that the paradigm of a commoditized education system is a relatively new one for the country, that the country is making a transition from an earlier system, where even the official perception of education recognized and even foregrounded its social role, to one where it is supposed only to produce the requisite labour-power for the market. The earlier perception, carried over from the days of the anti-colonial struggle, emphasized public funding of education, kept education in public institutions inexpensive, allowed for affirmative action in the form of reservations for marginalized groups, gave adequate importance to the humanities and social sciences, and provided scope for dissent, diversity, criticism and the practice of student politics on the campus. I do not wish to glorify it, but on the whole it provided intellectual space to students and teachers, and desisted from regimentation, both from the market forces and from vigilante groups backed or tolerated by the academic administration. Within this paradigm a number of institutions of excellence came up; and not surprisingly these are the very institutions whose students are in the forefront of the opposition to communal-fascism at present.

The one thing in common between all the institutions where students have been active in resisting the ascendancy of communal-fascism, whether it is Jawaharlal Nehru University, or Delhi University, or Jadavpur University, or University of Hyderabad, or Pune Film Institute, or the Fine Arts Department of Baroda's M.S. University, is that they are all publicly funded institutions. This is not to suggest that students from private universities have been unaffected by the goings on, but their participation has been fairly mute. And such participation as there has been, for instance, by way of joining demonstrations, has reportedly been opposed, not without effect, by their respective university administrations. The relatively freer atmosphere prevailing in the publicly funded educational institutions, has been conducive to student activism there.

There has been an additional factor at work. The policy of reservations for the *Dalits* and "other backward classes", practiced in these publicly funded institutions, has changed the social mix among the students there, resulting, on the one hand, in the emergence of a group of extremely articulate, effervescent and militant students coming from these marginalized segments, and, on the other, a greater degree of sensitivity towards the conditions of these marginalized segments among the other students. Publicly funded educational institutions, not all of them but some who have not yet been choked through a curtailment of funding, by providing scope for such interaction and for greater freedom of thought and expression, have been sites of struggle for the upholding of democracy and secularism. Not surprisingly they have been the ones facing attacks from the communal-fascist elements backed by the central government. And they have also been the ones where some voices against neoliberalism and the hegemony of finance capital have been raised in the past and continue to be raised till today.

There is in short a convergence of interest, between globalized finance capital and the domestic communal-fascist elements, in destroying whatever free space exists in publicly funded educational institutions. This is sought to be achieved directly, by changing the nature of these institutions themselves and introducing greater regimentation there through the appointment of hand-picked hatchet-men with little academic distinction as their administrative heads; it is also sought to be achieved through the more general policy of privatizing and commoditizing the entire educational system itself.

A view is often expressed that the contemporary phenomenon of globalization is an instrument of social progress, that it strengthens the advance towards democracy and inclusiveness, and has the effect of restraining the appeal of narrow-minded, bigoted, exclusivist and inward-looking ideological positions. This is an erroneous view. True, large-scale violence against people cannot be practiced in any country today without the world knowing and doing something about it; but a more quiet and silent fascism from what the thirties and the forties had seen not only can prevail with impunity today, but is even advantageous from the point of view of globalized finance. The convergence of interest between globalized finance, on the one hand, and communal-fascism, on the other, in the Indian case only illustrates this point.

III

On reviving higher education

The preceding discussion suggests that a necessary condition for reviving higher education in the country is to ensure that it remains predominantly publicly funded and allows space for students and teachers to think and express themselves freely without fear of State repression or attacks by vigilante groups. There is, however, a substantial private sector in the sphere of higher education, consisting not only of philanthropic institutions, and minority institutions falling under the purview of Article 30 of the Constitution, but also of commercial outfits that have mushroomed in recent years, which often deny their own commercial status by arguing that the surplus they earn through these institutions are all ploughed back to the same institutions. Even if the public institutions are strengthened henceforth, this large private sector which has come into being cannot just be wished away. What is minimally necessary with regard to this private sector is enforcing on them the reservation policy followed in public institutions, and also State control over their fees, admission procedure, curriculum, course content, and recruitment policy, subject of course to the condition that the rights guaranteed under Article 30 must not be violated. (An effort by the LDF government in Kerala in 2006 to introduce such control through legislation ran into trouble with the judiciary, on the grounds that the legislation violated Article 30.)

The argument usually adduced against the public sector in the economic sphere, namely that it is "inefficient", which itself lacks validity, cannot even be raised in the sphere of higher education – since the finest institutions of higher education in the country are mainly in the public sector. The argument that would be used instead is that the public sector lacks the resources for spending on higher education. This, however, is a spurious argument. India is among the lowest-taxed countries in the world, with a tax-GDP ratio that is lower than not just European countries but even the United States, despite the latter's proverbial hostility to "large government". Raising larger resources to spend on education in general (where even the target of 6 percent of GDP suggested by the Kothari Commission years ago has remained a far cry!), and higher education in particular, should not therefore be difficult for a government committed to it.

But larger public expenditure alone will not prevent the juggernaut of commoditization of the sphere of higher education. The Russian proverb "What is cooked in the kitchen is not decided in the kitchen" is particularly apposite in the case of higher education: what happens in this sphere is determined by the overall trajectory of development in the economy as a whole. And if the current economic trajectory is pursued, then a spread of public institutions providing inexpensive higher education would result more in the subsidization of a group of self-serving members of a would-be elite than in the creation of a socially sensitive group of "organic intellectuals of the people". This is not the place to outline what such an alternative economic trajectory should look like; but, at the very least, as even Social Democratic economists like Anthony Atkinson and Thomas Piketty have been arguing, income and wealth inequalities, which have been growing alarmingly in India, must be brought down. This would require not just capital controls (to prevent capital flight in response to the measures for reducing income and wealth inequality), but also a system of compensation to the State

The commoditization of education

by those members of the trained and educated set who choose to emigrate abroad because of the lure of higher salaries. I believe that even this limited objective of reducing income and wealth inequalities cannot be realized unless it becomes part of a dialectics of transition to an altogether different social order transcending neoliberal capitalism. But whether or not this belief is shared by others, there should at least be an agreement on this egalitarian objective itself.

Notes

1 The argument which follows in this paragraph has been developed at greater length in Prabhat Patnaik, "Affirmative Action and the Efficiency Argument" in Zoya Hasan and Martha Nussbaum ed., *Equalizing Access: Affirmative Action in Higher Education in India, United States and South Africa*, Oxford University Press, New Delhi, 2012.
2 The argument that follows has been developed at greater length in Prabhat Patnaik, "Two Concepts of Nationalism" in Rohit Azad, Janaki Nair, Mallarika Sinha Roy and Mohinder Singh eds., *What the Nation Really Needs to Know: The JNU Nationalism Lectures*, Harper Collins, New Delhi, 2017.

11 Neoliberal savagery and the assault on higher education as a democratic public sphere

Henry A. Giroux

Across the globe, a new historical conjuncture is emerging in which attacks on higher education as a democratic institution and on dissident public voices in general – whether journalists, whistleblowers, or academics – are intensifying with alarming consequences. Neoliberalism or market fundamentalism has put higher education in its cross hairs and the result has been the ongoing transformation of higher education into an adjunct of rich and powerful corporate interests.[1] Marina Warner has rightly called these assaults on higher education, "the new brutalism in academia" (Warner 2014). It may be worse than she suggests. In fact, the right-wing and corporate defence of the neoliberal dismantling of the university as a site of critical inquiry is more brazen and arrogant than anything we have seen in quite some time.

Just as democracy appears to be fading in the United States, so is the legacy of higher education's faith in and commitment to democracy. Higher education is increasingly abandoning its role as a democratic public sphere, as it aligns itself with corporate power and market values as well as the dictates of the surveillance state and military-industrial complex (Giroux 2007), while at the same time succumbing to a range of right-wing religious and political attacks. Instead of being a space of critical dialogue, analysis, and interpretation, it is increasingly defined as a space of consumption, where ideas are validated in instrumental terms and valued for their success in attracting corporate and government funding. As the culture of research is oriented towards the needs of corporate culture, faculty and students find their work further removed from the language of democratic values and their respective roles modelled largely upon entrepreneurs and consumers.

The dire threat neoliberalism poses to higher education and its commitment to democracy has been intensified under the presidency of Donald Trump. Under the Trump administration, the dark winds of fascism have returned to the United States. Educating young people with the tools of critical thinking, a robust historical consciousness, and the spirit of democracy is now viewed as dangerous to the neo-fascists and alt-right groups who have been emboldened by Donald Trump's authoritarian populism. In the face of expressions of ultra-nationalism, racism and xenophobia in populist movements across the United States, education is increasingly being used to produce, circulate and legitimate neo-fascist idioms of hate and violence. For instance, there has been a notable increase in white supremacists mobilizing on college campuses in the form of holding events, handing out racist posters and leaflets, and organizing rallies calling for defending white power and promoting "the heritage, identity and future of people of European descent".[2] Right-wing institutes, such as the David Horowitz Freedom Center, are heavily funded by conservative billionaires and are now flooding American campuses with defamatory posters linked to a vast array of websites that purport to identify left-academics as terrorists because of their criticisms of Israeli policies towards Palestinians (Mitchell 2018). These right-wing trolls have mastered the new media and present a clear and palpable threat to both non-tenured professors on the left as well as to academic freedom.

At the same time, conservative billionaires such as the Koch brothers are flooding college campuses with money in order to establish conservative institutes, think tanks, endowed chairs, academic courses, and student groups that promote neoliberal views. Alex Kotch, a writer for the *International Business Times*, reports that Koch foundations "gave over $51 million to higher education institutions in 2016".[3] What the Koch brothers deeply understand is that education is not only a site of intense struggle, it is also a sphere where matters of desire, identity, consciousness and agency are shaped. They understand that education is at the heart of politics, and have been highly successful in undermining the public's faith in higher education as a crucial space for nurturing democratic values. While Hannah Arendt (2003: 159) did not address directly the importance of critical pedagogy as being central to politics, she did grasp that in its absence monstrous deeds are often committed and that such deeds have less to do with an abstract notion of evil than with the production of civic illiteracy, thoughtlessness, and an "authentic inability to think", make judgments, and assume a sense of social and ethical responsibility. This is a lesson the left has not fully grasped yet.

As corporate power gets more concentrated and is less regulated by the Trump administration, right-wing politicians and ideologues have been emboldened in their efforts to turn universities into training centres, equipping young people with skills that will enable them to work in the global economy and instrumental values that undermine their capacity to become critically literate citizens indispensable to a democracy. For instance, Wisconsin legislators have passed a bill that basically weakens tenure so as to remove its protections for faculty. Lawmakers in Missouri are trying to pass legislation that would outlaw tenure to faculty members hired after January 1, 2018 (Zamudio-Suaréz 2017). House Bill 266 was introduced by State Rep. Rick Brattin, a Republican who argues that tenure is un-American and that the purpose of education is to prepare young people for real world jobs. In this stripped down version of the mission of education, knowledge-acquisition amounts to nothing more than training students for the workforce while denuding academics of any power in terms of faculty governance or in working in disciplines that promote democratic values, civic literacy, and critical thinking. Legislation being considered in Iowa would end tenure both for existing faculty and for those hired in the future (Charis-Carlson and Petroski 2017). In Arizona, conservative lawmaker Rep. Bob Thorpe proposed House Bill 2120, which would ban "virtually every college event, activity or course which discusses social justice, skin privilege, or racial equality. Violating the law would allow the state of Arizona to levy multimillion-dollar fines and penalties against universities – removing at least 10% of their state aid" (King 2017).

These attacks on higher education, tenure and academic freedom are not new, but under the power of right-wing Republicans who now control most state legislators and all branches of the United States government they will accelerate. But, of course, the assault on critical thinking, civic literacy, and the work of critical and public intellectuals does not only happen in spaces where formal schooling takes place. Such assaults are increasingly waged on those public spheres and cultural apparatuses actively engaged in producing knowledge, values, subjectivities and identities through a range of media and sites. This applies to a spectrum of creative spaces including art galleries, museums, diverse sites that make up screen culture, and various elements of mainstream media (Giroux 2011). What the apostles of neoliberalism have learned is that the educational force of culture and its diverse public apparatuses can be a threat to established orthodoxy. Such apparatuses can produce modes of public pedagogy that can change how people view the world, and that pedagogy can be dangerous because it holds the potential for not only creating critically engaged students, intellectuals and artists but can strengthen and expand the capacity of the imagination to think otherwise in order to act otherwise, hold power accountable, and imagine the unimaginable.

Since the 1970s, the United States has been in the grip of a neoliberal ideology that believes that the market should shape all social relations, that profit making and unabashed consumption are the essence of citizenship, and that the social contract is a pathology. Couple these ideological beliefs with the notion that economics should drive politics, that everything should be privatized, that markets must regulate themselves, the welfare state should be dismantled, and that self- interest is the highest ideal along with the competitive attitudes it promotes; and a society is created ripe for authoritarianism. The consequences of such a poisonous ideology, set of values, policies and mode of pedagogy are hard to miss.

Money has corrupted politics at the state and national levels. Civic culture and civic literacy have been undermined paving the way for the erosion of any sense of public trust, truth and shared citizenship. The aesthetics of vulgarity now drives the spectacle that makes up politics and degrades the culture of entertainment. The assault on public and higher education has produced a new kind of stupidity in which the line between fact and fiction is blurred, giving rise to empty and deceptive slogans, fake news and post-truth. As language is emptied of any substantive meaning, moral relativism provides support for a culture of immediacy, self-absorption, and privatization. Is it any wonder that Trump rode to victory in the presidential race to mark the collapse of any commanding democratic vision in America?

As education in all public spaces comes under attack, we are witnessing an attack on memory, the production of policies of extermination, and a terrifying new horizon in which politics is removed from any sense of justice and the ethical imagination. Totalitarian forms are with us once again, and as Hannah Arendt once observed "the aim of totalitarian education has never been to instill convictions but to destroy the capacity to form any" (2001: 468).

What we see unfolding in the United States and in many European countries is a planned desiccation of universities not because they are failing, but because they are public. This is not just an attack on political liberty but also an attack on dissent, critical education and any public institution that might exercise a democratizing influence on the nation. In this case, the autonomy of institutions such as higher education, particularly public institutions, is threatened as much by state politics as by corporate interests. How else to explain in neoliberal societies such as the U.S., U.K. and India the massive defunding of public institutions of higher education, the raising of tuition for students, and the closing of areas of study that do not translate immediately into profits for the corporate sector?

The hidden notion of politics that fuels this market-driven ideology is on display in a more Western-style form of neoliberalism in which the autonomy of democratizing institutions is under assault not only by the state but also by the rich, bankers, hedge fund managers, and the corporate elite. In this case, corporate sovereignty has replaced traditional state modes of governance that once supported higher education as a public good. That is, it is now mostly powerful corporate elites who despise the common good and who – as the South African Nobel Prize winner in literature J.M. Coetzee points out – "reconceive of themselves as managers of national economies who want to turn universities into training schools equipping young people with the skills required by a modern economy" (Coetzee 2013). Viewed as a private investment rather than a public good, universities are now construed as spaces where students are valued as human capital, courses are defined by consumer demand, and governance is based on the Walmart model of labour relations. For Coetzee, this attack on higher education, which not only is ideological but also increasingly relies on the repressive, militaristic arm of the punishing state, is a response to the democratization of the university that reached a highpoint in the 1960s all across the globe. In the past twenty years, the assault on the university as a centre of critique, as also on intellectuals, student protesters, and the critical formative cultures that provide the foundation for a substantive democracy, has only intensified (ibid.).

Coetzee's defence of education provides an important referent for those of us who believe that the university is nothing if it is not a public trust and social good; that is, a critical institution infused with the promise of cultivating intellectual insight, the civic imagination, inquisitiveness, risk-taking, social responsibility and the struggle for justice. Rather than defining the mission of the university by mimicking the logic of the market in terms of ideology, governance and policy, the questions that should be asked at this crucial time in American history might raise the following issues: how might the mission of the university be understood with respect to safeguarding the interests of young people at a time of violence and war, the rise of a rampant anti-intellectualism, the emerging spectre of authoritarianism, and the threat of nuclear and ecological devastation? What might it mean to define the university as a public good and democratic public sphere rather than as an institution that has aligned itself with market values and is more attentive to market fluctuations and investors than educating students to be critically engaged citizens? Or, as Zygmunt Bauman and Leonidas Donskis write: "how will we form the next generation of . . . intellectuals and politicians if young people will never have an opportunity to experience what a non-vulgar, non-pragmatic, non-instrumentalized university is like?" (2013: 139) As public spheres – once enlivened by broad engagements with common concerns – are being transformed into "spectacular spaces of consumption" (Miles 2001: 116), financial looting, the flight from mutual obligations and social responsibilities have intensified and resulted in not only a devaluing of public life and the common good, but also a crisis of the radical imagination, especially in terms of the meaning and value of politics itself (Kurlantzick 2013).

What I am suggesting is that the crisis of higher education is about much more than a crisis of funding, an assault on dissent, and a remaking of higher education as another institution designed to serve the increasing financialization of neoliberal societies; it is also about a crisis of memory, agency and the political. As major newspapers all over the country shut down and the media become more concentrated in the hands of fewer mega corporations, higher education becomes one of the few sites left where the ideas, attitudes, values and goals can be taught that enable students to question authority, rethink the nature of their relationship with others in terms of democratic rather than commercial values, and take seriously the impending challenges of developing a global democracy.

The apostles of predatory capitalism are well aware that no democracy can survive without an informed citizenry. Consequently, they implement a range of policies to make sure that higher education will no longer fulfil such a noble civic task. This is evident in the business models imposed on governing structures, defining students as customers, reducing faculty to Wal-Mart workers, imposing punishing accounting models on educators, and expanding the ranks of the managerial class at the expense of the power of faculty.

As politics is removed from its political, moral and ethical registers – stripped down to a machine of social and political death for whom the cultivation of the imagination is a hindrance – commerce becomes the heartbeat of social relations, and the only mode of governance that matters is one that rules Wall Street. Time and space have been privatized, commodified and stripped of human compassion under the reign of neoliberalism. We live in the age of a new brutalism marked not simply by an indifference to multiple social problems, but also defined by a kind of mad delight in the spectacle and exercise of violence and what the famed film director, Ken Loach, has called "conscious cruelty" (Blandy 2016). America is marked by a brutalism that is perfectly consistent with a new kind of barbaric power, one that puts millions of people in prison, subjects an entire generation to a form of indentured citizenship, and strips people of the material and symbolic resources they need to exercise their capacity to live with dignity and justice.

For those of us who believe that education is more than an extension of the business world and the new brutalism, it is crucial that educators, artists, workers, labour unions, and other cultural workers address a number of issues that connect the university to the larger society while stressing the educative nature of politics as part of a broader effort to create a critical culture, institutions, and a collective movement that supports the connection between critique and action and redefines agency in the service of the practice of freedom and justice. Let me mention just a few.

First, educators can address the relationship between the attack on the social state and the transformation of higher education into an adjunct of corporate power. As Stefan Collini has argued, under the regime of neoliberalism, the "social self" has been transformed into the "disembodied individual", just as the notion of the university as a public good is now repudiated by the privatizing and atomistic values at the heart of a hyper-market-driven society.[4] Clearly, in any democratic society, education should be viewed as a right, not an entitlement. This suggests a reordering of state and federal priorities to make that happen. Much needed revenue can be raised by putting into play even a limited number of reform policies in which, for instance, the rich and corporations would be forced to pay a fair share of their taxes, a tax would be placed on trade transactions, and tax loopholes for the wealthy would be eliminated. It is well-known that the low tax rate given to corporations is a major scandal. For instance, the Bank of America paid no taxes in 2010 and "got $1.9 billion tax refund from the IRS, even though it made $4.4 billion in profits" (Snyder 2013).

In addition, academics can join with students, public school teachers, unions and others to bring attention to wasteful military spending that, if eliminated, could provide the funds for a free public higher education for every qualified young person in the country. While there is growing public concern over rising tuition rates along with the crushing debt students are incurring, there is little public outrage from academics over the billions of dollars squandered on a massive and wasteful military budget and arms industry. As Michael Lerner has pointed out, democracy needs a Marshall Plan in which funding is sufficient to make all levels of education free, while also providing enough social support to eliminate poverty, hunger, inadequate health care, and the destruction of the environment. There is nothing utopian about the demand to redirect money away from the military, the powerful corporations, and the upper 1 percent.

Second, addressing these tasks demands a sustained critique of the transformation of a market economy into a market society along with a clear analysis of the damage it has caused both at home and abroad. Power, particularly the power of the largest corporations, has become more unaccountable and "the subtlety of illegitimate power makes it hard to identify" (George 2014: 8). Disposability has become the new measure of a savage form of casino capitalism in which the only value that matters is exchange value. Compassion, social responsibility, and justice are relegated to the dustbin of an older modernity that is now viewed as either quaint or a grim reminder of a socialist past. This suggests, as Angela Davis, Michelle Alexander, and others have argued, that there is a need for academics and young people to become part of a broader social movement aimed at dismantling the repressive institutions that make up the punishing state. The most egregious example of this is the prison-industrial complex, which drains billions of dollars in funds to put people in jail when such funds could be used for expanding public and higher education. We live in a country in which the police have become militarized, armed with weapons from the battlefields of Iraq and Afghanistan (Nelson 2000; Balko 2013). The United States prison system locks up more people than any other country in the world, and the vast majority of them are people of colour (Alexander 2010). Moreover, public schools are increasingly modelled after prisons and are implementing policies in which children are arrested for throwing peanuts at a school bus or violating a dress code (Giroux 2012). The punishing state is a dire threat to both public and higher education and democracy itself. The American public does not need more prisons; it needs more schools, free health services, and a living wage for all workers.

Third, academics, artists, journalists and other young people need to connect the rise of subaltern, part-time labour – or what we might call the Walmart model of wealth and labour relations – in both the university and the larger society to the massive inequality in wealth and income that now corrupts every aspect of American politics and society. No democracy can survive the kind of inequality in which

> the 400 richest people . . . have as much wealth as 154 million Americans combined, that's 50 percent of the entire country [while] the top economic 1 percent of the U.S. population now has a record 40 percent of all wealth and more wealth than 90 percent of the population combined.
>
> (DeGraw 2011)

Senator Bernie Sanders provides a statistical map of the massive inequality at work in the United States. In a speech to the U.S. Senate, he states:

> Today, Madam President, the top 1% owns 38% of the financial wealth of America, 38%. And I wonder how many Americans know how much the bottom 60% own. They want people to think about it. . . . The answer is all of 2.3%. . . . [T]here is one family in this country, the Walton family, the owners of Wal-Mart, who are now worth as a family $148 billion. That is more wealth than [of] the bottom 40% of American society. . . . That's distribution of wealth. That's what we own. In terms of income, what we made last year, the latest information that we have in terms of distribution of income is that from 2009–2012, 95% of all new income earned in this country went to the top 1%. . . . [W]hich tells us that when we talk about economic growth, which is 2%, 3%, 4%, whatever it is, that really doesn't mean all that much because almost all of the new income generated in that growth has gone to the very, very, very wealthiest people in this country.
>
> (Sanders 2014)

Democracy in the United States, and many other countries, has been hijacked by a free-floating class of ultra-rich and corporate powerbrokers and transformed into an oligarchy "where power is effectively wielded by a small number of individuals" (McKay 2014). At least, this is the conclusion of a recent Princeton University study, and it may be much too moderate in its conclusions.

Fourth, academics need to fight for the rights of students to get a free education, health care, and public transportation. They need to be provided with educational institutions and opportunities that offer them a formidable and critical education not dominated by corporate values. Education as the practice of freedom must provide opportunities for students to become critical and autonomous citizens, capable of self-reflection and the ability to call power into question. Moreover, they need to have a say in the shaping of their education and what it means to expand and deepen the practice of freedom and democracy. In many countries such as Germany, France, Denmark, Cuba and Brazil, post-secondary education is free because these countries view education not as a private right, but as a public good. Yet, in some of the most advanced countries in the world such as the United States and Canada, young people, especially from low income groups have been excluded from getting a higher education and, in part, this is because they are left out of the social contract and the discourse of democracy. They are the new disposables who lack jobs, a decent education, hope, and any semblance of a life better than the one their parents inherited. They are a reminder of how finance capital has abandoned any viable vision of a better future for young people. Youth have become a liability in the world of high finance, a world that refuses to view them as an important social investment.

Fifth, there is a need to oppose the ongoing shift in power relations between faculty and the managerial class. Too many faculty are now removed from the governing structures of higher education and as a result have been abandoned to the misery of impoverished wages, excessive classes, no health care, and few, if any, social benefits. As political scientist Benjamin Ginsburg points out, administrators and their staff now outnumber full time faculty, producing two-thirds of the increase in higher education costs in the past twenty years. This is shameful and is not merely an education issue but a deeply political matter, one that must address how neoliberal ideology and policy has imposed on higher education an anti-democratic governing structure.

Sixth, it is important to stress once again that education must be viewed not simply as a practice endemic to schooling but happens across society through a range of cultural apparatuses extending from the mainstream media to various aspects of screen culture. Education is at the centre of politics because it is crucial to how agency is formed, how people view themselves and their relations to others. Educators and other cultural workers must acknowledge that domination is as much ideological as it is economic and structural. This means taking on the challenge of embracing the symbolic and ideological dimensions of struggle as part of the struggle against oppression and domination. Pierre Bourdieu speaks to this issue in his comment that the "left has underestimated the symbolic and pedagogical dimensions of struggle and have not always forged appropriate weapons to fight on this front" (1998: 11). The late Stuart Hall goes further and argues that the left "has no sense of politics being educative, of politics changing the way people see things" (Williams 2012). Democracies cannot survive without informed citizens and as Gayatri C. Spivak has pointed out, "Without the general nurturing of the will to justice among the people, no just society can survive" (Spivak 2016). If pedagogy is to become central to politics, that is, if it is to make the political more pedagogical, educators not only will have to gain a critical understanding of how everyday troubles connect to wider systemic and structural issues, but will also have to learn how to translate such issues to a broad and diverse audience in a language that is both accessible and in which people can recognize the nature of their problems. People have to invest something of themselves in the discourses, narratives and stories progressives and educators want them to hear.

Educators need to launch pedagogical campaigns aimed at dismantling the common sense logic of neoliberalism: people are only consumers, government is the enemy, the market should govern all of social life, social bonds are a pathology, self-interest is the highest virtue, and last but not least, the market should govern itself. University faculty must join together and find ways to press the claims for economic and social justice and do so in a discourse that is aimed at multiple audiences and is both rigorous and accessible. Universities need to defend not only the idea of the university as a democratic public sphere, but also faculty as public intellectuals capable and willing to question authority, hold power accountable, and be critical of existing affairs. They must relentlessly pose questions such as: what should be the role of the university in a democracy? What responsibility does a university have in a time of terror and emerging authoritarianism? What constitutes a university that operates in the spirit of a democratic public sphere? How might universities create multiple spaces and sources in which students can combine the search for truths with the need to address the imperatives of economic, social and political justice? How might a university create governing structures that are democratic rather than excessively top-down, reductively managerial, and wedded to an audit culture? What policies can be put in place by faculty, administrators and students which guarantee full employment, autonomy and power to faculty? What might it mean to create a vocabulary that defines the university as a democratic public sphere, refuses the notion that students are consumers, values research and knowledge as more than a commercial activity, and views faculty as critically engaged and public intellectuals? What kind of conditions can be fostered in higher education that promotes research as a public good rather than a private gain?[5]

Finally, the fight to transform higher education cannot be waged strictly inside the walls of such institutions by faculty and students alone. As radical social movements more recently in Spain, Portugal and India have made clear, there is a need for new social and political formations among faculty, unions, young people, cultural workers, and most importantly social movements, all of which need to be organized in part for the defence of public goods and what might be called the promise and ideals of a radical democracy. Any struggle against the anti-democratic forces that are mobilizing once again all over the world must recognize that power is not global and politics is local.

A financial elite operates now in the flow and international spaces of capital, and has no allegiances to nation states and can impose its financial will on these states as we have seen recently in some European countries. Any viable form of resistance must address this new power formation and think and organize across national boundaries. Resistance on a global level is no longer an option, it is a necessity.

Neoliberal societies now further the shadow of the authoritarian corporate state, but the future is still open. The savagery of casino capitalism has undermined commanding visions rooted in the principles of economic and social justice. The totality of market relations has produced a massive retreat from any viable notion of civic education. Not only is politics being emptied out of any substantive value, the concept of truth is under siege in an age when the vocabulary of "fake news" and "post-truth" are peddled by politicians as legitimate terms rather than slogans designed to legitimate lies, deceits and falsifications – all of which is now embodied in the words and actions of Donald Trump. The age of greed and selfishness is reaching its endpoint in societies organized around the production of violence, hate, exclusion and rampant corruption by the financial elite. The time has come to develop a political language in which civic values and social responsibility – and the institutions, tactics and long-term commitments that support them – become central to invigorating and fortifying a new era of civic engagement. Real education and critical thinking must be embraced as part of a moral and political practice that allows young people and others to become immune to neoliberal seductions of privatization, consumerism, and unchecked greed. Education as the practice of freedom must be viewed as a struggle over a renewed sense of social agency, and part of a broader struggle for an impassioned international social movement with the vision, organization, and set of strategies capable of challenging the neoliberal nightmare that now haunts the globe and empties out the meaning of politics and democracy.

Notes

1 On neoliberalism, see David Harvey, *The New Imperialism* (New York: Oxford University Press, 2003); David Harvey, *A Brief History of Neoliberalism* (Oxford: Oxford University Press, 2005); Wendy Brown, *Edgework* (Princeton: Princeton University Press, 2005); Henry A. Giroux, *Against the Terror of Neoliberalism* (Boulder: Paradigm Publishers, 2008); Manfred B. Steger and Ravi K. Roy, *Neoliberalism: A Very Short Introduction* (Oxford University Press, 2010); Gerard Dumenil and Dominque Levy, *The Crisis of Neoliberalism* (Cambridge: Harvard University Press, 2011); Jonathan

Rutherford and Sally Davison, eds. *The Neoliberal Crisis* (London: Lawrence Wishart 2012); David Harvey, *Seventeen Contradictions and the End of Capitalism* (New York: Oxford University Press, 2014); Wendy Brown, *Undoing the Demos: Neoliberalism's Stealth Revolution* (New York: Zone Books, 2015); David Whyte and Jörg Wiegratz, eds., *Neoliberalism and the Moral Economy of Fraud* (New York: Routledge, 2017).

2 These activities have been documented by a number of sources; see Scott Jaschik, "Supremacists on Campus", *Inside Higher Education* (August 14, 2017). Online: www.insidehighered.com/news/2017/08/14/white-supremacy-turning-campus-speeches-and-leaflets (last accessed on 31 December 2017)

3 Alex Kotch, "Charles Koch Gave $50 Million to Higher Ed In 2016. What Did He Buy?" *International Business Times* (December 8, 2017). Online: www.ibtimes.com/political-capital/charles-koch-gave-50-million-higher-ed-2016-what-did-he-buy-2626269 (last accessed on 31 December 2017). The definitive work on the power and reach of the Koch brothers and their reach in American politics can be found in Jane Mayer, *Dark Money: The Hidden History of the Billionaires Behind the Rise of the Radical Right* (New York: Anchor, 2017).

4 These two terms are taken from Stefan Collini, "Response to Book Review Symposium: Stefan Collini, What Are Universities For", *Sociology 1–2* (February 5, 2014), Online: http://soc.sagepub.com/content/early/2014/02/14/0038038513518852 (last accessed on 31 December 2017)

5 Many of these issues are taken up in Christopher Newfield, *The Great Mistake: How We Wrecked Public Universities and How We can Fix Them* (Baltimore: Johns Hopkins University, 2016).

References

Alexander, Michelle. 2010. *The New Jim Crow*. New York: The New Press.
Arendt, Hannah. 2001. 'Ideology and Terror: A Novel Form of Government', in *The Origins of Totalitarianism*. New York: Houghton Mifflin Harcourt.
———. 2003. *Responsibility and Judgment*. (ed.) Jerome Kohn. New York: Schocken.
Balko, Radley. 2013. *Rise of the Warrior Cop: The Militarization of America's Police Forces*. New York: Public Affairs.
Bauman, Zygmunt and Donskis, Leonidas. 2013. *Moral Blindness: The Loss of Sensitivity in Liquid Modernity*. Cambridge: Polity Press.
Blandy, Fran. 2016. 'Loach Film on Shame of Poverty in Britain Moves Cannes to Tears', *Yahoo News*, May 13. Available at www.yahoo.com/news/loach-film-shame-poverty-britain-moves-cannes-tears-150546810.html (accessed on 31 December 2017).
Bourdieu, Pierre. 1998. *Acts of Resistance*. (trans.) Richard Nice. New York: Free Press.
Charis-Carlson, Jeff and Petroski, William. 2017. 'Iowa Lawmaker Looking to End Tenure at Public Universities', *Des Moines Register*, 12 January. Available at www.desmoinesregister.com/story/news/education/2017/01/12/iowa-lawmaker-looking-end-tenure-public-univerisities/96460626/ (accessed on 31 December 2017).

Coetzee, J. M. 2013. 'JM Coetzee: Universities Head for Extinction', *Mail & Guardian*, 1 November. Available at http://mg.co.za/article/2013-11-01-universities-head-for-extinction (accessed on 31 December 2017).
Collini, Stefan. 2014. 'Response to Book Review Symposium: Stefan Collini, What Are Universities For', *Sociology*, 1–2, February 5). Available at http://soc.sagepub.com/content/early/2014/02/14/0038038513518852 (accessed on 31 December 2017).
DeGraw, David. 2011. 'Meet the Global Financial Elites Controlling $46 Trillion in Wealth', *Alternet*, 11 August. Available at www.alternet.org/story/151999/meet_the_global_financial_elites_controlling_$46_trillion_in_wealth (accessed on 31 December 2017).
George, Susan. 2014. 'State of Corporations: The Rise of Illegitimate Power and the Threat to Democracy', in Nick Buxton (ed.) *State of Power 2014: Exposing the Davos Class*. Transnational Institute and Occupy.com. Available at www.tni.org/sites/www.tni.org/files/download/state_of_power-6feb14.pdf (accessed on 31 December 2017).
Giroux, Henry A. 2007. *The University in Chains: Confronting the Military-Industrial-Academic Complex*. New York: Routledge.
———. 2011. *On Critical Pedagogy*. New York: Bloomsbury.
———. 2012. *Youth in a Suspect Society*. New York: Palgrave.
King, Shaun. 2017. 'Arizona Lawmaker Proposes New Bill Banning Classes or Events Discussing Social Justice on College Campuses', *The New Yorker*, 13 January. Available at www.nydailynews.com/news/national/king-rep-ban-social-justice-events-arizona-schools-article-1.2945382 (accessed on 31 December 2017).
Kurlantzick, Joshua. 2013. *Democracy in Retreat*. New Haven: Yale University Press.
McKay, Tom. 2014. 'Princeton Concludes What Kind of Government America Really Has, and It's Not a Democracy', *Popular Resistance*, 16 April 16. Available at www.policymic.com/articles/87719/princeton-concludes-what-kind-of-government-america-really-has-and-it-s-not-a-democracy (accessed on 31 December 2017).
Miles, Steven. 2001. *Social Theory in the Real World*. Thousand Oaks, CA: Sage.
Mitchell, W. J. T. 2018. 'The Trolls of Academe: Making Safe Spaces Into Brave Spaces', *Los Angeles Review of Books*, January 5. Available at https://lareviewofbooks.org/article/the-trolls-of-academe-making-safe-spaces-into-brave-spaces/ (accessed on 5 January 2018).
Nelson, Jill. (ed.) 2000. *Police Brutality*. New York: Norton & Company.
Newfield, Christopher. 2016. *The Great Mistake: How We Wrecked Public Universities and How We Can Fix Them*. Baltimore: Johns Hopkins University Press.
Sanders, Bernie. 2014. 'A Threat to American Democracy', *RSN*, 1 April. Available at http://readersupportednews.org/opinion2/277-75/22830-focus-a-threat-to-american-democracy (accessed on 31 December 2017).
Snyder, Michael. 2013. 'You Won't Believe Who Is Getting Away with Paying Zero Taxes While the Middle Class Gets Hammered', *InfoWars.com*,

19 February. Available at www.infowars.com/abolish-the-income-tax-you-wont-believe-who-is-getting-away-with-paying-zero-taxes-while-the-middle-class-gets-hammered/ (accessed on 31 December 2017).

Spivak, Gayatri C. 2016. 'A Bit on Theory', *The European*, 15 June. Available at www.theeuropean-magazine.com/gayatri-c-spivak/10243-theory-and-education# (accessed on 31 December 2017).

Warner, Marina. 2014. 'Dairy', *The London Review of Books*, 36: 17. Available at www.lrb.co.uk/v36/n17/marina-warner/diary (accessed on 31 December 2017).

Williams, Zoe. 2012. 'The Saturday Interview: Stuart Hall', *The Guardian*, 11 February. Available at www.guardian.co.uk/theguardian/2012/feb/11/saturday-interview-stuart-hall (accessed on 31 December 2017).

Zamudio-Suaréz, Fernanda. 2017. 'Missouri Lawmaker Who Wants to Eliminate Tenure Says It's "Un-American"', *The Chronicle of Higher Education*, 12 January. Available at www.chronicle.com/article/Missouri-Lawmaker-Who-Wants-to/238886 (accessed on 31 December 2017).

12 The university in question

Ari Sitas

Academics, students and support staff the world over are in the midst of deeply emotive struggles in what has been identified as an assault on many fronts inaugurated by fiscal and political circuits of power on their (and, our) spaces' integrity.[1]

Whereas the fiscal assault attempted to treat the university as a corporate entity and to instil managerial structures that enforce productivity and a peculiar notion of excellence (Noble 2003), the political assault originated from movements and parties of authoritative restoration, trampling over areas of dissent and diversity.[2] The key problem has been that the struggles have been reactive and defensive and that they lack an alternative vision of what a University ought to be in the twenty-first century.[3]

The most unremarkable consequence has been the valorization of the past as a better time, better at least than what the contemporary pugilists in power insisted or have already forced into place – which is not entirely untrue but it is a capitulation to older forms of elitism and exclusion (Readings 1997).

At the same time, movements and more specifically student movements tend to bring forth new normative orientations, and there is much to be learnt about alternatives from students in India (JNU, Hyderabad) and South Africa (let alone Latin America, North Africa and so on). But their narratives and their moral underpinnings are still in formation and it would be premature to ascribe a closure to them or, worse, to read them as most scholars do, as a manifestation of our preferred theorist from Fanon to Ambedkar.

What we can do, though, is to look seriously at the university as a specific kind of institution that needs careful analysis. I would like to therefore outline twelve points that have to be taken up with some urgency if we are to seriously challenge the free-marketeers, the bean counters and the new cultural and authoritarian commissars:

1 Societies cluster people together to achieve certain goals – this is Sociology 101 – and these clusterings are institutions; and to continue this train of thought, the University is a remarkable institution which preceded the emergence of a capitalist world economy and which has been re-fashioned to play a vital role within it (Mielants 2007).
2 Knowledge and know-how were not and are not the sole preserve of the university and the system it operated within, but the university has established the right to be the arena that operates their formal accreditation.[4]
3 As an institution there is a tension between its character, its function, its knowledge project and its practices – how these are handled. These tensions reproduce and transform its authority in any social formation.
4 Due to the predominance of European powers in the long period between the fifteenth and late nineteenth centuries, the evolving university system in the world inherited the character, function, knowledge project and practices of the European experience.[5]
5 Its character: it involves a withdrawal from the world and its contaminations that survived from its old theocratic forms where the hermeneutic study of scripture was encouraged and civilizing languages were learnt – a withdrawal that was reinforced by the emerging scientific spirit of the seventeenth and eighteenth centuries, that used this space of withdrawal to argue its necessary autonomy from the world of the clergy and immediate power (Colish 1997: 267). Peerage trumped interest and therefore the origins of academic freedom to research and disseminate are to be found there.[6]
6 Its function: to create the quality of mind necessary to populate the steering and professional strata of society and therefore play a defining role in class and elite formation in society and to reproduce itself as such a marker (Soares 2002; Anderson 2009; Deresiewicz 2014). This was not only about the quality of mind of its graduates but also about the regimes of rule and discipline to groom such an elite,[7] which always carried a tension between an older apprenticeship system and a hierarchy of control – a tension at the heart of the bureaucratization of the system (McDonald 1995).
7 Its knowledge project: the academic community had to research what it taught, and research networks were created out of a range

of horizontal activities embedded in scientific and knowledge networks that were trans-institutional and transnational and often quite "deviant" – for example, although Descartes was highly respected in scientific and philosophical networks he had to be in exile in Amsterdam, Bernier who was his kindred spirit was in touch with the Mughal world of science, philosophy and medicine as much as the English, German and Dutch thinkers (Ari Sitas et al. 2013). Once the knowledge interest got normalized as a public good, the networks of science and scholarship and not the specific institution (that is, "My University") became the definers of, in the words of Kuhn, "normal science" (Kuhn 1962[1974]).

8 Practices: within each institution there are further tensions that finally shape its ethos and the way it works and educates students (Bourdieu 1984 [1990]). There is the perennial dissonance that each student and younger academic is considered to be a site of reason and yet the hierarchical professorate demands minimal challenge – rather it demands patriarchy, loyalty and mimicry (Deresiewicz op. cit.). There is also a dissonance between the relational dissemination of knowledge and the bureaucratic consensus that all should be equal as specific rule-guided "cases". The internal tensions and the tensions between autonomy and compliance create sites of contestation. In that we find differential traditions of freedom of expression and the right to serve non-elite interests and communities.[8]

9 By the late nineteenth century, Britain established its centrality not only as an economic but also as a symbolic imperial node (in culture, education and technology). Inter-imperial competition led to a transformed curriculum to articulate a civilizational prowess – the Canon (the synergy of Shakespeare and Newton), with France and Germany following suit, and the idea of it being the centre of excellence and progress got deeply entrenched (Sillars 2005). By implication, all colonial spaces had to be validated in and through its circuits of scholarly power (Hobsbawm 1987).

10 It is fair to say that the majority of the world's idea of and institutions of higher learning and the very university system itself owed in design and purpose to the European model. This is true of settler societies like the USA (Harvard with 9 students was established in 1636, the Rio de Janeiro University as a college for armaments and fortifications in 1792 or through British East India Company, the University of Calcutta in 1857 and the Imperial University of Peking in 1898). Most of the universities in the world during the

colonial and postcolonial period reflect a direct influence of the model (Barrington 2006).
11 Similarly, the creation and reproduction of elites and class differentiation relied on a world system of higher education whose apex was the imperial metropole. It was a sign of explicit distinction if from India you studied in Cambridge and if from Martinique, you studied in Paris (Selingo 2016).
12 Since the late nineteenth century pressure was exerted on the university systems of Europe and North America to become more relevant to corporate and state interests and a vast array of applied disciplines proliferated – including explicit work for the military-industrial complex in the West and the East (Rose 1985)! Furthermore the rise of scientific management in society, the separation of mental and manual labour in mass production and the need of new types of professionals in industry, commerce and the state, stimulated the enlargement of tertiary sectors – whose absolute demographic explosion occurred in the 1950s and 1960s (Braverman 1974; Burawoy 1996). The idea that universities and disciplines became servants of power gained traction in the 1960s (Baritz 1960).

It could be argued that there are exemplary models we should not lose: Harvard, for example, and its private endowments give it a remarkable peer-based autonomy and it is the arch-model of excellence and liberal education;[9] the Soviet Union and China, for example, created more inclusive systems but constrained the development of revolutionary science and critical literacy (Graham 2002); that Jawaharlal Nehru University created a remarkable system of diversity, autonomy and tolerance (Batabyal 2015); that the German system has had the best mix of high technology and philosophy and so on (Anderson 2004). There is much to be preserved and defended, the issue is about vision. Without it, it degenerates into a list of preferences.

There are a few questions that the contemporary fortunes of the university force on us, and with specific reference to its intersections with the state and the market. Would it be possible to transform the character of the university out of its monastic character and make it worldly and more engaged without surrendering its autonomy? Can the system operate outside the cycles of elite formation and class and other forms of differentiation? Is it an anachronism? Can a new knowledge project be found that is about human flourishing rather than about trade, production and war? Can a democratic ethos supplant the hierarchical systems of academic patronage and can freedom of experimentation and expression be guaranteed?

The only emancipatory project of modernity has been the search for a balance between freedom and equality, ideas that originated outside any university system (Sitas 2016). Has the university been a site for their enhancement and realization, or has it been the thinking workshop of unfreedoms?

Most certainly, the role, function and vision of the university will generate multiple contestations and pressures. The strongest pressure for change will involve a "cultural turn": whether this arises out of "decolonial" networks with a popular democratic leaning, or movements of authoritative restoration (a Huntingtonian civilizational argument with elite imperatives), and in the ways in which this re-organizes its character, curriculum and outcomes. It will go deeper than a semantic shift, adding a cultural appellation/identity to the word 'University'. The results will be uncertain: they could lead to more authoritarianism or they could lead to a restorative moment. In the latter case, it could be uncovering traditions and know-hows buried by colonial arrogance. This will no doubt lead in turn to polarizations over the "authentic" and "inauthentic", the "identity" (national, ethnic, religious, civilizational) and elite drivers versus the people-centred levellers.

The second pressure will be about knowledge as such: there will be an increasing divide between those who do not believe in the "universal" and who by implication will be searching for the "multi-versal" and connect with mobilizations around the first set of pressures. They will be emphasizing culturally sensitive ways of cultivating diversity of knowledges (and could even be critical of the essentialisms of some of the "cultural turn" protagonists). They will be in tension with those who would be arguing that the problem with the West's knowledge project was not universalism as such, but a false and self-serving version of it that needs a serious challenge and correction.

The third pressure will be around the "technological/productive forces" imperative. This change, it has been severally argued, is already underway which has meant that the University (and knowledge/science) is the driver of the new industrial revolution (third or fourth, it remains undecided). The mix between artificial intelligence, on the one hand, and the genetic and digital revolutions, on the other, are and will be transforming knowledge, work, life and our very mortality itself. This pressure to change will not be about rankings and mere mimicry of the West, but a drive to proactively embrace the new frontier. It will transform in a rapid way both our idea of education, disciplinary boundaries, professions and the labour market. The university "as is" will be seen as a bumbling dinosaur.

The fourth will be a continuation of the social justice imperative that defined the post-second world war period within the student movement everywhere, but to it would be added more aspects of historical forms of derogation from class, caste, gender, race, sexual preference and many more that are being added to our imaginary. There will be pressures for the redefinition of its vision, mission or relevance; there will also be attempts to break down the moat that separates the citadels of knowledge and the broader society. There would be pressures to do things differently, more dialogical in terms of broader society, more rewards for talent and not privilege. As long as there remain broader structures and institutions that produce inequality in a capitalist world and/or country, these pressures will rise and fall in effervescence.

The fifth will be an attempt to deepen the managerial and fiscal logic of the tertiary education sector. An intensification of the minutest patterns of performance is still possible and so are its concomitant resistances. New indicators of 'fitness' between what one does and what is demanded of one might proliferate through educational experts, and most certainly much of the academic activity could be outsourced, as the producers of knowledge and teaching have been turned into "cost to employer" categories. Unimaginable as yet but new areas of contestation will create new demands for alternative reward and measurement systems, until the university resembles more of a logistics warehouse rather than a supermarket.

Of course each one of us will be at the confluence of such pressures and finding meaning in their interstices and between their magnetic fields. Yet, unless the transformation and reconfiguration of the world's socio-economy is achieved, the university will continue being a serious source of social differentiation and inequality.

Notes

1 See Noam Chomsky (2011) Academic Freedom and the Corporatized University, Public Lecture: University of Toronto. Also, Nicolaus Mills (2012), The Corporatization of Higher Education. *Dissent*. Fall. Also for in-depth studies, see Geiger R. L. (2004), *Knowledge and Money, Research Universities and the Paradox of the Marketplace*. Stanford: Stanford University Press; and Berman E. P. (2012), *Creating the Market University: How Academic Science Became an Economic Engine*. Princeton and Oxford: Princeton University Press.

2 The assault on a range of institutions in India and the replacement of a democratic ethos based on tolerance about diversity and caste and its gradual supplanting with a Hindu-centric intellectual project is a case in point.

3 Save, of course, utopian views of what the digital revolution will accomplish, for example, Manuel Castells (2001), *The Internet Galaxy*: Oxford University Press.
4 See the fascinating study of the seventeenth century in England by Christopher Hills (1972), *The World Turned Upside Down: Radical Ideas During the English Revolution*, Harmondsworth: Penguin.
5 All theories of modernization converge on this point from Shlomo Eisenstadt.
6 See A. Sitas et al (2013), *Gauging and Engaging Deviance 1600–2000*, Delhi: Tulika Press, on articulatory deviance through the last 400 years.
7 Of course Pierre Bourdieu's work on the French Academy has been illustrative of these patterns of power and elite/class formation: see (1979/1990) *Reproduction in Education, Society and Culture* (London: Sage) and his (1984/1990) *Homo Academicus*, London: Polity Press. See also C. Wright Mills's work on elite formation, the middle-class and the Academy; *The Power Elite* (1956); *White Collar* (1951) and *The Sociological Imagination* (1959).
8 During the heyday of the anti-Apartheid struggle many universities in South Africa decided to transform their mandates of "relevance" with the University of the Western Cape trying to make itself a People's University with a clear anti-establishment agenda. See Gregory Anderson's (2002), *Building a People's University in South Africa: Race, Compensatory Education, and the Limits of Democratic Reform* (Bern: Peter Lang International Publishers).
9 Not only has this been a tremendous resource plus, but it is also punted as a successful investment model: see Mebane T Faber and Eric W Richardson (2011), *The Ivy Portfolio: How to Invest Like the Top Endowments and Avoid Bear Markets*, New Jersey: John Wiley, April 5, 2011

References

Anderson, Gregory. 2002. *Building a People's University in South Africa: Race, Compensatory Education, and the Limits of Democratic Reform*. Bern: Peter Lang International Publishers.

Anderson, Robert D. 2004. 'Germany and the Humboldtian Model', in *European Universities from the Enlightenment to 1914*. Oxford: Oxford University Press. Available at DOI:10.1093/acprof:oso/9780198206606.003.0004 (accessed on 31 December 2017).

———. 2009. *Universities and Elites in Britain since 1800*. Cambridge: The University Press.

Baritz, Loren. 1960. *Servants of Power: A History of the Use of Social Science in American Industry*. Middletown, CT: Wesleyan University Press.

Barrington, Lowell W. (ed.) 2006. *After Independence: Making and Protecting the Nation in Postcolonial and Postcommunist States*. Ann Arbor: The University of Michigan Press.

Batabyal, Rakesh. 2015. *JNU: The Making of a University*. New Delhi: Harper Collins.

Berman, E. P. 2012. *Creating the Market University, How Academic Science Became an Economic Engine*. Princeton, NJ, Oxford: Princeton University Press.
Bourdieu, Pierre and Passeron, Jean-Claude. 1979[1990]. *Reproduction in Education, Society and Culture*. (trans.) Richard Nice. London: Sage.
———. 1984[1990]. *Homo Academicus*. (trans.) Peter Collier. London: Polity Press.
Braverman, Harry. 1974. *Labor and Monopoly Capital· The Degradation of Work in the 20th Century*. New York: Monthly Review Press.
Burawoy, Michael. 1996. 'A Classic of Its Time', *Contemporary Sociology* 25(3): 296–9.
Castells, Manuel. 2001. *The Internet Galaxy: Reflections on the Internet, Business and Society*. Oxford: Oxford University Press.
Chomsky, Noam. 2011. 'Academic Freedom and the Corporatized University'. Public Lecture: University of Toronto.
Colish, Marcia L. 1997. *Medieval Foundations of the Western Intellectual Tradition, 400–1400*. New Haven: Yale University Press.
Deresiewicz, A. 2014. *Excellent Sheep: The Miseducation of an American Elite*. New York: Simon and Schuster.
Faber, Mebane T. and Eric W. Richardson. 2011. *The Ivy Portfolio: How to Invest Like the Top Endowments and Avoid Bear Markets*. Princeton, NJ: John Wiley.
Geiger, R. L. 2004. *Knowledge and Money, Research Universities and the Paradox of the Marketplace*. Stanford: Stanford University Press.
Graham, Loren. 2002. *Science and the Soviet Social Order*. Cambridge: Harvard University Press.
Hills, Christopher. 1972. *The World Turned Upside Down: Radical Ideas During the English Revolution*. Harmondsworth: Penguin.
Hobsbawm, Edward. 1987. *The Age of Empire, 1874–1915*. London: Weidenfeld and Nicolson.
Kuhn, Thomas S. 1962[1974]. *The Structure of Scientific Revolutions*. Chicago: University of Chicago Press.
McDonald, Keith M. 1995. *The Sociology of Professions*. London: Sage.
Mielants, Eric. 2007. *The Origins of Capitalism and the 'Rise of the West'*. Philadelphia: Temple University Press.
Mills, C. Wright. 1951 [2002]. *White Collar: The American Middle Classes*. Oxford, New York: Oxford University Press.
———. 1956 [2000]. *The Power Elite*. Oxford, New York: Oxford University Press.
———. 1959 [2000]. *The Sociological Imagination*. Oxford, New York: Oxford University Press.
Mills, Nicolaus. 2012. 'The Corporatization of Higher Education', *Dissent*, Fall.
Noble, David F. 2003. *Digital Diploma Mills*. Cambridge, MA: Harvard University Press.

Readings, Bill. 1997. *The University in Ruins*. Cambridge, MA: Harvard University Press.
Rose, Michael. 1985. *Industrial Behaviour: Theoretical Development since Taylor*. Harmondsworth: Penguin Books.
Selingo, Jeffrey J. 2016. 'Our Dangerous Obsession with Harvard, Stanford and Other Elite Universities', *The Washington Post*, 5 April. Available at www.washingtonpost.com/news/grade-point/wp/2016/04/05/our-dangerous-obsession-with-harvard-stanford-and-other-elite-universities/?utm_term=.665392cecb5e (accessed on 31 December 2017).
Sillars, Stuart. 2005. *Shakespeare and the Victorians*. Oxford: Oxford University Press.
Sitas, Ari. 2016. 'Freedom's Blind Spots: Figurations of Race and Caste in the PostColony', *South African Review of Sociology*, 47(4): 121–31.
Sitas, Ari et al. 2013. *Gauging and Engaging Deviance 1600–2000*. Delhi: Tulika Press.
Soares, Joseph A. 2002. *The Power of Privilege: Yale and America's Elite Colleges*. Palo Alto: Stanford University Press.

13 Revolutionary critical pedagogy
Staking a claim against the macrostructural unconscious[1]

Peter McLaren

Critical pedagogy exists today as precariously as a shabby lean-to room added to a typical American hall-and-parlour house. I'm referring to the type of house that formed the basic English prototype for the classic American building we see everywhere in New England and on the East Coast. If the hall-and-parlour house represents education in the main, then we critical educators are as rare as hen's teeth, shunted to the rear of the house, squatters huddled under a slanted roof, wearing fingerless gloves, clutching our tin cups of broth, spearing biscuits and dreaming of the day when we will become an official part of the architecture of democracy.

Those of us who practice revolutionary critical pedagogy, who comprise the night shift of critical pedagogy, are more marginalized still. Our push for democracy in U.S. schools is drowned out by the clamour of the parlours and chambers being enlarged above to make room for more policies such as No Child Left Behind, Race to the Top or even the current Common Core. Charter schools, while making up only a fraction of the overall schools in the country, are more accepted into the floor plan than are public schools in communities struggling with unemployment and urban infrastructure damage. And what happens when students exit those floor plans and enter into the university system? Here students enter a more ominous structure because they are given the appearance of having some autonomy over the process of their learning, of having some control of the production of knowledge and the formation of their own political subjectivity. Yet here, alas, wisps of consumer whimsy disguised as truth trickle out of the smokestacks of knowledge production; intellectual chloroform wafts from corporate furnaces towering over the entire system, anesthetizing young brains and putting dreams into deep sleep.

Life since Year Zero of the Capitalocene to the advent of techno-eco systems and their toxic and eutrophicating chemicals has not been a pleasant ride. Soon we will be fracking the noosphere of human thought in our lecture halls, making Freire's critique of banking education seem utterly tame. Teachers' work will be routinized and rationalized to that of stoop labourers (as Henry Giroux would put it) weeding celery fields. As far as job satisfaction goes within our inherited system of reactionary meritocracy, a Walmart cashier or a Best Buy clerk would feel more fulfilled. As any awake teacher is aware, we live at a time of intensified race and class warfare in U.S. society. The crisis is epidemic and readily visible in our schools. As each generation tries to move forward on the path to liberation, we are held back, ensepulchred in the vault of hubris like insects frozen in amber, while the trees are filled with green whispers of perturbation.

The world is being transformed into a single mode of production and a single global system and bringing about the integration of different countries and regions into a new global economy and society (Robinson 2004, 2014, 2016b). As William I. Robinson notes, the revolution in computer and information technology and other technological advances have helped emergent transnational capital to achieve major gains in productivity and to restructure, "flexibilise", and shed labour worldwide. This, in turn, has undercut wages and the social wage and facilitated a transfer of income to capital and to high consumption sectors around the world that provided new globalized flexible market segments fuelling growth. A new capital-labour relation emerged that was based on the deregulation, informalization, deunionization and the subordination of labour worldwide. More and more workers have swelled the ranks of the "precariat" – a proletariat existing in permanently precarious conditions of instability and uncertainty. In saying this, we need to recognize that capitalist-produced social control over the working-class remains in the hands of a single powerful state – what Robinson (2004, 2014, 2016a, 2016b) calls the core institution of the transnational state that serves the interests of the transnationalist capitalist class. This transnational capitalist class (TCC), according to Robinson, constitutes a polyarchy of hegemonic elites which trade and capital have brought into increasingly interconnected relationships and who operate objectively as a class both spatially and politically within the global corporate structure. This corporate structure has congealed around the expansion of transnational capital owned by the world bourgeoisie. Robinson here is referring to transnational alliances of owners of the global corporations and private financial institutions who control the worldwide means of production and manage – through the consolidation of the transnational corporate-policy networks – global rather than national circuits of production. Robinson describes these groups as operating in clusters scattered throughout the globe, clusters that cohere and increasingly concentrate their wealth through mergers and acquisitions. This transnational capitalist class struggles for control over strategic issues of class rule and how to achieve regulatory order within the global capitalist historic bloc. According to Robinson, there are clear empirical indicators that transnational capital is integrating itself throughout the globe and some of these include the spread of TNCs, the sharp increase in foreign direct investment, the proliferation of mergers and acquisitions across national borders, the rise of a global financial system, and the increased interlocking of positions within the global corporate structure. Robinson essentially argues that capitalism is now participating in a global epochal shift in which all human activity is transformed into capital. All social relationships are becoming privatized as part of the global circulation of capital.

I remember my "Junior Fellow" days at Massey College in Toronto, a site of higher learning patterned after All Souls College, University of Oxford, that reproduced and maintained the cognitive command structures of the Canadian ruling elite. Swaddled in my academic gown (required for all meals) I would drink port at high table dinners (mainly to distract me from the smell of wood polish) with brown-nosed boffins and beanpole and bemused graduates from Upper Canada College who seemed to have been born with a charismatic self-possession and system-loyal élan much like the votaries of capitalism that taught them. These slick-witted harbingers of a capitalist technofuture, this microclass of the Canadian power elite, would captivate us with topsy-turvy and scintillating stories of their champagne-drenched lives that flowed effortlessly from their mirth-filled prime of life, forcing those of us who had shaved their adolescent faces in the porcelain basins of working-class apartments to palisade our dreams behind looming towers of regret.

Later in life I was fortunate enough to be able to replant my bread crumb memories in new, subversive soil away from the imperialist nostalgia of the Canadian haute bourgeoisie. Out of the rubble of the world-shaking revolution of 1968 had emerged counter-memories that helped some of us to challenge our sabotaged lives and reorganize patterns of political subjectivization and resistance. True, many of these counter-narratives were captured in a sound-byte rebelliousness and expressed in guerrilla-style readymades, but the zeitgeist of revolution was unceasing in its ability to illuminate the hierarchies of power and privilege that served to stabilize the social system. Those memories were still there in the 1980s when I needed them. It was this history that helped me to shake off the cigar and brandy days of my 'higher' learning. Today I don't need a barstool nostalgia or acid kickback to dial back the years and remember the counter-narratives that guided my life in 1968. The red bones of my memories suffice and there is enough foot room in my mind to find the right ones. And there is also the raised part of my forehead courtesy of the Metropolitan Police flashlights my skull encountered repeatedly in a jail cell when I was nineteen.

The macrostructural unconscious

As Peter Hudis and other Marxist humanists have argued, the drive to increase material wealth is *not* the *fundamental* problem. The fundamental problem is the drive to increase value – which is not the same as material wealth. It is important to understand that wealth is a physical *quantity* that has limits to its expansion whereas value (i.e., surplus value or profit) is a non-physical quality that can be expanded indefinitely. The creation of more millionaires does not mean there will be less poor; the truth is more likely to be the reverse.

In our struggles alongside our many comrades – ecosocialist, anarchist, socialist feminist, autonomist Marxist, and Marxist humanist – we must work together to fight the transnationalist capitalist state in all of its hydra-headed relations of exploitation and alienation by developing a philosophy of praxis.

In their struggle for a social alternative to capitalism's value form of labour, revolutionary critical educators have challenged the lissome grandeur of postmodern theory and its fear of universal values and its inevitable retreat behind the tombstones of a sepulchral bargain-bin secularism. Whether revolutionary critical pedagogy's push for a socialist alternative will make an impact on the field of education in the near future is unclear, especially at a time in which right-wing populism and fascism continue to predominate across the political horizon of the country.

It is acutely painful to reflect upon the tragic irony of the current crisis of education that leads Stan Karp (2011) to characterize it as follows:

> If you support testing, charters, merit pay, the elimination of tenure and seniority, and control of school policy by corporate managers you're a 'reformer'. If you support increased school funding, collective bargaining, and control of school policy by educators you're a 'defender of the status quo'.

Largely as a result of huge marketing campaigns in the corporate media, it is the ideological right-wing that now claims the mantle of reformer, and progressive teachers and defenders of public schooling have been placed on the defensive. The right-wing educational reform movement, so dangerous to our democratic pretensions, must erelong bear potential surplus value returns for the capitalist class. That is the whole point. Critically minded educators are not so easily fooled and we will not meekly and fruitlessly submit to the tenor of the times.

Decades ago I sounded a little-heeded alarm that urban education in the U.S. increasingly was susceptible to the intentions of neoliberal capitalism and a jaundiced corporate-infused perspective. Today, in a world where capitalism has monopolized our collective imagination as never before, befouled our bodies through a frenzied pursuit of narcotizing consumption and turned education itself into a subsector of the economy, such a remark would be read by most critical educators as a gross understatement. Because today, more than at any other time in human history, the perils of capitalism have been exposed. It is no longer controversial among many of us in the teaching profession to acknowledge that "governments seek to extend power and domination and to benefit their primary domestic constituencies – in the U.S., primarily the corporate sector" (Chomsky 2013). The contradictions that for so long have been held in check by the violent equilibrium of market regulation have unchained themselves and as a consequence the mythic unity of capitalism and democracy has been exposed as a trussed-up fraud.

Yet in the academy few have chosen to speak about the crisis of democracy and instead are self-admiringly recapitulating all the articles they wrote before getting tenure, that is, before they decided to overhaul what is left of the pursuit of knowledge so that it fits better into the corporate brand of their institution. They even might be working on university-Pentagon joint partnerships on crowd control or cyber warfare. The good professors don't bother to offer up any excuses for not jumping into the public fray other than maintaining that they are still collecting "data" and aren't ready to make any judgment calls about politics.

As I have written elsewhere about some of the professional researchers that I have met in the academy over the past twenty years:

> Many of my academic colleagues, looking for some final vantage point from which to interpret social life, remain politically paralyzed, their studied inaction resulting from a stubborn belief that if they wait long enough, they surely will be able to apprise

themselves of a major, messianic, supra-historical discourse that will resolve everything. Presumably this ne plus ultra discourse will arrive on the exhausted wings of the Angel of History! There seems to be some naïve belief that a contemporary codex will eventually be announced (no doubt by a panjandrum at an Ivy League university) which will explain the quixotic mysteries and political arcana of everyday life. At this moment intellectuals will have the Rosetta Stone of contemporary politics in their possession, enabling them to know how to act decisively under any and all circumstances. Establishment academics under the thrall of technocratic rationality act as if the future might one day produce a model capitalist utopia in the form of an orrery of brass and oiled mahogany whose inset spheres and gear wheels, humming and whirring like some ancient clavichord melody, will reveal without a hint of dissimulation the concepts and practices necessary to keep the world of politics synchronized in an irenic harmony. All that would be necessary would be to keep the wheelworks in motion.

(McLaren 2008: 474–5)

The tendrils of capitalism's poisonous vine are spreading into all the spaces and virtual spaces of potential capital accumulation and we need cadres of teachers to speak out and to create spaces where their students can assume roles as razor-tongued public instigators for the social good. Globalized finance capitalism is the most widespread authoritarian structure in the history of civilization, giving the rich even greater riches and forcing the dispossessed to set up markets on moonlit streets to augment their exiguous incomes. We might be living in what is now called the "age of greed" but we should not be fooled that the current crisis of capital is linked mainly to the greed of corporate capitalists captured by Hollywood figures such as Gordon Gekko, since we believe that it is endemic to the system of capitalism itself.

The free-market economy is championed as the protector of democracy, like the fierce Chinese guardians or warrior attendants in a Tang dynasty temple. They protect us from any competing alternative, such as dreaded socialism. The new citizens of this tilt-a-whirl domain of American politics remain functionally unaware, studiously refusing to see capitalism as a means of the exploitation of the labour-power of the worker and even less as accumulation by dispossession. As David Harvey (2010) puts it, accumulation by dispossession "is about plundering, robbing other people of their rights . . . capitalism is very much about taking away the right people have over their natural resources"

(Harvey 2010: 99). Accumulation by dispossession is interrelated with neoliberalization or institutional reforms that are premarket and pro-privatization and against state interventions into the marketplace and so on.

Those who do not want to talk critically about capitalism should keep quiet about the barbarism we are witnessing all around us. Be my guest and keep complaining about violence in schools, and how poorly teachers teach, and how immigrants are spoiling the country, but we don't need your advice. Can't you hear the earth shuddering in agony beneath your spit-and-polished jackboots? People aren't falling on the streets like spent bullets in crime ridden neighbourhoods. Violence is more than a metaphor. People are falling in the street *because* they have been shot with bullets! And these are disproportionately people of colour. Is it so difficult to connect this destruction systematically to capitalist relations of production rather than simply foisting it off as the result of greedy capitalists (we are tired of psychologizing what is clearly a structural crisis built into the dynamics of value production under capitalism)?

In our world of hand sanitizers, wilfully disenfranchised youth, high-gloss reality shows, television commentaries on world events that have as much analytical depth as sparkle dust sprayed from a vintage-style perfume bottle, and benign varieties of televised adolescent rebellion with fast-food marketing tie-ins, we try in vain to find a way out. But that proves as difficult as asking your eyeball to stare back at itself. Or Benjamin's Angel of History to turn her head and face the future. Yet even against logo-swathed backdrops and image-based commentaries of daunting corporate grandeur, we keep ransacking Marx's tomb, especially when an economic crisis hits that demands some kind of explanation not afforded by the pundits of the *Wall Street Journal*. Everywhere it seems – perhaps especially in education – you find Marxism being derided with a leering flippancy or galvanized indifference. You can't escape it, even in coffee shops for the urban literati, as a recent visit to a popular Los Angeles establishment taught me. There, among the hard-nosed espresso drinkers, a stranger approached me, waving heavy hands. Bobbing over a thin nose and a pair of succulent lips was a pair of tarsier eyes, as if they had been clumsily plopped onto plump, fleshy stumps that sprung out ominously from deep within his sockets. Escaping his overly caffeinated oral cavity was a stage-whispered admonition delivered with requisite theatrical intensity: "Oh, you're McLaren, the one that writes that Marxist shit". I responded with a simple retort, as quickly as if I had rehearsed it in advance: "I assume you're already so full of capitalist shit that I wonder how you noticed mine". Today's capitalism is spawned in a petri dish of virtual Faustian space, as dank and suffocating as the inside of a hot air balloon. Capitalism dresses itself up in corset-like vocabularies of common sense. It can adapt to and absorb any language – even the language of the Left. It works its discourse in the service of its self-expansion, having no master to serve but itself. Its favourite language is the language of mystification, of progress, of democracy. By fashioning itself out of the contradictory logic of progressivism and traditionalism, it can confuse and obfuscate unobstructed.

The discourse of the state – that positions the "other" as irredeemably evil, as a monolithic alien species that is so barbaric as not to merit the rule of law – along with the functional existence of the state as an instrument of exploitation and repression, clearly need to be overcome. How can this be possible? Cold War ideology prevails and U.S. citizens in the main bear the ideological marks of their times. The term "American empire" is being championed by the Right out of a sense of noblesse oblige – to be part of an empire is a duty and a responsibility that comes with being the leader and protector of the "free" world. With their paternalistic toy trumpets, and their willingness to jettison their critical faculties in favour of embracing an iron certainty and ineffable faith that the United States has a providential mission in the world, the far right boasts that free-market democracy has to be delivered to the far corners of the earth (by bombing runs, if necessary) if civilization is to prevail on the planet.

Is it too late to re-enchant the world, to remould the planet in mytho-poetic terms, to create a past dreamtime, a mystical milieu in the present, to give ourselves over to dream divinities, to live in the eternal moment, to mould sacred totems from the clay of the riverbed? And while we ponder this possibility, the armies of the night march on, sneering at the pious surrender of the oppressed.

Because through the medium of experience the ego-driven individual is mistaken as the source of social practices, this process of misidentification has become a capitalist *arche*-strategy that marginalizes collectivity and protects the individual as the foundation of entrepreneurial capitalism. As a consequence, the well-being of the collectivity is replaced by the "politics of consumption" that celebrates the singularities of individuals by valorizing the desire to obtain and consume objects of pleasure. Experience in this view becomes non-theoretical and beyond the realities of history. This is why we need to locate all human experience in a world-historical frame, that is, within specific social relations of production. Revolutionary critical pedagogy, as we have been trying to develop it, attempts to create the conditions of pedagogical possibility that enable students to see how, through the exercise of power, the dominant structures of class rule protect the practices of the powerful from being publicly scrutinized as they appropriate resources to serve the interests of the few at the expense of the many (Ebert and Zavarzadeh 2008).

While we do not seek to live life with caprice or with an insouciant smirk, our project is anti-normative as long as schools seek to normalize students to an unjust world of stultifying toil for the labouring classes. We challenge this natural attitude of capitalist schooling and its moralizing machinery by climbing out of our spiritually dehydrated skin and re-birthing ourselves into relations of solidarity and comunalidad. Critical pedagogy has done much to inspire dissidents to engage culture in the agonistic terrain of the cultural imaginary so as to break with dominant relationships of power and privilege through forms of pedagogical subversion. While some dimensions of subversion have led to interventions and new communal relationships of solidarity and struggle, others have been dominated by forms of postmodern self-absorption and self-fashioning where the embattled agent engages in acts of symbolic inversion within the contradictions of consumptionist capitalism. What interest me are the ethical imperatives driving such acts of subversion. Is the protagonist subject not codetermined by discourses of resistance and possibility, as Henry Giroux might put it? If this is the case, then I would argue that within the field of critical pedagogy today, there is a disproportionate focus on the critique of identity formation at the expense of examining and finding alternatives to existing spheres of social determination that include institutions, social relations of production, ideologies, practices and the cultural imaginary – all of which are harnessed to value production.

Solving the problem of inequality: the market is not a sustainable or liveable community

If we want to participate in educational reform, then it becomes necessary to challenge the proponents of the competitive market whose corporate outlawry is driving the reform initiatives of education today.

We see the wake of capitalism's devastation in the privatization of public schooling following Hurricane Katrina in the Gulf Coast to myriad ways that 'No Child Left Behind' and 'Race to the Top' transform public schooling into investment opportunities – not to mention trying to turn New Orleans into a city of white yuppies. We see it in the retooling of colleges in order to serve better financial and military-industrial interests, in overuse and exploitation of contingent faculty, in the growth of for-profit degree-granting institutions and in rising tuition and student debt (student debt in the U.S. now exceeds that of credit cards, totaling over $1 trillion; see Cauchon 2011), not to mention the assault on critical citizenship in favour of consumer citizenship. The crisis of the "free" enterprise system today, the naked money-grabbing practices that might accurately be described as gangster capitalism, or drive-by capitalism, lacks any sincere connection with human dignity and is reconstructed as a mere "greed-is-good" formalism and proffered to the American people as self-protection: a harsh and unavoidable reality of the times. This legally unrestrained self-initiative that enables all barriers to the market to be dismantled in the interests of profit making by the few is built upon a negative definition of freedom – the freedom from having to enter into the necessary conversations with humanity that permit the full development of human capacities for fairness and social justice.

But the market is not a community. It is possible to realize your humanity only if you are educated in an authentic community. And how do we achieve true community? Only by analysing and understanding the distinction between how the social system understands itself, and how it exists in objectivity, that is in reality. In other words, only by working through false consciousness towards critical consciousness, towards a more dialectical understanding of how capitalism affects the very way we approach social problems, including educational problems. At present there is a huge disconnect between the two; that is, there is a tremendous gap between how U.S. society comprehends itself and how it is structured to be co-extensive with inequality. In a community, social wealth is distributed by means of the principle of equality in response to need. For me, education is about creating community in a society that has forgotten the meaning of the term.

Critical pedagogy is strongly assertive of its epistemologies and premises, its obligations and its practices, as well as its normative prescriptions and prohibitions with respect to engaging with *others* in the world. Even though critical pedagogy has been on the scene for decades, it is still argued by many in the educational establishment that the problem with working-class families has to do with the culture of poverty, in which it is assumed that there is an egregious deficit in working-class culture when read against the values and cultural capital of bourgeois culture.

But for critical educators, this is taking what is fundamentally a structural problem – capitalist-produced inequality – and turning it into a cultural problem: the problems of values, attitudes and the lack of high culture and preponderance of low or middlebrow culture within working-class families, which suggests erroneously that class privilege and educational success have something to do with individual merit and intrinsic self-worth. It reflects a ruthlessly instrumentalized and paternalistic presumption implicit in contemporary school reform approaches, namely, that the poor lack the proper 'civilized' attitudes and cosmopolitan values to help them realize their full humanity and succeed in consumer capitalist society.

Of course there is a racial dimension to all of these measurable inequities, when examining the statistical facts of gaps between the outcomes of students disaggregated by race and affluence and comparing them with the statistical facts of disproportionate numbers of teachers among races. Moreover, when you compare these to the realities of the school-to-prison pipeline, and the resegregation of schools, we see a national trend. Consider the following statement from Dr. Martin Luther King, Jr. (2009):

> We have come a long way in our understanding of human motivation and of the blind operation of our economic system. Now we realize that dislocations in the market operation of our economy and the prevalence of discrimination thrust people into idleness and bind them in constant or frequent unemployment against their will. The poor are less often dismissed from our conscience today by being branded as inferior and incompetent. We also know that no matter how dynamically the economy develops and expands it does not eliminate all poverty.

Relatos salvajes (wild tales): the illogicality of the market

The fact that the logic of the market is a regulatory principle of life within capitalist societies is now commonplace. Over time, this regulatory principle has led the state to react harshly to fomenting opposition, especially from the current generation whose futures seem, in the words of Henry Giroux, disposable. This has led to various incarnations of "soft fascism" that we saw increase exponentially throughout the U.S., especially after September 11, 2001, and the global slump of 2008. We have witnessed the militarization of the police, the often fatal assaults on black men by the police, harsh sentences for whistleblowers, etc. and the push to privatize public spaces such as schools and universities where dissent can be more effectively controlled by private owners and conservative and well-heeled boards of trustees.

Clearly, the corporatocracy is worried about political dissent. Capitalism is in the process of reconstituting itself transnationally. And those who are hit hardest are learning from alternative sites in the social media to see through the veil of deception and lies of the corporatocracy. They know that the state is recalibrating its plans for reacting to hostile opposition from the poor, from students saddled with debt, and from those who are committed to the process of democratization in all spheres of public and private life. They have been aided by critical educators who are intent on helping their students read both the word and the world dialectically, recognizing power as a constitutive dimension of both pedagogy and politics.

I am often struck by the fact that analyses of universities often do not consider educational institutions, curricula and policy-making that occur before students begin to attend colleges or universities. After all, university life is part of a continuum, and students who enter colleges and universities have been "formed" out of political necessity by classrooms that began with pre-school, home-schooling or kindergarten and ended after completing their SAT exams in their senior year of high school. Students are producers, yes, but they are also products of policies put in place by federal law, state law, and the mission statements of the schools that they attended throughout their lives. Students in my generation who attended compulsory public schools in the 1950s and 60s, were implicated not only in particular educational policies but as part of the larger socio-economic, geographical, topographical and historical lineaments that shaped those years. In the U.S., Martin Luther King, Malcolm X, the Black Panthers, the Young Lords, and other individuals and groups were engaged in fighting for civil rights, the desegregation of schools, and the end to the Vietnam War, as well as other issues relevant to the times. They were also the objects of surveillance and assassination by the covert activities of COINTELPRO (an acronym for COunter INTELligence PROgram) run by the United States Federal Bureau of Investigation (FBI) which undertook a campaign of infiltrating, criminalizing and destroying political organizations that had gained national attention in the media and wider public. But there were a few victories. In the *Mendez vs. Westminster* court case of 1947, the 9th Circuit Court of Appeals held that it was unlawful and unconstitutional to segregate Mexican American students into Mexican-only schools. At the time Mexican Americans were classified as white, but the court ruling recognized that "Mexican schools" did not have the same standard of education provided to other groups. In *Brown v. Board of Education of Topeka*, the Supreme Court in 1954 declared state laws establishing separate public schools for black and white students to be unconstitutional. And there was the *Civil Rights Act* of 1964 which banned segregation in public places and outlawed employment discrimination on the basis of race, class, colour, religion, gender or sexual origin. Yet despite these significant achievements, the struggle for desegregation continues to this day. This struggle rarely includes any mention of how the context of the Cold War between the U.S. and the Soviet Union impacted the struggle against segregation. Dean MacCannell, now professor emeritus at UC Davis's Department of Human Ecology, published an article in 1984 that posited a controversial thesis – that U.S. military strategic planners, unified in the belief that the Soviet Union would engage in a "first strike" against U.S. cities, decided against protecting cities and its urban inhabitants which mainly consisted of African Americans, Latin/os and other people of colour. Using work by Lacan, Freud and sociologists such as Talcott Parsons, MacCannell put forward a provocative thesis that maintained that after the nuclear attacks on Japan by the United States military, military strategic planners developed an unconscious desire to see the inhabitants of their own American inner cities destroyed in a Soviet "first strike". He maintained that this was part of what he called "the nuclear unconscious" (part of what I refer to as the "macrostructural unconscious"). These planners felt that the inner cities were expendable, and that programmes of nuclear deterrence should put most of their energy in convincing white populations to leave the cities and settle in suburban areas or small towns near agricultural areas.

With the dismantling of the Soviet Union, the threat of nuclear war diminished, and urban renewal programmes began to expand. Nevertheless, inequality persists and the country continues to be segregated by race and class. According to Christopher Petrella (2017), racial disparities have intensified over the past 40 years between white communities and communities of colour. Petrella refers to this as systematic resegregation. This systematic resegregation has grave implications for access to health care services, education and accumulation of wealth. Low-income African Americans who become ill cannot afford to receive assistance from major teaching hospitals, according to a report issued by the Harvard Medical School and the Boston University School of Medicine. Petrella also reports that minorities "are more likely to be exposed to sulfate, a powerful respiratory irritant, and nickel, a possible carcinogen" (Petrella 2017). He also notes a 2014 University of Minnesota study that revealed that people of colour "are exposed to almost 50 percent more hazardous pollutants. Such communities, for example, inhale 46 percent more nitrogen dioxide, a pollutant linked to increased heart disease, lung cancer, asthma and premature births" (Petrella 2017). Since 2001, there has been an expansion of the proportion of high-poverty, majority black and Latino schools, where "the number of black and Latino students enrolled in resource-poor K-12 public schools – where 75 percent to 100 percent of students qualify for price-reduced lunch – increased 11 percent from 2001 to 2014" (Petrella 2017). The practice of school secession has grown. This is a practice "by which wealthy white communities around the country choose to 'break away from their public-school districts to form smaller, more exclusive ones'" (Petrella 2017).

Petrella points to reports which reveal that white people do not wish to share their communities with African Americans, regardless of their income. He also shares the grim reality that the median white family holds 13 times as much net wealth as the median black family. And the median white family holds 10 times as much wealth as the median Latino family. Petrella believes that the vocabulary of racial inequality isn't working to help people of colour. He urges us to focus instead on the reality of growing racial resegregation. He writes:

> Not only does the idiom of racial resegregation help remove the notion of 'whiteness' as the reference point on which formal equality is measured, it also guards against the stigmatising 'culture of poverty' behavioral arguments that many conservatives routinely marshal.
>
> (Petrella 2017)

Given the grim reality of segregation and racial inequality in U.S. schools today, I have advised university administrators and teachers to make the study of the topic of capitalism paramount both within and without schools and colleges of education. The university should put a sustained emphasis on encouraging sustainability and efficiency protocols when studying how to recreate an economy not based on the production of value (I am using the term "value" to mean monetized wealth), but rather as a socialist alternative to capital's law of value. What could be more important for universities than to initiate projects revolving around localized energy production – ensuring that professors are working from principles of cooperation rather than competition. The purpose of universities should be to transform society in the interests of those who suffer most from conditions of scarcity not of their own making. In working to remake society, I would urge university officials to think about saving the planet. What could be more important than this! Research should be directed at developing solar power, small wind-harvesting systems, to reimagine mass transit networks for large urban environments using sustainable resource allocation strategies. The entire world needs a new generation of industrial designers – and universities should be at the forefront of producing this generation. Where are the courses in engineering that research how to harvest energy from the airflow of airplanes and ocean currents? I would point to a recent book by Peter Joseph – *The New Human Rights Movement* (2017) – which advocates using an "integrated systems approach" to achieve key sustainable energy abundance and underscores the importance of using wind farms, solar fields, and ocean hydropower. Joseph notes that harnessing energy from open ocean currents could power the entire planet. New technology is now available to reuse piezo-engineered floors and sidewalks and even rail systems that can capture energy from passing train cars through pressure. In short, can universities place more emphasis on curricula that enable students to involve themselves in projects where they explore new forms of small scale and large-scale energy production, especially ocean-based energy sources – that is, ocean thermal energy conversion – that can drive turbines? Unfortunately, incentivizing cooperation over competition and the creation of a cultural commons that is equipped to help the planet survive brushes against the grain of the logic of capital and its price-oriented financial system that is choking the life out of our planet. Clearly, we need a revolutionary critical pedagogy to take on such a task.

Revolutionary critical pedagogy has attempted to give substance to the lie that the U.S. is fighting evil empires around the globe in order to protect its vital interests, interests that must be met for it to continue as the prime defender of the 'free' world. Critical educators assume the position that equality is both a precondition and outcome for establishing community, and a community is a precondition for deep democracy. This demands that students question the various roles played by the U.S. on the stage of history and nurture a radical imagination where they can consider other forms of organizing society and collectively providing for themselves and others their economic, social, cultural and spiritual needs.

Critical pedagogy

A revolutionary critical pedagogy, then, is both a reading practice where we read the word in the context of the world, and a practical activity where we write ourselves as subjective forces into the text of history – but this does not mean that making history is only an effect of discourse, a form of metonymy, the performative dimension

Revolutionary critical pedagogy 261

of language, a rhetorical operation, a tropological system. No, reality is more than textual self-difference. Praxis is directed at engaging the word and the world dialectically as an effect of class contradictions. A critical pedagogy is a way of challenging the popular imaginary (which has no "outside" to the text) that normalizes the core cultural foundations of capitalism and the normative force of the state. In other words, the ruling capitalist ideology tells us in numerous ways that there is no alternative to capitalist social relations.

Critical pedagogy is illuminated by an insight made foundational in the work of Paulo Freire: that politics and pedagogy are not an exclusive function of having the right knowledge via some kind of "ah-ha" awakening of the revolutionary soul. Critical consciousness is not the root of commitment to revolutionary struggle but rather the product of such a commitment. An individual does not have to be critically self-conscious in order to feel the obligation to help the poor and the dispossessed. In fact, it is in the very act of struggling that individuals become critically conscious and aware. Praxis begins with practice. This is the bedrock of revolutionary critical pedagogy's politics of solidarity and commitment. While radical scholarship and theoretical ideas are important – extremely important – people do not become politically aware and then take part in radical activity. Rather, participating in contentious acts of revolutionary struggle creates new protagonistic political identities that become refined through theoretical engagement and refreshed in every moment by practices of critical reflexivity. Critically informed political identities do not motivate revolutionary action, but rather develop as a logical consequence of such action. And the action summoned by revolutionary critical educators is always heterogeneous, multifaceted, protagonistic, democratic and participatory – yet always focalized – anti-capitalist struggle.

For the guardians of our cognitive plutocracy, making critical interventions into the lives of the oppressed is rendered, if not unacceptable, then at least less legitimate than developing rubrics, criteriologies, architectonics or systems of intelligibility for studying 'others' or than itemizing epistemological issues that might be inherently problematic for unspecified research protocols. In other words,

> the neoliberal academy and its clerisy wedded to the establishment of official channels and the principles of the new managerialism as rule-creators, rule-enforcers and moral entrepreneurs trained for appropriate decisional responses, has brutally cleaved dialectical engagement into two, deracinating its hermeneutical potential by focusing only on one half of what constitutes the dialectic

of critical consciousness; such a brutal sundering of the potential for critical analysis is accomplished by validating theory as a discrete entity that should stand on its own, as somehow existing in antiseptic isolation from its dialectical companion: practice. This prohibits any real critical and transformative engagement – any authentic praxis – to emerge from collaboration with living and breathing human beings and promotes a radical disjuncture with everyday life. This is the very opposite of how a university should function.

(McLaren, in press)

As I shared during a recent discussion of the neoliberal university:

Years ago, it was Paulo Freire and Chavista activists in Venezuela who taught me the importance of orthopraxis over orthodoxy, that is, the necessity of understanding praxis as the foundation and bellwether of theory. In this instance, theoretical clarity is not necessary before we engage in an active living commitment to the poorest and most marginalized in society. We must live our politics in fidelity with our obligation to help marginalized and oppressed communities before we can arrive at a correct or orthodox understanding of critical theory. That does not mean that theoretical understanding is unimportant. Far from it. Being informed by relevant critical theories admittedly is very crucial in social justice education as these theories can help to refine and fine-tune concrete practices of intervening in the world rather than simply positioning us as passive observers trained only to transpose reality onto a factory foreman's ledger and judge it on the basis of inputs and outputs. But to restrict our theories to or value them mainly for their sumptuous appearance in high status journals is to reduce the role of the educator to that of an academic.

(McLaren, in press)

Not all, but many academics see their time spent on university campuses as part of a 'career' and in doing so excise their subjectivity from any ethical commitments to and activist-interventionist involvement with others. They often remain professionally cautious and walk tremulously past proscribed domains of discourse that involve, for instance, participatory action research-methodologies that might have inveigled their way into their research domains as doctoral students. They refrain from taking any adversarial stance towards capitalism and avoid visiting those research enclaves populated by scholars who agitate for social transformation in their scholarly work. They studiously avoid taking a position that might suture their subjectivity to a larger political framework that commits them to addressing the need of the oppressed. They do so by, among other things, dogmatically defending their work under the banner of investigative objectivity. They reframe, rephrase, resituate and rearticulate aspects of their work that might create a "red flag" to their superiors so that their research becomes acceptable to more conventional canons of scientific research concerning the vexed questions of what is possible, what is politically safe and what is 'really' real in the field of social science research. Their fidelity to the ideology of materialism – while not a bad thing in itself – sometimes becomes so fetishized and triumphalist in a metaphysical sense that it automatically positions them to reject indigenous ways of knowing and the cosmovisions of non-Western, colonized peoples. Especially when dealing with those in their department who serve as research initiatrixes, new faculty are poised to be uncomplainingly seduced by those systems of interpretation that predominate in the field, those that have been academically certified and have been granted the imprimatur of the sanctioning body of regnant scientific authorities.

A critical pedagogy is about the hard work of building community alliances, of challenging school policy, of providing teachers with alternative and oppositional teaching materials. It has little to do with awakening the "revolutionary soul" of students – this is merely a re-fetishization of the individual and the singular under the banner of the collective, and serves only to bolster the untruth fostered by capitalist social relations and postpone the answer to the question: Is revolution possible today? It falls into the same kind of condition that critical pedagogy had been originally formulated to combat. It diverts us from the following challenge: can we organize our social, cultural and economic life differently so as to transcend the exploitation that capital affords us?

Within U.S. capitalist society, academics continue to hide behind a politics of neutrality. I believe that it is not only possible but imperative that academics and researchers make a "commitment" as public intellectuals to a specific action or consider as an "obligation" their actions regarding the relationship between a specific premise and their concluding interpretations and explanations. That, of course, depends upon whether or not they agree to consider both creatively and dialectically the idea that our interpretation of the world is inseparable from our transformation of the world – both are linked socially and ethically. As such, a dialectical and critical self-consciousness of the relationship between being and doing (or being and becoming) becomes a part of the very reality one is attempting to understand and requires an ethical rather than an epistemological move, which is why ethics always precedes epistemology in the field of critical pedagogy. Only an ethics of compassion, a commitment to ending the horror of neoliberal capitalism through the creating of a social universe outside of value production, and respect for diversity can guide us out of the neoliberal capitalist impasse that we face. Such critical self-consciousness steeled by a commitment to the oppressed becomes revolutionary if, for instance, your analysis is placed within the class perspective of the oppressed, that is, within the class perspective of the proletariat, cognitariat, precariat, etc. Logic and reason must be anchored by values and virtues that are grounded in an obligation to help the most powerless and those who suffer most under the heel of capitalism.

As I have maintained elsewhere:

> We need to address these questions urgently. Especially since recent research indicated that young people born between 1980 and 1994 are more polarized politically that Generation X'ers and Baby Boomers, with millennials more likely identifying as conservatives, compared to the 1980s (Howard 2016). In fact, 23% of millennials are identified as leaning far right (Howard 2016). We need to understand better how universities shape and are shaped by disciplinary regimes of power and privilege that often overshadow their critical role. Here I am referring to courses, programs, faculty hires and tenure decisions that include criteria such as race, class, gender, disability, and LGBT issues. But we should also be concerned with how universities in our society contribute to the social reproduction of capitalism with its entangled antagonisms such as racism, sexism, patriarchy, homophobia, white privilege and the colonial imperatives of the white settler state. We need to ask: What is the source of our responsibility as public pedagogues and activists who reject the consumer model of education and who, as agents and agitators of social change, view our role as cultural workers carrying out our decolonizing projects in spaces both inside and outside the university? How can we better understand the role played by universities in the production, circulation and consumption of cognitive and informational capitalism? How is academic labor and productivity assessed in a setting where digital education and communication technologies are blurring the distinction between students' and professors'

professional and personal lives in our "always on" culture? What role do universities play today in advancing and legitimizing capitalist development? What role do they play in strengthening the military industrial complex and the development of cyber technologies used to control information, in creating ideological submission for the masses to particular political and cultural views, or in supporting research by biotech companies committed to creating weapons technologies used to increase the "kill ratio" of our military? How are faculty and students engaged in or prevented from making decisions about how university financial investments are made? Are decisions about student tuition costs and admissions arrived at collectively? How is value produced in the process of academic labor and how does this affect both permanent and adjunct faculty as well as graduate assistants? How is freedom of speech protected in a world where social media is obliterating the distinction between public and private lives? These are only a few of the crucial questions that must be raised.

(McLaren, in press)

The falcon is "turning in the widening gyre", beware! Do you not hear Yeats's anguished cry as "things fall apart", as the centre collapses like a sunken lung? Beware the Spiritus Mundi, blackened with pitch and winter catarrh, carrying portents from lost scrolls hidden in the damp abode of billionaires' yachts. A new messiah is being spawned from the curdling afterbirth of history's raw defeat, its spine bent forward like a twisted compass, pointing to Silicon Valley. This "rough beast", this "rising Sphinx" with a smile of infinite bandwidth and burning fibre optic eyes encoded with apocalypse wades slowly through deep deposits of NSA data, gleefully sinking in the muck of its own creation. It is up to us to fight this beast and to fight it with every means that we have. I think it was the poet June Jordan who said, "we're the ones we've been waiting for", a line made famous in a song by Sweet Honey in the Rock. Well, what can I say except, "we're the ones we've been waiting for!" The time for the struggle is now. And it is a struggle that will tax both our minds and bodies. It will be fought in the seminar rooms, in the picket lines, and on the streets. Let's get ready for a revitalized revolutionary critical pedagogy.

A revolutionary critical pedagogy operates from an understanding that the basis of education is political and that spaces need to be created where students can imagine a different world outside of the capitalist law of value, where alternatives to capitalism and capitalist institutions can be discussed and debated, and where dialogue can occur about why so many revolutions in past history turned into their opposite (McLaren and Rikowski 2000). It looks to create a world where social labour is no longer an indirect part of the total social labour but a direct part of it, where a new mode of distribution can prevail not based on socially necessary labour time but on actual labour time, where alienated human relations are subsumed by transparent ones, where freely associated individuals can work towards a permanent revolution, where the division between mental and manual labour can be abolished, where patriarchal relations and other privileging hierarchies of oppression and exploitation can be ended, where we can truly exercise the principle 'from each according to his or her ability and to each according to his or her need', where we can traverse the terrain of universal rights unburdened by necessity, moving sensuously and fluidly within that ontological space where subjectivity is exercised as a form of capacity-building and creative self-activity within the social totality (see Hudis 2012).

We continue to struggle in our educational projects to eliminate rent-seeking and for-profit financial industries; we seek to distribute incomes without reference to individual productivity, but rather according to need; and we seek to substantially reduce hours of labour and make possible, through socialist general education, a well-rounded and scientific and intercultural development of the young (Reitz 2013). This involves a larger epistemological fight against neoliberal and imperial common sense, and a grounding of our critical pedagogy in a concrete universal that can welcome diverse and particular social formations (San Juan 2009) joined in class struggle. It is a struggle that has come down to us not from the distant past, but from thoughts that have ricocheted back to us from the future.

Note

1 This is a revised version of a chapter from Peter McLaren's *Pedagogy of Insurrection* (Education and Struggle Series, Volume 6), New York: Peter Lang, 2015.

References

Cauchon, D. 2011. 'Student Loans Outstanding Will Exceed $1 Trillion This Year', *USA Today*, 11 October. Retrieved from http://usatoday30.usatoday.com/money/perfi/college/story/2011-10-19/student-loan-debt/50818676/1 (accessed on 31 December 2017).

Chomsky, N. 2013. 'A Roadmap to a Just World [Web log comment]', *Reader Supported News*, 17 August. Available at http://readersupportednews.org/

opinion2/277-75/18946-focus-a-roadmap-to-a-just-world (accessed on 31 December 2017).
Ebert, T., & Zavarzadeh, M. 2008. *Class in Culture*. Boulder, CO: Paradigm Press.
Harvey, D. 2010. 'An Interview with David Harvey', in A. L. Buzby (ed.) *Communicative Action: The Logos Interviews* (pp. 99–105). Lanham, MD: Lexington Books.
Howard, Jacqueline. 2016. 'Millennials More Conservative Than You May Think', *CNN*, 7 September. Available at www.cnn.com/2016/09/07/health/millennials-conservative-generations/index.html (accessed on 31 December 2017).
Hudis, P. 2012. *Marx's Concept of the Alternative to Capitalism*. Chicago: Haymarket Books. Available at http://dx.doi.org/10.1163/9789004229860 (accessed on 31 December 2017).
Joseph, Peter. 2017. *The New Human Rights Movement: Reinventing the Economy to End Oppression*. Dallas, TX: BenBella Books, Inc.
Karp, S. 2011. 'Challenging Corporate School Reform and 10 Hopeful Signs of Resistance', *Rethinking Schools*, 25 October. Available at www.commondreams.org/ view/2011/10/25–1?print (accessed on 31 December 2017).
King, M. L. 2009. 'Martin Luther King on Guaranteed Income Social Dividend', *The Progress Report*. Available at www.progress.org/2009/05/03/martin-lutherkingon-guaranteed-income-social-dividend/ (accessed on 31 December 2017).
MacCannell, Dean. 1984. 'Baltimore in the Morning . . . After: On the Forms of Post-Nuclear Leadership', *Diacritics*, 14(2): 32–46.
McLaren, P. 2008. 'This Fist Called My Heart: Public Pedagogy in the Belly of the Beast', *Antipode*, 40(3): 472–81.
———. forthcoming. 'Afterword', in Marc Spooner and James McNinch (eds.) *A Critical Guide to Higher Education: Resisting Colonialism, Neoliberalism, and Audit Culture*. Regina: The University of Regina Press.
McLaren, P. and Rikowski, G. 2000. 'Pedagogy for Revolution Against Education for Capital: An E-Dialogue on Education in Capitalism Today', *Cultural Logic*, 4(1). Available at http://clogic.eserver.org/4-1/mclaren%26rikowski.html (accessed on 31 December 2017).
Petrella, Christopher. 2017. 'The Resurgence of Resegregation of America', *NBC News*, 3 December. Available at www.nbcnews.com/think/opinion/resegregation-america-ncna801446 (accessed on 31 December 2017).
Reitz, Charles. 2013. 'Introduction', in *Crisis and Commonwealth: Marx, Marcuse, McLaren* (pp. 1–18). Lanham, MD: Lexington Books.
Robinson, W. I. 2004. *A Theory of Global Capitalism: Production, Class, and State in a Transnational World*. Baltimore: Johns Hopkins University Press.
———. 2014. *Global Capitalism and the Crisis of Humanity*. New York: Cambridge University Press.
———. 2016a. Reform Is Not Enough to Stem the Rising Tide of Inequality Worldwide. *Truthout*, 1 January. Available at www.truth-out.org/news/item/

34224-reform-is-not-enough-to-stem-the-rising-tide-of-inequality-world wide (accessed on 31 December 2017).

———. 2016b. 'Sadistic Capitalism: Six Urgent Matters for Humanity in Global Crisis', *Truthout*, 12 April. Available at www.truth-out.org/opinion/item/35596-sadistic-capitalism-six-urgent-matters-for-humanity-in-global-crisis (accessed on 31 December 2017).

San Juan, Jr., E. 2009. '*Critique and Social Transformation: Lessons from Antonio Gramsci, Mikhail Bakhtin and Raymond Williams*. New York: The Edwin Mellen Press.

Index

Note: Page numbers in *italic* indicate a figure and page numbers in **bold** indicate a table on the corresponding page.

Abbasid Empire 132
Ability Enhancement Compulsory Courses (AECC) 196
academic community 238–9
academic excellence 47–8
academic freedom 163–80; assault on 163; collegiality 178–80; Delhi University photocopy case 163–74, 175; intellectual property 163, 165, 167, 176–80; overview 29
academic journals *see* journals
Academic Performance Index (API) 137
academic publishing 163
academic restrictions 176
Academie Royale des Sciences in Paris 133
accumulation by dispossession 251–2
action research 156
Act No. 27 of 2012 171
AECC *see* Ability Enhancement Compulsory Courses (AECC)
African Americans 258, 259
Agamben, Giorgio 87
age of greed 251
agonism of social relations 20
Ahmed, Najeeb 79
Alexander, Michelle 229
Ali, Syed Imdad 136

Aligarh Muslim University 48, 103n9
All Souls College, University of Oxford 248
Althusser, Louis 183, 192–3
Ambani, Mukesh 4, 52
Ambani-Birla Report 4
Ambedkar, B. R. 106
Ambedkar University, Delhi 154
"American empire" 253
Analysis of the Experiment in Education Made at Egmore, near Madras, An (Bell) 188, *189*
Analyst's Discourse 150–1
Ananthamurthy, U. R. 50, 56
Andrews, C. F. 13
anti-capitalism 155
anti-intellectualism 53–7
API *see* Academic Performance Index (API)
Archimedes 133
Arendt, Hannah 223
Aristotle 132–3, 151, 161n16
Arizona 224
artificial intelligence 138, 241
ASEAK *see* Association of Students for Equitable Access to Knowledge (ASEAK)
Ashoka University 79
askesis 156, 157

Index

Association of Students for Equitable Access to Knowledge (ASEAK) 164
audit of public university 47–8
authoritarian populism 223

Badiou, Alain 201, 205n20
Bah Doyle Act of India 180
Bal Basappa 49
Banaras Hindu University 48, 101, 103n9
Banerjee, Mamata 78
Bangalore University 51
Bank of America 228
Barry, Andrew 197
Barthes, Roland 204n18
Bauman, Zygmunt 226–7
Bell, Andrew 187–90
Bengal National College 97–8
Benjamin, Walter 1–2, 8, 10, 11, 16, 23
Bentham, Jeremy 190
Bentinck, William 95
Berman, Marshall 157
Bernier, F. 239
Beyond Good and Evil (Nietzsche) 191–2
Bhabha, Homi J. 116
bhadralok communities 9
Bharat Electronics Limited 56
Bharat Ratna 106
Bhattacharya, K. C. 68
Bhide, V. G. 115–16
Bihar Scientific Society 136
Birla, Kumarmangalam 4, 52
black money 33
boosa agitation of 1973 51
bootlegging of education 175
Born, Georgina 197
Bose, Jagadish Chandra 106, 107, 137
Bose, Satyendra Nath 106, 107
Boston University School of Medicine 258
Brattin, Rick 224
Brihadaranyaka Upanishad 56
Brown, Wendy 199, 204n17, 233n1
Brown v. Board of Education of Topeka 257–8

bureaucratization of academy 27
Butler, Judith 56

Calhoun, Craig 48
Cambridge University Press 163
Canada 248–9
capitalism 249–54; accumulation by dispossession 251–2; democracy and 250; globalized finance 251; greed 251; neoliberal 250; perils of 250; social alternative to 249; virtual Faustian space 253
capitalist schooling 254
casino capitalism 229, 233
caste-based affirmative action policies 128–9
caste identities 51
CBCS *see* Choice Based Credit System (CBCS)
CCSU *see* Cotton College State University (CCSU)
Centre for the Study of Discrimination and Exclusion (CSDE) 194
Centres for Study of Social Exclusion and Inclusive Policy (CSSEIP) 194, 196
Chakrabarty, Dipesh 63
Chaplin, Charlie 150
Charter Act of 1813 94–5
charter schools 246
Chatterjee, Bankim Chandra 100
Chatterjee, Partha 100
Chaudhuri, Supriya 27
China 240
Choice Based Credit System (CBCS) 196, 198
Chomsky, Noam 242n1
Chrestomathia (Bentham) 190
Chrestomathic Day School 190
citizen science 138–9
Civil Rights Act of 1964 258
class differentiation 240
Coetzee, J. M. 74–5, 83–4, 88–9, 226
COINTELPRO 257
Cold War 177–8, 253, 258
Coleridge, S. T. 96
colleges: conversion into universities 111–13, **113**; engineering **114**,

Index   271

114–15; *see also* historic colleges; university
Collini, Stefan 228
communities of specialists 134–5
concept of duty 1
Conflict of the Faculties (Kant) 177
conscious cruelty 227
Constantinople 133
corporate media 250
corporate powerbrokers 230
corporatocracy 257
cosmopolitics 15
Costello, Elizabeth 75
Cotton College State University (CCSU) 111–12, 113
Country Paper 100–2
Court of Directors of East India Company 95
creative destruction 56
crisis of public university 27, 74–90
critical pedagogy 31–2, 246–66
Critique of Pure Reason (Kant) 186
crowdsourcing 138
CSSEIP *see* Centres for Study of Social Exclusion and Inclusive Policy (CSSEIP)
cultural turn 241
cultural unity 99–100
culture: re-invention of 99–102
Curzon, Lord 97

Dabholkar, Narendra 79
Dalit 6, 26, 41, 45, 46, 51, 79, 106
Dalit Sangarsh Samiti 56
Darnton, Robert 176
Darwin, C. 134
Das, Chittaranjan 14–15
data collection or analysis 138–9
David Horowitz Freedom Center 223
Davis, Angela 229
Dawn 97
decolonization 62–72; intellectual 69–70; language 70–2; overview 27
deconstruction 152–3
Deleuze, Gilles 67, 200
Delhi University 6, 116–17, 175; Four Year Undergraduate Programme (FYUP) 21, 196; photocopy case 163–74, 175
demonetization drive 33
Derrida, Jacques 152–3
Descartes, R. 239
Deshpande, Sudhanva 175
Development Practice 154–8
Dhar, Anup 29
dharma nirapekshata see secularism
discipline: growth of 184–7; knowledge categorized into 134; overview 183–4; political economy 187–90; scientific 184–7
Discourse of the University 149–54
Doctor Faustus (Marlowe) 184
Dongerkery, S. R. 99
Donskis, Leonidas 226–7
Downing, David 178–9
doxa 184
Draft Educational Policy 2016 6
dropout rates 76
duty, concept of 1

early nationalist ideas of university 97–9
'Eastern University, An' (Tagore) 18
East India Company 94–5
Ecole Normale Superieure 192–3
Economic and Political Weekly 71
Education Cess 78
education loan 129–31; repayment of 130
Eliot, T. S. 53
elites 240
Elizabeth Costello (Coetzee) 75, 88–9
Elmhirst, Leonard 17, 19, 22–3
employment discrimination 258
employment opportunities 130–1
English 46–7, 131
English education 9, 95–6
English medium Public Schools 131
Enlightenment 2, 94
entrepreneurial vocationalism 2
Essence of Christianity, The (Feuerbach) 156
Euclid 133
Euro-American academy 193–4

Europe 240
European model of university 239-40

faculty 231
Faraday, Michael 136
fascism 249
Faust, Johann Georg 184
feudalism 71-2
Fichte, Johann Gottlieb 187
First World War 16
Foreign Educational Institutions (Regulation of Entry and Operations) Bill 2010 5
Foreign Education Providers Bill 2013 5
Foucauldian strain 200
Foucault, Michel 150, 156, 157, 200, 205n19
Four Year Undergraduate Programme (FYUP) 21, 196
free enterprise system 255
free-market economy 251-2
free software movement 180
fundamental problem 249
'Future of the Liberal Arts, The' 85

Galaxy Zoo 138
Gandhi, Mahatma 13, 100, 106
Geddes, Arthur 19
Gekko, Gordon 251
General Agreement on Trade in Services (GATS) 2-3
GER *see* Gross Enrolment Ratio (GER)
Germany 239, 240
Ghose, Aurobindo 98
Giant Metrewave Radio Telescope (GMRT) 119
Ginsburg, Benjamin 231
Giroux, Henry 30-1, 247, 254
GMRT *see* Giant Metrewave Radio Telescope (GMRT)
Goldberg, David Theo 42
Golinski, Jan 184
Government Brahmana 51
Government of Assam Act No. XXII of 2017 112
grants 75
Great Dictator 150

Gross Domestic Product 130
Gross Enrolment Ratio (GER) 3, 76, 127
Guattari, F. 200
Gujarat Riots (2002) 94

Habermas, Jürgen 54-5, 80-1, 90
Hall, Stuart 231
Halliday, F. J. 96
Harper, William Rainey 120
Harvard Medical School 258
Harvard University 129, 240
Harvey, David 251-2
Heidegger, M. 55, 87, 151, 156-7, 159n6, 159n8, 161n15
"Heidegger's Hut" 151, 161n15
heteronormativity 201
Higgins, John 74
higher education 127; alumni contributions 129; Gross Enrolment Ratio (GER) 3, 76, 127; growth 127; industry and 129; language 131; loan 129-31; neoliberalism and 222-33; private sector 129; state withdrawing from 129; under-represented sections 128; vocationalization 20-2; *see also* public university; university
Higher Education Act (2017) 78
"Higher Education in India: Vision and Action" 100
Hindi 70-2
Hinduism 98
Hindutva athava Hind Swaraj (Ananthamurthy) 50, 56
Hindutva forces 28
Hindutva nationalism 94
historic colleges: engineering, technological institutions on 114, 114-15; universities on foundation of 111-13, 113
HMS Beagle 134
Hooke, Robert 133
hostels 50-2; caste-specific 50, 51; post-independence 51; students mobilization 51
Hudis, Peter 249
humanities 85-90; employment opportunities 130

Index 273

Human Resource Development (HRD) 7
Humboldt, Wilhelm von 187, 202n5
Hurricane Katrina 254
Hyde, Lewis 178
hyper-specialization 135
Hysteric's Discourse 150–1

IACS *see* Indian Association for the Cultivation of Science (IACS)
Ibn Sina 67
The Idea of the University (Jaspers) 80
IIEST Shibpur 114
IIT Bombay 115
IIT Guwahati 115, 118
IIT Kanpur 115
IIT Madras 6, 115
IIT Roorkee 114–15, 118
Imperial University of Peking 239
India: cultural unity 99–100; early nationalist ideas 97–9; East India Company 94–5; missionaries/English education 95–6; Nehruvian vision of 99–100; utilitarian ideas 94–7; Western education 96–7; *see also* higher education; public university; university
India: A National Culture? (Sen) 94
Indian Association for the Cultivation of Science (IACS) 136–7
Indian Copyright Act 175
Indian Education Service (IES) 76
Indian Institute of Science (IISc) 105, 107, 111, 116, 118
Indian Institute of Science Education and Research (IISER) 115–16
Indian Institute of Technology (IIT) 26, 114–15, 116
inequality 254–6
Institute of Rural Reconstruction *see* Sriniketan
intellectual decolonization 69–70
intellectual property 29, 163, 165, 167, 176–80
Intellectual Property Agreements 179
inter-curricular training 198

interdisciplinarity 190–3; agendas 197–9; ethico-political practice 201–2; recent developments 193–7; social justice 199–202; state-sanctioned projects 197–8
Interdisciplinarity: Problems of Teaching and Research in Universities (OECD) 193
Interdisciplinarity: Reconfigurations of the Social and Natural Sciences (Barry and Born) 197
Interdisciplinarity and Social Justice (Parker and Samantrai) 200
inter-imperial competition 239
International Business Times (Kotch) 223
International Monetary Fund (IMF) 3
invented national culture 101–2
Irani, Smriti 55

Jadavpur University 6, 195
Jaspers, Karl 80
Jawaharlal Nehru Centre for Advanced Scientific Research (JNCASR) 111, 116, 118
Jawaharlal Nehru University (JNU) 6, 48, 117, 240
job-oriented course 130
Johns Hopkins University 120
Joseph, M. 107, 108
Joseph, Peter 260
Joshi, Murali Manohar 100
journals 134; communication between specialists 135; publishing 176; scientific societies 134

Kalburgi, M. M. 79
Kannada University, Hampi 49, 51
Kant, Immanuel 29, 176–7, 185–7, 202n4
Karp, Stan 249
Kasahara, Kim Taro 19
Kasturirangan, K. 119
Kautilya 68
Khan, Mosarrap Hossain 27–8
Khan, Syed Ahmed 136
Kind, Jonathan 178
King, Martin Luther, Jr. 256

knowledge: diversity 241; multiversal 241; universalism 241
knowledge commons 90, 179
knowledge economy 42, 77
Kohler, Robert 184
Kotch, Alex 223
Krishnan, K. S. 137
Kumar, Kanhaiya 46

Labour Bureau Surveys 21
Lacan, J. 258; Discourse of the University 29; meeting Tagore at Sriniketan 149–54
language 46–7, 131; decolonization 70–2
Latif, Nawab Abdul 136
Latin, as language of science 133
Lerner, Michael 228
Letter on Humanism (Heidegger) 87
Liang, Lawrence 29
liberal arts 5, 27, 79, 85–6
liberalism 2
"Life of Students, The" (Benjamin) 1
Lingayats 50
linguistic alienation 9
linguistic handicap 131
The Lives of Animals (Coetzee) 88
loan scheme *see* education loan
lokavidyas 148
Lok Shiksha Sansad 19

Macaulay, Thomas 95–6, 97
MacCannell, Dean 258
macrostructural unconscious 249–54
Madras system 187–90
Mahajan, Shobhit 28–9
Malagatti, Arvind 51
Manipur University 195
Marathon Man 79–80
marketing campaigns 250
Marlowe, Christopher 184
Marshall Plan 228
Marx, Karl 156–7
Marxism 252
Marxist humanists 249
Massey College in Toronto 248
Master's Discourse 29, 149–53
mathematics 133
matsyanyaya 68

Mauss, Marcel 178
McSherry, Corynne 176–7, 180, 181n7
measurement systems 242
Menon, Dilip 102n3
Mignolo, Walter 64
Mill, James 96
Miller Committee Report of 1919 50
Minimum Course Curriculum Document (UGC) 196, 198
Ministry of Skill Development and Entrepreneurship (MSDE) 21–2
minorities 258; exposure to hazardous pollutants 258–9
Minto, Lord 95
Minute on Indian Education (Macaulay) 95–6
missionaries 95–6
Modern Review 13
Mohammedan Literary Society 136
monitorial system 188
Mukherjee, Satish Chandra 97–8
Murugan, Perumal 79
Muslims: Gujarat Riots (2002) 94; university system 96
mutual tuition 187, 190

Nair, Janaki 26
Nalanda University 42, 55, 56, 100, 101
nation: in place of state 3–8; re-imagining 8–17; in university 1–3
National Capital Region of Delhi 128
National Commission for Higher Education and Research 76
National Commission of Scheduled Castes (NCSC) 196
National Council for Educational Research and Training (NCERT) 71
national culture 94, 98–9; Hindu nationalism 94; invented 101–2
National Institute of Science Education and Research (NISER) 109, 111, 116
National Institutional Ranking Framework (NIRF) 6–7

Index 275

National Knowledge Commission (NKC) 4–5, 62, 63
National Policy on Education 62, 76, 78, 119, 129–30
National Policy on Skill Development 21
National Sample Survey (NSS) 129
National Skills Qualification Framework 22
National Translation Mission 131
national university 8–17
nation-building 1
NCERT *see* National Council for Educational Research and Training (NCERT)
Nehru, Jawaharlal 54, 99–100, 106
neoliberal capitalism 250
neoliberalism 222–33
neoliberal savagery *see* neoliberalism
neo-nationalist anti-intellectualism *see* anti-intellectualism
networks of collaboration 118
New Human Rights Movement, The (Joseph) 260
Newman, John Henry 53, 135–6
Nietzsche, F. 191–2
Nigam, Aditya 27, 175
NIRF *see* National Institutional Ranking Framework (NIRF)
NISER *see* National Institute of Science Education and Research (NISER)
NITI Aayog 196
No Child Left Behind 246, 254
North America 240
nuclear war 258

Oakeshott, Michael 41, 50
O'Brien, Peter 67
OECD *see* Organisation for Economic Cooperation and Development (OECD)
offshore campuses of foreign universities 5
oligarchy 230
On the Constitution of the Church and the State (Coleridge) 96
"On the Internal and External Organization of the Higher Scientific Institutions in Berlin" (Humboldt) 187
Ooru keri (Siddalingaiah) 51
Ooty Radio Telescope 119
The Open: Man and Animal (Agamben) 87
optimistic deconstruction 152–3
Organisation for Economic Cooperation and Development (OECD) 193
Osmania University 51
O'Sullivan, Simon 200
Other Backward Classes (OBCs) 127
Oxford University Press 132, 163

'Palli-Seva' (Tagore) 19
Panjab University (PU) 7, 117
Partition of Bengal (1905) 97
Patnaik, Prabhat 30
pedagogical campaigns 232
pedagogy 231–2
periodicals 134
pessimistic deconstruction 153
Petrella, Christopher 258–9
Philosophical Transactions of the Royal Society 134
"Philosophy Course for Scientists" (Althusser) 193
photocopy case of Delhi University 163–74, 175
phronesis 156, 157
Planning Commission of India: abolition of 196; Tenth Five-Year-Plan (2002–2007) 195; Twelfth Five-Year Plan (2012–2017) 195, 196
post-capitalism 155
praxis 29, 147, 148, 155–6
Prime Minister's Council on Trade and Industry 4
prison system 229
private universities 85
Private Universities (Establishment and Regulation) Bill 3–4
privatization 52–3
Ptolemy 133
public university 41–57; academic excellence 47–8; anti-intellectualism 53–7; assaults on 53; audit culture 47–8; crisis of

74–90; hostel 50–2; language 46–7; obligation 126–7; politics of presence 45–6; privatization 52–3; as public space 89; rankings 48; transforming power 49–50; as undeserved privilege 52; universal access 127
publishing industry 175–6
Punjab Science Institute 137

Quarterly Review of Education (UNESCO) 193

Race to the Top 246, 254
racial discrimination 258–9
Radhakrishnan, Sarvepalli 106
Radhakrishnan Commission (1948–9) 62–3
radio astronomy 119
Rajagopalachari, Chakravarti 106
Ramaiah, K. 56–7
Raman, C. V. 106, 107, 137
Raman Research Institute 85
Ramanujan, Srinivasa 106
Rameshwari Photocopiers 163–4
Ram Janmabhoomi Movement 103n8
Ramjas College 77
Randel, Don Michael 120
rankings 48
Ravenshaw College, Cuttack 112
Ravenshaw University Act 2005 112
Rege, Sharmila 47
research 132–9
reservation policies 43, 52, 127–8; caste composition 128–9
residential university *see* hostels
righting wrongs 156
rights of students 230–1
Right to Education Act of 2009 76
right-wing educational reform movement 250
right-wing populism 249
Rio de Janeiro University 239
Robinson, A. 107, 108
Robinson, Rowena 28
Robinson, William I. 247–8
rogue institutions 6
Rothenstein, William 12
Roy, Arundhati 79

Roy, Raja Rammohan 95
Royal Geological Society 134
Royal Society, London 133, 136

Saancha 71
Sadhana 9
Saha, Meghnad 106, 107
Saikia, Dhruba Jyoti 28
samant/tantra 71
samantvaad 71–2
Sanders, Bernie 230
sangharsh 155
Sarkar, Jadunath 15
Schaffer, Simon 183, 184
Schawinski, Kevin 138
Scheduled Castes 127
Scheduled Tribes 127
Schumpeter, Joseph 56
science: citizen 138–9; employment opportunities 130; as independent discipline 187; Latin as language of 133; research (*see* scientific research); self-governing condition 186; as system 184–7; in universities and other institutes of higher learning 106–9
scientific research 28–9, 105–21, 132–9; high-quality research output 109–17; newer institutes 115–16; well-established universities 116–17
scientific revolution 133
scientific societies 133–6
Scientific Society of Aligarh 136
Search for Extra-terrestrial Intelligence (SETI@home) 138
Second World War 135
secularism 72
Sen, Amartya 33
Sen, Geeti 94
Shankanapura, Mahadev 49
Shantiniketan 15
Sharma, Ruchi Ram 137
'Shikshar Her-pher' (Tagore) 9
Shiksha Satra 19
Siddalingaiah, D. 51
Sircar, Mahendralal 136–7
skill development and training 21–2
Sloan Digital Sky Survey 138
Slow Man (Coetzee) 88

Index   277

social discrimination 201
social inclusion 17–23
socialism 251
social justice 199–202, 242
Society for Promoting Educational Access and Knowledge (SPEAK) 164
South Africa 237
Soviet Union 240; Cold War 258; dismantling of 258
SPEAK *see* Society for Promoting Educational Access and Knowledge (SPEAK)
specialists, communities of 134–5
Spivak, Gayatri C. 183, 201, 205n21, 231
Sriniketan 18–19, 29, 147–9, 156–8; Lacan meets Tagore at 149–54; objectives of 148–9; transformative social praxis 148
students: caste composition 128–9; rights of 230–1; socio-economic profile 129
studia humanitatis 88
Subramanian Committee *see* T.S.R. Subramanian Committee Report on New Education Policy (2016a)
swaraj in ideas 67–70
Swarup, Govind 116, 119
systematic resegregation 258

Tabb, William 2–3
Tagore, Rabindranath 8–20, 22, 106; 'Eastern University, An' 18; idea of university 8–20, 22; Lacan meets 149–54; 'Palli-Seva' 19; Visva Bharati 14–17, 18, 22; *see also* Shantiniketan; Sriniketan
Takshashila 101
Tapas Majumdar Committee Report of 2005 121
tapovan ashram 11, 154
Tata Institute of Fundamental Research (TIFR) 111, 116
Tata Institute of Social Sciences (TISS) 194
taxpayer 51–2
Taylor and Francis Routledge 163
TCC *see* transnational capitalist class (TCC)
teaching 127–32
technological institutions **114**, 114–15
technological/productive forces 241
Telegraph, The 112
Tenth Ministerial Conference of WTO (2015) 5
textbooks 131
Tezpur University 113
Thorpe, Bob 224
TIFR *see* Tata Institute of Fundamental Research (TIFR)
Tilak, Bal Gangadhar 98
TISS *see* Tata Institute of Social Sciences (TISS)
transformation 154–5
transformative social praxis 148
Translation Society 136
transmissible knowledge 151
transnational capitalist class (TCC) 247–8
transnational corporate-policy networks 247–8
Trump, Donald 31, 222–3, 225, 233
T.S.R. Subramanian Committee Report on New Education Policy (2016) 6, 119–21

UGC *see* University Grants Commission (UGC)
UNESCO 193
United States: brutalism 227–8; Cold War 258; democracy in 222, 230; neoliberalism 222–33; policies 246; prison system 229; providential mission 253
universal access 127
universalism 241
university: careful analysis and consideration 237–40; defending 24–5; definitions/meanings 56–7; early nationalist ideas of 97–9; on foundations of historic colleges 111–13, **113**; idea of 32–3; importance in national life 99; liberal-democratic 2; medieval description 42; national-modern phase 42; nation in 1–3; politics of future 23–4; pressures 241–2; Readings on 93, 94; social

inclusion 17–23; social mobility 42–3; as space of training 52; Tagore on 8–20, 22; utilitarian idea of 94–7; Western incarnation 42; *see also* public university
University Grants Commission (UGC) 3, 76, 194–6
University in Ruins, The (Readings) 93
University of Berlin 187
University of Calcutta 239
University of Cape Town 74
University of Chicago 120
University of Hyderabad 6, 26, 117, 218
University of Paris 132
University of Pune 47
University of Roorkee 115
University of Wittenberg 184
"University Without Culture?, The" (Readings) 93
Upper Canada College 248
upper castes 52
urban education, US 250
Urdu 70
utilitarian idea of university 94–7

value 1; as non-physical quality 249
Vemula, Rohith 46, 79
violence 252
virtue 1
Visva Bharati 14–17, 18, 22
vocationalization of higher education 20–2
vocational/skill training 21–2
Vyapam scam 52

Wall Street Journal 252
Walmart model 31, 226, 229
Warner, Marina 222
"Washington Consensus" of 1989 3
wealth: as physical quantity 249; *see also* capitalism
Western education 96–7; production of civility 102n5
Wilhelm, Frederick, III 2
Williamson, John 3
Women in the Beehive: A Seminar with Jacques Derrida 152
Wood, Charles 96
World Bank 3
World Trade Organization (WTO) 2–3
WTO *see* World Trade Organization (WTO)

Yashpal Committee Report (2009) 62, 195

Printed in the United States
By Bookmasters